T0413395

The
RETURN *of*
CRITICISM

www.royalcollins.com

The
RETURN *of*
CRITICISM

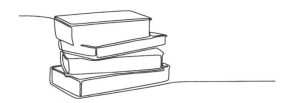

Written by **He Ping**

Translated by **Daniel McRyan**

Books Beyond Boundaries

ROYAL COLLINS

The Return of Criticism

Written by He Ping
Translated by Daniel McRyan

First published in 2025 by Royal Collins Publishing Group Inc.
Groupe Publication Royal Collins Inc.
550-555 boul. René-Lévesque O Montréal (Québec)
H2Z1B1 Canada

ISBN: 978-1-4878-1272-0

To find out more about our publications,
please visit www.royalcollins.com.

Contents

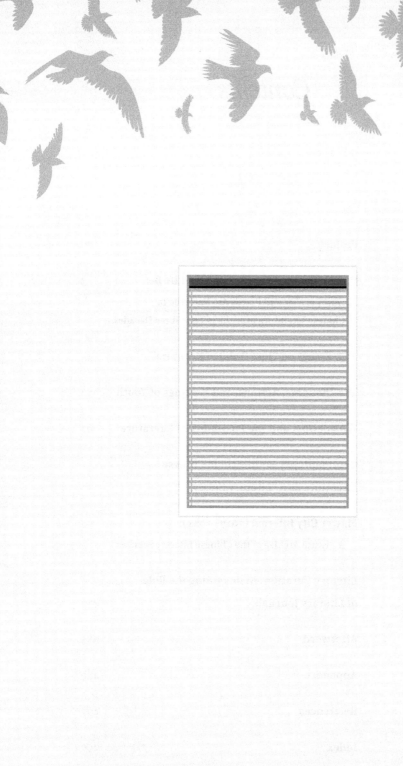

Preface

Return: Literary Criticism That Rebuilds Dialogue and Action

At the turn of the century, the boundaries and connotations of literature underwent significant changes. Although these changes have roots and families in the history of modern Chinese literature, the literary market share, power discourse, and reader influence have acquired characteristics of the new times. The literary landscape, established from the May Fourth Movement to the mid-1930s and characterized by literary nomenclature, distinctions between high and low culture, and hierarchical order, dramatically contracted following the marketization of the 1990s and the subsequent influx of capital into new Internet media. This shift saw an aesthetic downgrade in exchange for the explosive growth of the literary population. While this seemed to flatten the literary hierarchy, it also led to the distinction and governance of literary types based on media, literary views, readers' interests, and various production and consumption methods.

Notably, for the publication and dissemination of literature, even within the same media, significant differences exist. For example, in print, there is an obvious distinction in style between traditional literary journals and revised publications like *Mengya, Fiction World, Youth Literature,* and *China Literature Today,* and latecomers *Chutzpah!, ZUI Found, NEWRITING, Sinan Literary Journal,* and between traditional publishing houses and new ones such as Ideal Country, Houlang, Wenjing, Motie, Fenghuang Liandong, Boji Tianjuan, Chuchen Culture, Fuben Zhizuo, Lianbang Zouma, and Readers. Similarly, on the Internet, personal blogs, social media platforms like Weibo and WeChat, BBS forums, Douban's literary community, individual writing, and commercial literary websites controlled by large capital each follow their distinct paths and occupy different network spaces. Consequently, it is nearly impossible for a literary critic to be well-versed in the diverse literary geography within China, let alone place contemporary Chinese literature in a global context and the wider real world.

In other words, the writing and commentary across the nation, propelled by the burgeoning influence of Internet media, may increasingly splinter into stratified and tribalistic factions. This division and tribalization have permeated every facet of literary creation and consumption. The current literary landscape, marked by such divisions and tribal identities, allows professional critics to operate within narrow circles defined by their own specialization, readership, and authors. Critics aspiring to transcend these boundaries, to cross into unfamiliar territories and articulate perspectives beyond their immediate circles, face the daunting task of comprehending the diverse works produced by various divisions and tribes. Undoubtedly, this presents a significant challenge to critics' cognitive agility, critical insight, and breadth of knowledge resources.

The revolution in media has led to another consequence: a cacophony of voices, but this cacophony may not necessarily foster dialogues of harmony and semantic enrichment. Instead, it could cause self-referential dissolution and dissipation. In the short essay I wrote for the eighth anniversary of *Literature Journal: New Criticism*, I said, "In an era of information overload, chaos, and inundation, the constant dissemination of information and drifting of meanings lead to each individual viewpoint being drastically altered through secondary and even multiple processes like appropriation, distortion, and selective quoting. Fragmentation seems almost inevitable for thoughts and concepts in the age of mass media. Thus, in the literary arena of the mass media age, can traditional literary criticism continue in its conventional sense? And how will it proceed? How can the scattered fragments of information hastily gathered by authors, media practitioners, ordinary readers, and even the authors themselves be orderly integrated in the process? In short, can we organize the literary logic of our time based on continuous historical logic, articulate the aesthetic new quality of our time, and give it a name?"

In contrast, there have been subtle shifts in the composition of professional literary critics. Most notably, since the turn of the new century," "academic criticism" has gradually gained prominence. This trend can be vaguely discerned from the column arrangements in literary journals. For instance, starting in 1999, *Zhongshan* introduced the section Doctoral Perspectives, which was discontinued in the third issue of 2000 and replaced by a highly influential new section called Gazing at Stars, which persisted for many years. The authors of Gazing at Stars are primarily teachers of contemporary Chinese literature in major universities. While categorized as "authorial discourse," these essays differ from general intuitive authorial discourse by placing greater emphasis on the systematic application of theoretical resources and the assessment of literary values within the context of literary history. They are endowed with rigorous scholarly rigor.

Following the wave of "academic criticism," apart from a few literary journals such as *Zhongshan*, *Mountain Flowers*, *Shanghai Literature*, *Tianya*, *Flower City*, *Writer*, and *The Great Wall* that have maintained consistent literary criticism traditions and good relations with academic critics, for a long time, most literary journals found it difficult to attract high-quality submissions from top-tier university faculty members. As a result, literary criticism sections in many journals could only symbolically sustain themselves through contributions from emerging and amateur practitioners.

The current issue is whether the literary scene, which is increasingly expansive and complex, matches the conceptual, intellectual, visionary, technical, methodological, and stylistic capabilities of professional literary critics concentrated in universities and specialized research institutions. Particularly, do the new-generation academic critics who entered the scene in the 1980s, 1990s, and beyond have significant differences in their developmental paths, intellectual makeup, knowledge structures, and critical paradigms? Unlike earlier critics who experienced "wild growth" and long-term freedom in critical writing styles, these new critics have been disciplined from the outset within the knowledge-network-based CNKI (China National Knowledge Infrastructure) academic writing system of university institutions. In fact, literary criticism cannot simply equate to academic research. The new-generation literary critics of the twenty-first century do not necessarily possess, nor do they require, a comprehensive understanding of literary aesthetics or the capability to engage with and grasp the literary scene. Instead, they often transform literary criticism into "papers" using electronic resources such as CNKI.

Observing the history of modern Chinese literature, literary critics were not predominantly based in universities and specialized research institutions as they are now. Instead, many were involved in literary-related work such as newspapers, periodicals, book editing, and publishing. Furthermore, looking at the contemporary academic system in China, such stringent academic standards have only emerged in the past one or two decades. In reality, not just literary criticism but academic research as a whole during times of relatively relaxed academic regulations in universities was not entirely as structured as it is today.

However, it is unfair to blame the current detachment of literary criticism from the literary scene solely on the university academic system. Even in the present university academic environment, compared to research in humanities and social sciences, there still exists ample space for the growth of literary criticism.

For instance, a rigid criterion of the university academic system is the so-called core journal paper. I have observed that present literary criticism publications are not as restrictive as imagined and can accommodate a diverse range of literary critiques. Most of the so-called "C journals" recognized by universities and the core journals of Peking University can publish various types of literary criticism that we can conceive, not just the format of a sole academic journal paper. Even core journals like *Contemporary Writers Review*, *Southern Cultural Forum*, *Yangtze River Literature Review*, *Novel Critique*, *Literary Disputes*, and *Shanghai Culture* do not impose strict format requirements for keywords and abstracts. Compared to this seemingly relaxed literary criticism publication ecology, if we observe the writings of the same author in these literary criticism publications and in publications requiring keywords and abstracts such as *Literary Review*, *Studies in Modern Chinese Literature*, *Literary Studies*, *Contemporary Cultural Forum*, and even journals and other humanities and social science publications, there is no clear distinction in their "literary form."

In their understanding, literary criticism is simply a form of "academic paper." This directly results in today's literary criticism publications being transformed by their authors into something that is not "literary criticism." Therefore, while emphasizing the disciplinary influence of the academic system on literary criticism, literary critics have effectively precluded themselves from the full freedom offered by most literary criticism publications. This abandonment extends not only to textual formats, rhetoric, and language style but also to the intellectual, thinking, and spiritual aspects of literary practitioners. Looking at the modern tradition of literary criticism since the May Fourth Movement, at a spiritual level, literary criticism is

implemented as "criticism." One should be aware of the inherent relationship between modern literary criticism and intellectuals. The fundamental
starting point of this relationship is aesthetic criticism, and from aesthetic
criticism, one can extend to what Lu Xun referred to as social criticism and
civilization criticism.

Considering the objective existence of the university academic system,
the disciplinary positioning of literary criticism cannot be merely confined
to the research domain of modern Chinese literary history and become its
appendage. Can literary criticism draw on the practical spirit and research
paradigms of social science research to rebuild legitimacy within the university academic system? Social science research emphasizes field investigations and hands-on actions, and literary criticism can similarly handle
its relationship with the literary scene: critics can impact the literary scene
through their literary criticism practice. Particularly memorable are stages
of literary journals like *Shanghai Literature, People's Literature, Mountain
Flowers,* and *Zhongshan,* where critics such as Chen Sihua, Cai Xiang, Ding
Fan, Li Jingze, Shi Zhanjun, Zhang Qinghua, and Wang Gan were involved
in literary journal editing, shaping the tastes and selection criteria of the
publications.

In 2017, I began collaborating with Flower City Interest, a column of
Flower City hosted by critics. Since its debut in 2017, it has released 30 issues, focusing on hundreds of novelists, prose writers, playwrights, and
poets, with two-thirds of them not receiving adequate attention from critics and traditional literary journals. The 30 special topics covered in the 30
columns include possibilities in directing and fiction, the imagination in
literature, limitations of generational descriptions, literary returns in drama scripts, young writers and their hometowns, science fiction and reality,
literary boundaries and multi-ethnic writing, the "innocent" starting point
of poetry writing, fieldwork in proses, overlapping subjects in prose writing,
"story retelling" and "reinterpreting," overseas Chinese literature, rock and
folk music, creative writing, early styles of young writers, the expansion of

literature into other artistic categories, intimate relationships between native urban writers and new urban literature, impacts in counties, rural museums, global time zones, spiritual tree holes, youthful impacts, journal interests, local illusions, ideals of short story masters, machine-made literature, literary tribes, and cross-border travel, among others.

Flower City Interest dedicates each of its columns to specific critiques addressing the current nature and sense of the literary scene, using the potential and future prospects of Chinese literature as criteria for selecting writers. Under this philosophy, heterogeneous texts deviating from aesthetic norms naturally receive more "attention," and room for discussion and questioning is reserved for biases in the program. Inspired by art exhibitions and activities, I introduced the concept of "literary curation" to Flower City Interest.

The literary journal environment and the role of critics have changed around the turn of the century. Journals in the 1980s and 1990s consciously organized literary production, which is evident in their engagement with every trend and the growth of every classic writer. However, contemporary literary publications rarely produce and innovate literary concepts like those from the 1980s and 1990s, nor do they consciously drive literary trends. Scheduled literary publications have gradually devolved into collections of author works. Concurrently, critics' ability to consciously engage in the literary scene has also deteriorated, where enriched literary criticism practices almost equate to thesis writing. Therefore, proposing the concept of "literary curation" aims for critics to learn from art curators, consciously engaging more in the literary scene to discover new growth points in contemporary Chinese literature.

Unlike traditional literary editors, literary curators serve as connectors, facilitators, and sharers rather than dogmatic literary missionaries. In fact, every literary publication, including media, resembles a form of "curation." Similar to public spaces like museums and art galleries hosting art exhibitions, literary journals serve as bustling "skywalks." Just as art events at museums and art galleries are curated, critics are most likely to become literary curators. Thus, envisioning the Flower City Interest column as a public art gallery with a curator role aligns with my envisioned role of critics intervening in literary production and moving toward editing. For me, hosting the column is critiquing. Through hosting, I express approval or disapproval of current Chinese literature, highlighting my aesthetic judgments and literary perspectives as a critic.

Flower City Interest does not deliberately create literary topics or produce literary concepts—short-term tactics that might attract attention but could also foster literary bubbles. Instead, it emphasizes critics' deep immersion in the literary scene to identify issues, thus continuing the spirit of literary criticism since the 1980s and the entirety of modern literary criticism to some extent.

In recent years, the interaction among literary journals, literary criticism, and literary critics has seen a revival and become more active. On the one hand, critics such as Xie Youshun, Jin Li, Wang Chunlin, Zhang Xuexin, Gu Jianping, Li Denan, Chen Peihao, Fang Yan, Huang Dehai, Zhang Li, Shao Yanjun, among others, have been hosting columns in multiple literary journals. Some of these columns have been running for years, such as Wang Chunlin's Literary Focus, Zhang Xuexin's The Art of Short Stories, and Li Hao's The Possibilities of Novels in *The Great Wall*; Xie Youshun's New Criticism and Gu Jianping's New Power in *Young Writers*; Huang Dehai's Commercial Exchange Record in *Youth Literature*; and Li Denan's Journal Observations in *Literature Port*, etc.

On the other hand, traditional literary journals not known for their strength in contemporary Chinese literary criticism, such as *Jiangnan, China Literature Today, Literature and Art of Guangzhou, Yalujiang Literature Monthly, Youth Literature, Sinan Literary Journal, Harvest,* and *Works,* have dedicated significant space to literary criticism. Notable examples include Bright Stars in *Harvest*, Survey of Contemporary Young Writers on 115 participants born after 1985 in *China Literature Today*, Observations in *Jiang-*

nan, Keywords in Contemporary Literature in *Literature and Art of Guang-zhou*, Classic Post-70s Generation in *Works*, and Youth City, New Youth in *Yalujiang Literature Monthly*.

Moreover, young critics like Zhang Dinghao, Liu Daxian, Jin Li, Huang Ping, Huang Dehai, Yang Qingxiang, He Tongbin, Fang Yan, Li Denan, and Yue Wen have consciously strengthened the dialogues between literature and the times, enhancing the intellectual depth of literary criticism.

The literary criticism of action and practical engagement is not just about reaching the literary scene but being "in the literary scene" itself; or, to put it another way, it is "being an indispensable part of the literary scene." Critics involved in such practices participate in the production of contemporary literature, thereby shaping their own identities as critics. Being "in the literary scene" involves exploring nascent possibilities and discovering new literary qualities, contributing to the exploration and invention of "new literature."

An increasing number of critics are hosting columns in literary journals and publishing literary critiques. This not only revives the tradition of literary journals balancing creation and criticism but also plays a crucial role in securing unique academic territories and dignity for literary criticism within the university academic system. This correction is significant in countering the tendency to diminish and sideline literary criticism in favor of more closely related disciplines like literary history and theory. In fact, the academic advancement of literary history and theory relies heavily on the support of literary criticism.

The involvement of literary criticism in the literary scene is certainly more than just participating in the editorial practices of literary journals. Figures like Ding Fan, Chen Fumin, Wang Binbin, Wang Yao, Li Jingze, Zhang Qinghua, Zhang Xinying, Zhang Ning, Liang Hong, Zhang Dinghao, Huang Dehai, Mu Ye, Li Yunlei, Xiang Jing, and Fang Wei, among others, not only engage in literary criticism but also write various forms of literature such as novels, poetry, and prose. This dual engagement is indeed an important tradition in modern Chinese literature.

In fact, the "action" and practical significance of literary criticism as a "verb" are not confined to "essays" alone. Apart from hosting columns and interdisciplinary writing, it can also encompass literary education, editorial selections, rankings (for example, critic Wang Chunlin publishes an annual "personal novel list"), and so on. Even within the realm of "essays," it does not necessarily adhere strictly to formal academic standards. On top of literary publications and critical journals, in the age of the internet, platforms like online communities, WeChat, and Weibo have opened various avenues and new forms of critical discourse.

Let us believe, for the moment, that today's literary critics all possess their own literary values and positions. In this regard, one can refer to the column Critics Today in *Southern Cultural Forum*. This column is perhaps the oldest and continuously running section in literary criticism publications. Influential literary critics born after the 1950s have almost all been introduced through this column, and each featured critic in Critics Today expresses "my critical view." Perhaps in contemporary Chinese literary criticism, there is no shortage of "my critical view," but are we aware that the more "my critical view" there are, the more necessary it becomes to debate, question, and name in order to establish literary "consensus"?

For a healthy literary ecology, dialogue should not only occur between critics but should naturally expand to between critics and writers, as well as between critics and various sectors of society. Therefore, contemporary literary criticism needs not only to revive the tradition of field investigations reaching the literary scene and "being in the scene" but also to rebuild the dialogical nature of literary criticism. In fact, genuine awareness of problems and polyphonic literary dialogues have largely been lost in our era, leaving behind superficial literary exchanges, literary events, literary conferences, and public literary performances as "pretend dialogues."

The essay published at the end of the twentieth century, *Collective Work*, is a full record of a "gathering" held on November 3, 1998. Participants included young writers at the time, such as Li Jingze, Qiu Huadong, Li Er, Li Feng, and Li Dawei. They did not discuss literary gossip or lightly support a writer and their work but directly addressed significant contemporary literary issues: personal writing and grand narratives, everyday life, tradition and language, imagination and the avant-garde, and other "literary issues"—real and significant issues. (What do young writers and critics gather to discuss now?) Their recorded literary "gathering" should be like this: "The dialogue took place at Li Dawei's home, starting in the morning and continuing late into the night." "Li Er made a special trip from Zhengzhou. Due to the lively atmosphere on-site and the noise of voices, so as not to miss a single person's speech, everyone carried small tape recorders, passing them to each person sitting or standing, much like passing and sharing something tasty."

In the 1980s and 1990s, especially after 1992, it was truly an era of literary "gatherings." Looking back at the periodicals of that time—*Readings, Literary Disputes, Book House, Shanghai Literature, Flower City, Tianya, Lotus, Zhongshan, Mountain Flowers, Beijing Literature, Literature Review, Writers' Daily, Literary Arts Daily,* and *Eastern Culture Weekly*—how the literary and intellectual circles loved these "gatherings" and discussions! It is worth mentioning that these "gatherings" related to literary criticism or initiated by literary criticism almost never limit themselves to internal literary discussions. Participants spanned almost all fields of humanities, social sciences, and the arts. For example, the Critics Club of *Shanghai Literature* addressed "the crisis of literary and humanistic spirit," "the value norms of contemporary intellectuals," and "the fate and choices of humanists." Modern Trends and Flower City Forum of *Flower City* tackled cutting-edge issues like cities and popular culture. New Ten Critiques of *Zhongshan* focused on the spiritual ruins brought by the commercial era. *Mountain Flowers, Lotus,* and *Tianya* devoted their enthusiasm and concern to literature and contemporary avant-garde art. Among these, Writer's Position and Research and Criticism of *Tianya* are rare columns that have consistently focused on "big literature" up to today.

Based on the reconstruction of literature and the big literature and art, the reconstruction of literature and the intellectual community, and the reconstruction of literature's connections with the wider society, and based on the expansive imagination opened up by the complex and multidimensional connections of literary criticism, in 2017, Jin Li from Fudan University and I initiated a long-term project "Shanghai-Nanjing Dual Cities Literary Workshop."

Every year, alternating between Fudan University and Nanjing Normal University, we convened critics, publishers, novelists, artists, playwrights, and poets to collaboratively complete themed workshops with a conscious awareness of issues. The aim is to revive the tradition of dialogical literary criticism, which is not seminars, work discussions, and research forums taking place in universities, writers' associations, and research institutions. Instead, it is a more open and potentially boundary-crossing "dialogue."

This dual cities workshop has held five sessions, with the following themes: "Literary Provocation and Youth Writing" (2017, Shanghai), "The City as Seen and Displayed" (2018, Nanjing), "World Literature and Youth Writing" (2019, Shanghai), "Chinese Nonfiction and Nonfictional China" (2020, Nanjing), and "Literature and Public Life" (2021, Shanghai).

In addition, over the past two years, Chen Qiuhan and I initiated the "Nanjing Forum of Chinese Science Fiction Literature," and Li Hongwei, Li Qiang, Fang Yan, and I launched the "2019 New Fiction."

The current relationship between writers and critics in the Chinese literary realm is overly "sweetened." Perhaps rarely in any time have writers cared so much about how critics view them. Reading Writer Interviews from *The Paris Review*, I noticed that familiar figures like Hemingway, García Márquez, and Vladimir Nabokov all maintained sufficient caution and "distrust" toward critics. Of course, a writer's "care" could potentially form a tense dialogue relationship if it solely concerns literature. However, in reality, this so-called "care" is often not about the critic's honest literary insights and aesthetic abilities but rather their power in selection, historiography, awards, and rankings.

Reconstructing the dialogical nature of literary criticism essentially means returning literature, through criticism's discoveries and voices, to the realm of public relevance or at least to aspects relevant to national aesthetics rather than engaging in a hollow ritual. The starting point is that literature critics, especially young critics, should aspire to be protectors, discoverers, and supporters of those writers who challenge aesthetic norms. They should function as critics who are contemporaries of the writers they critique. There is no need to look far back into tradition for this; in the 1980s and 1990s, critics were willing to act so.

However, in recent years, apart from a minor debate last year between Zhang Dinghao and Huang Ping in *Literature and Arts* about new Northeastern novelists, can we recall any literary dialogues that pinpoint the real issues, major problems, symptomatic issues, or pathological issues of our literary times? Many young critics have become inheritors and conservators of certain rigid literary doctrines. The 1980s was a time of intellectual trends, while the 1990s saw a tendency toward "de-intellectualization." In 2010, I penned an article titled "The Problem of Re-individualization in the Times of Individual Literature," discussing the advent of individualistic times in literature around the turn of the century. Today, it is impossible to integrate fragmented literary scenes according to different intellectual trends, as was the case in the 1980s.

Literary transformation is driven by a few exploratory individuals rather than adherence to inherited literary conventions. Since the reform and opening up period, Chinese literature has continued to progress because some people were dissatisfied with existing literary norms, challenged and offended them, constantly opening themselves up and becoming more acute. Today, it is not that such traditions have disappeared or that individuals with the exploratory spirit no longer exist; instead, the over-saturation, fragmentation, and lowering of aesthetic standards in literature have sub-merged distinctive literary qualities, making it difficult to clarify them.

Therefore, contemporary literary criticism must, on the one hand, have the courage and insight to name truly innovative literature. On the other hand, it must decisively reject so-called literature that relies on capital and new media, among other non-aesthetic powers. Hence, the purpose of literary criticism is to return to rediscovering each unique individual, exploring the relationships between these individuals' writings, those of their contemporaries, and their historical logic, thereby considering what new possibilities they bring to contemporary Chinese literature.

PART I

Only in Such a Place Can Such a Life Be:

How Locality and Places Are Narrated in Chinese Literature over the Recent Three Decades

Not all writers need to fixate on a single place to succeed; outstanding writers are not necessarily obligated to depict a specific locality. However, it is undeniable that the portrayal of places in literature has been an important tradition in Chinese novels over the past three decades. How are places depicted in literature? One basic premise is whether, within our unified multi-ethnic national community, there exist aesthetic differences in "places." Liu Zhenyun once said, "Hometown is a country."[1]

---

1   Liu Zhenyun, "The Overall Hometown and Its Specifics," *Literary and Artistic Contention*, No. 1, 1992.

In anthropology and sociology studies, local experiences within the political community of China have been experienced and disclosed since the first half of the twentieth century by scholars like Fei Xiaotong, Lin Yaohua, Du Zhanqi, and Zhuang Kongshao. In terms of literature, as people have recognized through experience, "Mainland China's literature, which is primarily political, is actually a collection of diverse voices. For instance, how can a northern writer like Mo Yan from Shandong understand the works Li Rui wrote in Shanxi or *Qinqiang* written by Jia Pingwa in the local dialect of Shaanxi? Language itself is constantly evolving. Not to mention writers like A Lai, who has a Tibetan background, adding many complex factors to the mix."[2]

Language certainly constitutes a significant "local" factor, but "local" encompasses more than just language. What about the places themselves, as depicted by writers? Su Tong recently wrote, "Xiangchun Street and Fengyangshu Village are geographical markers in my works."[3] It is not only Su Tong's "Xiangchun Street and Fengyangshu Village." In Chinese literature of the past three decades, there are also "Big Nur" (by Wang Zengqi), "Shangzhou" and "Qingfeng Street" (by Jia Pingwa), "Lesser Khingan Mountains" (by Zheng Wanlong, Ureltu), "Xizang" (by Tashi Dawa, Ma Yuan), "Ujimqin Grassland" (by Zhang Chengzhi), "Bao Town" and "Shanghai Alleys" (by Wang Anyi), "Jitou Village" and "Maqiao" (by Han Shaogong), "Gechuan River" (by Li Hangyu), "Lüliang Mountains" (by Li Rui), "Taihang Mountains" (by Zheng Yi), "Qingping Bay" (by Shi Tiesheng), "Gaomi Northeast Township" (by Mo Yan), "Wenjiayao" (by Cao Naiqian), "White Deer Plain" (by Chen Zhongshi), "Shangtang" (by Sun Huifen), "Yanjin Old Town" (by Liu Zhenyun), "Balou Mountains" (by Yan Lianke), "Wangjia Village" (by Bi Fei-

---

2   Li Fengliang, "The Concept and Operation of Chinese Language Literature—Interview with Professor Wang Dewei," *Flower City*, No. 5 (2008).

3   Su Tong, "About or Not about Writing," *Yangtze Jiang Literary Review*, No. 3 (2009).

yu), "Clumsy Flower Village" (by Tie Ning), "Tianmenkou" (by Liu Xinglong), "Wangzha" (by Lin Bai), "Ji Village" (by A Lai), "Beiji Village" and "Erguna River Right Bank" (by Chi Zijian), "Dongba" (by Lu Min), "Xietang" (by Bi Yu), "Majiabao" (by Dong Jun), and so on. When writers depict these places, it is evident that they are not merely decorative cultural landscapes or geographical labels.

However, it should be noted that, on the one hand, places have frequently appeared in Chinese literary writing over the past three decades; on the other hand, not all these local places have become literary places revered by Chinese writers like William Faulkner's Yoknapatawpha County, Gabriel García Márquez's Macondo, or the literary places in Chinese literature such as "Lu Town," "Xiangxi" (western Hunan), "Orchard City," and "Hulan River." In other words, a local place has not necessarily become the literary world of a writer.

— Literary Local Narratives Started by Wang Zengqi —

O nce literature becomes history, new problems emerge. As we talk about the literature of the new era through the lenses of "wounds," "reflection," and "reform," we find hardly any mention of Wang Zengqi, although the first two years of the 1980s were almost the "years of Wang." Influential magazines like *Beijing Literature* and *Yuhua* from the north and south respectively published his works such as *Buddhist Initiation* (*Beijing Literature*, 1980, Issue 10), *Special Gift* (*Yuhua*, 1981, Issue 1), *A Tale of Big Nur* (*Beijing Literature*, 1981, Issue 4), *Migration* (*Beijing Literature*, 1981, Issue 10), and *Fellow Townspeople* (*Yuhua*, 1981, Issue 10).

Wang's writing was not included in literary history. For writings excluded from literary history, the current approach is to awkwardly fit them into a category. For example, many literary history books classify Wang's works as regional or everyday novels. However, in fact, his novels should be recognized as distinct from regional novels by contemporaries such as Lu Wenfu, Deng Youmei, and Chen Jiangong. Therefore, looking back now, it would be more proper to consider him as the beginning of another tradition in the literature of the new era.

In his preface to Li Hangyu's *The Last Fisherman*, Wang Meng wrote, "Traditionally, Chinese novels do not seem to pay much attention to geography and nature ... They focus more on social, political, and ethical interpersonal relationships."[4] Prior to Li Hangyu, Wang Zengqi's novels like *A Tale of Big Nur* paid attention to "geography and nature," marking a significant

---

4   Wang Meng, "Preface: Charm of Gechuan River," in Li Hangyu, *The Last Fisherman*, (Beijing: Peoples Literature Publishing, 1985).

aspect of the new-era literature. Wang excelled in depicting the "geography and nature" of places. In this regard, he continued the modern literary tradition of Fei Ming and Shen Congwen in the new-era literature. His continuation or initiation of this literary tradition represents another kind of literature that exists alongside "wounds," "reflection," and "reform" within the same historical and literary context. Wang himself said, "This is *siwuxie* [an innocent mind], a state of mind in the *Book of Songs*. I write this under the deep influence of the liberation of thought since the Third Plenary Session. For years, we have suffered from restrictions on our thoughts."[5]

> This place has a peculiar name, Anzhao Village. Zhao is because most residents in the village are surnamed Zhao. It is called a village, but people live scattered, with a couple of families here and there. They can be seen from far away, but walking takes a while as the main roads wind through the fields. The An [temple] is Puti An, but everyone got it wrong and called it Biqi An.
>
> (*Buddhist Initiation*)
>
> This place has a peculiar name, Big Nur. Few in the entire county recognize the word Nur. Within the county, there is no other place named Nur. It is believed to be Mongolian. So, this name probably dates to the Yuan Dynasty. Earlier than that, it remains unknown whether this place existed and what it was called.
>
> (*A Tale of Big Nur*)

From the beginning, Wang was aware that the stories he told were "local" and "peculiar." But this "peculiarity" is how others see it; for Wang himself, the place he wrote about is simply his hometown. "Deep impressions make me remember it clearly," "I'm rather familiar with many industries.

---

5   Wang Zengqi and Shi Shuqing, "Prose-Style Novels as Lyrical Poetry—a Conversation with Mainland Chinese Writers No. 4," *Shanghai Literature*, No. 4 (1998).

Like the pharmacy Baoquan Tang in *Special Gift*, which my grandfather owned, I used to roam around there all day as a child. When I wrote about these characters, some were slightly exaggerated based on real experiences. How can a monk marry a wife and bring her to the temple, and the little monk calls her *shiniang* [teacher's wife]? How can monks gamble, play cards, and slaughter pigs in the main hall? All of these are true. I lived in this small temple for six months; Yingzi even served as my younger brother's nanny ... In *A Tale of Big Nur*, those young girls and married women dared to go skinny-dipping in the river. People question, 'How is that possible?' Well, I have seen it with my own eyes."[6]

How does literature depict locality? Primarily, it is about respecting and adhering to the diversity of places. Local experiences often struggle to find their way into public discourse. As depicted by Wang Zengqi in *A Tale of Big Nur*, "The colors, sounds, and smells here differ from those in the city streets. The people here, too. Their lives, customs, moral standards, ethical concepts, and the people who walk the streets chanting Confucius are completely different." This inspired Wang to write *Buddhist Initiation*.

Minghai was called Xiaomingzi at home. He decided to become a monk from an early age. In his hometown, it is not called "entering Buddhist practice" but "becoming a monk." In his hometown, monks are produced, the same as some places produce butchers, some produce mat weavers, some produce barrel makers, some produce cotton-pickers, some produce gardeners, some produce prostitutes ... The Second Master, Renhai, has a wife who stays here for a few months every spring and autumn because the temple is cool. There are six people in the temple, and one of them is this monk's family member. Renshan and Rendu call her sister-in-law, and

---

6   Wang Zengqi and Shi Shuqing, "Prose-style Novels as Lyrical Poetry—a Conversation with Mainland Chinese Writers No. 4," *Shanghai Literature*, No. 4 (1998).

Minghai calls her *shiniang*. This couple stresses hygiene, doing cleanings all day long. In the evening, they sit in the courtyard to cool off, and during the day, they stay indoors.

Monk Rendu sings folk songs:

"She is so pretty, her breasts so perky. I want to do some grabbing; my heart is racing."

The monks slaughter a pig in the temple:

In this temple, there are no strict rules, and no one even mentions these words ... They do not hide the fact that they eat meat and even slaughter pigs during the year-end. The pig is slaughtered right in the main hall. It is the same as laypeople, with boiling water, wooden barrels, and sharp knives. When the pig is tied, it screams loudly. Unlike laypeople, there is an additional ritual where they recite the *Amitabha Pure Land Rebirth Dharani* for the pig about to die, always solemnly by the senior monk: "All born from the womb, eggs, or breath, come from emptiness and return to emptiness. Rebirth and reincarnation, all should rejoice. Namo Amitabha!" The Third Master Rendu makes a single slash, and fresh, red pig's blood sprays out with lots of froth.

The novel ends as follows:

Xiaoyingzi suddenly puts down the oar, walks to the stern, and leans close to Mingzi's ear, whispering, "Do you want me to be your wife?"

Mingzi widens his eyes.

"Say something."

"Mm," Mingzi responds.

"What does 'mm' mean? Yes, or no?"

Mingzi shouts, "Yes!"

"Why are you shouting?"

Mingzi whispers, "Yes ..."

"Only in such a place can such a life be."[7] In *Buddhist Initiation* by Wang Zengqi, the love of youngsters and the breaking of religious precepts are unrelated but relevant to the locality. Therefore, the attempt to discover the revolutionary subtext at the end of the novel certainly contradicts Wang Zengqi's original intent.

The significance of local narratives in the 1980s literature since Wang lies in their multifaceted nature and the most important is discovering the value of locality and establishing the legitimacy of local narratives. However, Wang's narrative of locality at that time did not delve into the complex conflicts between the nation and locality, grand history and local history, and Chinese experience and globalization, as later Chinese literature did. He simply honestly wrote about the "place" in his old dreams and memories, and the hijacking and appropriation of local narratives should be seen as a later development.

However, objectively speaking, Wang's narrative of locality and its detachment from mainstream writing can also be observed as a form of "apolitical" politics, developing a consciousness within literature itself. Looking back 30 years later, regardless of whether one is influenced by Wang or not, the emphasis on the "peculiarity" and "oddity" of locality in subsequent literary narratives after Wang undoubtedly contrasts or confronts the imagined center. Without a nation, where would localities be? It is for this reason that Wang's presence in the 1980s of "wounds," "reflection," and "reform" is both accidental and inevitable.

---

7   Wang Zengqi, "Postscript: Reading 'Can't Help Thinking of You at Night,' Cao Naiqian,"
     Cao Naiqian, *Can't Help Thinking of You at Night*, (Wuhan: Changjiang Literature and Art
     Publishing House, 2007), 232.

The Aspiration of Local Narratives Appropriated — by Educated Youth

The way places are depicted inherently implies a basic premise: who depicts these places? Are places in traditional China truly the silent, motionless China we imagine? This question is worth pondering. At the very least, in traditional China, narrators of places consist of folk artists, clan leaders, gentry, and other local intellectuals. They used oral literature, genealogies, clan records, and privately compiled local chronicles to depict places. However, the highly centralized and grassroots-oriented political structure of contemporary China inevitably leads to the marginalization of such narrators. This marginalization directly results in the narrative of places being completed only by the "others" of those places.

Around 1985 was the "Great Discovery of Geography" in Chinese literature. Reading *New Fiction in 1985* by Wu Liang and Cheng Depai, one can feel the frenzy of geographical discoveries by writers during that time: *Bababa*, *Swing Frame*, *Xizang: The Secret Years*, *The Yellow Mud Hut*, *Heavenly Dog*, *Bombing Graves*, *Dog Head Gold*, *Five Women and a Rope*. If we include those not selected to avoid repetition with the selected works like *Bao Town* and *Transparent Radish*, more than half of the selected stories narrate "places."

Let us take a look at the composition of these authors. In this literary trend, known in literary history as "root-seeking," many of them have a background in "educated youth literature." Furthermore, most of these narrators of places were either returnees or educated youth sent to the countryside. Even if they were not, they entered these places as modern intellectuals. Therefore, it should not be a problem to say that the narrators of places around 1985 were a group of educated new youth born in the People's

Republic of China. What no one expected was that one day, these educated youth who ate, lived, and worked alongside farmers would become narrators of local stories.

Cao Naiqian wrote, "In the last year of the Cultural Revolution, I was sent to the remote Beiwenjiayao Village to lead a group of educated youth to the countryside ... I stayed there for a year. The feelings I had during that year were extremely strong. The profound experience and intense shock came primarily from their begging tunes that cut deep into the bone and heart. Twelve years later, I suddenly thought of writing about them, about that place, about my own *Wenjiayao Scenery*, and decided to use the lamentation 'I Can't Help Thinking about You at Night' sung by Er Ming as the emotional tone to govern my series of novels."[8]

Li Rui also stated, "Hadn't I lived in the remote and desolate mountain gullies of Lüliang Mountain for six years, hadn't I farmed with those unknown mountain people for six years, I would never have been able to write these novels."[9] The "educated youth sent to live and work in the mountains and countryside" meant various fates and experiences for each individual, but collectively, it was an unprecedented cultural relocation and transformation campaign in modern and contemporary China. Its objective result was that educated youth received reeducation from poor and lower-middle peasants, and in return, these "mountains" and "countryside" places were transformed by them.

In understanding the literature on seeking roots, some argue it is a form of "apolitical" resistance writing,[10] while others see it as a writing of escap-

---

8   Cao Naiqian, "Appendix: You Become a Fox and I a Wolf—Me and the Folk Songs of the Northern Frontier," *Can't Help Thinking of You at Night*, 238–239

9   Li Rui, "Thick Soil" in *The Reward of Life* (Beijing: Peoples Literature Publishing House, 2008), 215.

10 Li Qingxi, "Rethinking Root-Seeking Literature," *Shanghai Culture*, No. 5 (2009).

ism and withdrawal from the world.[11] In reality, it is the two sides of one coin. Escapism is its surface, but on the other side, it is a subtle form of resistance. The local narratives around 1985 clearly represent a deliberate shift in collective writing strategy. "The greatest achievement of seeking roots literature is its emphasis on national culture, not confined to political events or social issues, but bringing literature back to its literary significance."[12] Revisiting these works today, we indeed see a facade of museum-like folk culture. But is this truly "national culture" or a "return to literary significance"? We need to think about these questions. More importantly, this group of people narrating about places may not genuinely understand those places, nor do they intend to. They are transient in these places, perhaps even strangers and antagonists to these places themselves.

King of Chess, *King of Trees*, and *King of Children* by A Cheng can serve as samples for interpreting the local narratives' stance of these people. Even as they root their culture in the places, here, writing from the margins, non-mainstream, the "worship of knowledge," "worship of enlightenment," and "worship of modern civilization" remain the latent texts for observing and interpreting the margins. Therefore, in their view, the nobility of the so-called humble ones has its limits. Writers like Zhang Chengzhi, who declared to write "for the people," later could not avoid conforming to the norm of writers who sought refuge in the people at that time.

On the one hand, he acknowledges, "I once lived deep in the Mongolian grasslands, hat brim turned back, robe tattered, riding horse crookedly, bathing once a year." "No matter how shocking the wounds we once suffered, how disrupted our life's pace and order, how we still sigh over youth to this day; I still believe that we are a uniquely blessed generation, that we are pio-

---

11 Wang Xiaoming, "Disbelief and Unwillingness to Believe: On the Creations of Three Root-Seeking Writers," *Literary Review*, No. 4 (1998).

12 Jia Pingwa and Xie Youshun, *Dialogues between Jia Pingwa and Xie Youshun* (Suzhou: Suzhou University Press, 2003), 59.

neers." "In adversity, in labor, in remote villages and at the bottom of society, in the processes of reflection, enjoyment, comparison, and abandonment, in the revelations of historical shifts, we have also found true insights; found something that still moves us and warms ourselves." "I can never forget the many people, scattered across the vast northern land I love, perhaps diverse in language and race yet sharing the same fate." "And not only never do I regret, but I will forever adhere to the principle of 'for the people' that I have believed in since the first time I picked up a pen."[13]

On the other hand, when he began to structure his own novels, things became different.

> ... Perhaps it is because the habit of reading for several years has grad-
> ually cultivated another character of mine; perhaps it is precisely because,
> fundamentally, I am not a native-born herdsman; I noticed the differences
> between myself and this place. I could not tolerate the habits of the grass-
> lands that Grandma had grown accustomed to, nor its natural laws, despite
> my deep affection for it. In the darkness, I embraced Gangga Hala's neck,
> enduring terrible torment within. No matter how desperately I tried to stop
> myself, no matter how the river of past events overwhelmed the sparks of
> temptation, a fresh desire had already been born in pain. It summoned me
> and compelled me to pursue a life that is purer, more civilized, more re-
> spectful of humanity, and richer in career allure.
>
>   (*Black Steed*).

An undisclosed fact is that many of our critics have identified the anxieties these writers harbor between traditional and modern civilizations,
which might seem mundane to the local narrators of root-seeking literature.

---

13   Zhang Chengzhi, "Postscript," in *Old Bridge* (Beijing: Beijing October Literature and Art
Publishing House, 1984), 304–306.

They leave their places, yet in the cities where they live, they become surplus and superfluous. "After living in the city for a long time, that small mountain village hidden in the Taihang Mountains becomes increasingly unfamiliar and distant, while six years of life among the peasants, intertwined with their flesh and blood, has built a deep bond. Like in the old days, I rode my bicycle and climbed seventy *li* of mountain roads, returning to the small adobe where I lived for six years, where I met Uncle Yang."[14]

Earlier on, Jia Pingwa's "Shangzhou" series straightforwardly originated from a hurried rural field investigation. Thus, it is no wonder that in their perspective, places became showcases of "exoticism" in "strange tales from distant lands." For example, in *The First Chapter about Shangzhou*, he writes,

It went dark, and the host let the traveler sleep on the *kang* [bed with fire pits underneath] [...] But after the door was closed, the host took off his shoes and got on the *kang*, and so did his wife. It is just that the host slept in the middle, acting as a divider.

When the host went out,

He put a pole in the middle of the *kang* ... An hour later, the *kang* was so unbearably hot that the traveler had to toss and turn like a pancake being baked. As he was suffering, the host returned. Seeing the pole on the *kang* and the traveler, he brought a bowl of cold water for him to drink. If he drinks it, the host would feel relieved and offer wine, thus seeing him truly a learned person. If he doesn't, the host would believe that he must have done

---

14   Zheng Yi and Shi Shuqing, "Pastoral Songs of Taihang Mountain," *Shanghai Literature*, No. 4 (1989).

something wrong, thus give him a good beating, and chase him out of the door, without returning his luggage placed on the *kang.*

(*The First Chapter about Shangzhou · Heilongkou*)

These are place explorers, nostalgias, tourists, thrill-seekers, and, of course, the predominant group, root-seekers, each with their own axe to grind, their own territories to open, and their own battles yet collaborating and networking. Despite their differences in stance, perspectives, linguistic styles, and rhetoric, one thing is certain: they are all appropriators and hijackers of places. As Li Rui put it, "Actually, the 'literature' concocted by literati and the 'history,' 'eternity,' 'truth,' and 'ideal,' among other concepts created by literati are more or less the same thing and have little to do with farmers."[15] "Poor places also nurture good culture"[16] is almost their common narrative perspective. Here, "good culture" can certainly be replaced with "good morality," "wise people," and so on.

So, what exactly is "good culture" in their writing perspective? It is "the 'residue' abandoned by civilized society, such as ancient myths, and Xu Wenchang's stories. In ancient times, humans had no distinction between high and low, and literature was not divided into elegant and vulgar. It is chaotic, blending history, belief, education, natural observation, primitive ethics, and racial continuity. It is also a channel for emotional exchange, information dissemination, and knowledge transmission, expressed through songs and dramas."[17] It is "traditional culture condensed in rural areas, mostly belonging to the non-standard category. Colloquialisms, unofficial histories, legends, jokes, folk songs, supernatural stories, customs, sexual

---

15   Li Rui, *The Reward of Life.*

16   Han Shaogong and Wang Yao, *Dialogue between Han Shaogong and Wang Yao* (Suzhou: Suzhou University Press, 2003).

17   Li Hangyu, "On 'Seeking a Way Out': On the Problem of Seeking 'Roots,'" *Zhongshan*, No. 1 (1986).

practices, and so on, most of which are rare in classics and do not conform to norms."[18] It is "the 'non-traditional' cultures of various ethnic minorities outside the norms."[19]

Therefore, it is hardly surprising that some works of root-seeking literature have turned into a show, selling oddity and "three-day tours of folk customs."[20] From the outset, their local narratives have been inclined toward the mysterious and exotic, showcasing spectacles of wonders and freaks.

In the decades following the great discoveries of places in Chinese literature around 1985, today the local narrators have fully seized cultural resources and discursive power. "Root-seeking," along with neo-Confucianism, cultural conservatism, modernization, Chinese experiences, globalization, and other alliances, has been molded into a great cultural event of the 1980s. But I cannot help but ask: to what extent do these avant-garde cultural strategies, in becoming part of present "narratives of oddity," actually "narrate the places"? Works like *Bababa, Thick Soil, Wenjiayao Scenery, Amorous Everywhere, Strange Tales from a Foreign Land*, etc., treat places as cultural specimens sampled according to predefined criteria. They are used to measure and compare different cultures. Representative works in recent years, such as *Wolf Totem* and *Luokan Village*, similarly compare agrarian cultures to nomadic cultures, or Chinese culture to Western culture. Within the influence of root-seeking literature, it has become the past to treat literature as academic papers.

---

18   Han Shaogong, "The 'Roots' of Literature," *Writers*, No. 4 (1985).

19   Li Hangyu, "Sort Out Our 'Roots,'" *Writers*, No. 9 (1985).

20   Han Shaogong and Wang Yao, *Dialogues between Han Shaogong and Wang Yao*, 60.

─ The Local History Narrative of "Feigned History" ─

o Yan, Ma Yuan, and Su Tong's rise in the mid-to-late 1980s could have effectively corrected the scholarly "cultural fetishism" of root-seeking literature. To this day, their local narratives from the mid to late 1980s remain the most technically challenging and imaginative parts of Chinese literature. However, their local narratives, which rely on their unique talents, imagination, and creativity, are impossible to replicate. Their local narratives did not become a literary trend, either.

Due to the inspiration from the new realistic literature at the end of the 1980s, the 1990s saw a sudden increase in local historical narratives of "micro history" in Chinese literature. I refer to these novels as local history narratives of "feigned history." "Feigned history" refers to fiction posing as truth in history. In recent creative and critical practices discussing these novels, restoring historical truth and historical scenes have been important criteria. Leaving aside whether truthfulness is the natural criterion for literature, an evident fact is that these novels not only won Mao Dun Literature Prizes, such as *White Deer Plain*, *The Song of Everlasting Regret*, and *Qinqiang* but also scholarly evaluations of such works are rather positive and the ambition to be an epic novel is well-received.

The local narratives of "feigned history" carry out a tradition in contemporary literature. Li Tuo pointed out that *The Three Chapters of Shangzhou* by Jia Pingwa "seems to attempt to combine novels and history, but he is not writing historical novels; he imbues his novels about Shangzhou with the value of local history."[21] A decade later, apart from a few novels such as *Daily Conventions in Hometown*, the local narratives of "feigned history" in the 1990s were particularly interested in Chinese modern and early Republican history, the resistance war, land reform, and the Cultural Revolution. In the interpretation of new historicism criticism, these local narratives, taking the "subtext" of the Red Classics of the People's Republic of China, employ local experiential narratives imitating local chronicles to deconstruct the grand narrative of the state.

The narrative of history first involves the origin of history itself. The local narratives of "feigned history," which assumes fake history as true history and unofficial history as official history, certainly do not find a definite contemporary national historical origin like national narratives. Therefore, the local historical origin in local narratives of "feigned history" often becomes unofficial. Hence, we can observe a genealogical connection between this narrative of local historical origins and the root-seeking literature of the "narrative of oddity" in the 1980s. Take two representative works of root-seeking literature, *Bao Town* and *Bababa*, as examples:

> In the ancient annals of Bao Town, the forebears held lofty positions, entrusted by the Imperial Court to safeguard against floods. They labored tirelessly for 999 days alongside 9,999 workers to erect the Baojia Dam, an engineering marvel encompassing 99,999 *mu* of fertile land, providing respite for the populace. Yet, fate took an unforeseen turn one year when torrential rains persisted for 77 consecutive days. The deluge breached the stout dam, cascading like an overflowing basin, transforming it into a vast lake.

---

21 Li Tuo. "Cultural Consciousness and Aesthetic Consciousness in Chinese and Western Literature—Preface to 'Shangzhou Sanlu' by Jia Pingwa," *Shanghai Literature*, No. 1 (1986).

Three years later, the lakebed finally dried up. The ancestral steward of Bao Town faced demotion from his esteemed rank. Despite his earlier diligence, the Imperial Court, moved by his past efforts, spared him from the execution. Overwhelmed with remorse for his perceived failure to protect the people, he sought redemption with his family, resettling beneath the shadow of the Bao family dam. There, amid the lowest reaches, he endeavored to rebuild their lives. Thus began a resurgence, and from this humble beginning, Bao Town burgeoned into a thriving village, nurturing several hundred souls.

[...] Encircled snugly by gentle mountains, with Bao Mountain standing sentinel, it delineated the inner sanctum from the outer realms.

This saga evolved into a legendary tale passed down through generations, initially steeped in ancient lore and later embellished in posterity's retelling. Some narratives hailed the ancestor as a descendant of Yu the Great, attributing the Bao clan as heirs to Yu's legacy. Others said though of Yu's lineage, Bao's ancestor lacked his legendary spirit—Yu left his wife three days after marriage to manage the flood and did not return home despite passing it thrice, even after hearing the cry of his newborn son. Married and fathering three sons and one daughter during his dam-building, this ancestor bore the weight of karmic consequences.

These tales, blending history with folklore, now serve as both entertainment and a testament to the resilience and adaptability of Baotown's progenitors.

(Wang Anyi, *Baotown*)

Deep in the embrace of mist-laden mountains, the village resides, ensconced within ethereal clouds.

[...]

Drop by drop, a warm stream of urine disappeared into the white clouds. What happened under the cloud layers seemed unrelated to the villagers. Once designated Qianzhong Commandery in the Qin Dynasty and later Wuling Commandery in the Han Dynasty, and the bureaucratization of indigenous officials ... All these tales were told by the voices of traders who traversed the mountains, dealing in cowhides and opium. But whatever they said, one can only sustain oneself through farming.

[...]

The village's origins remain enigmatic, with claims placing it in both Shaanxi and Guangdong, though the definitive answer eludes grasp. Their dialect diverges sharply from that of Qianjiaping down the mountains. Here, "seon" is favored over "see," "specan" over "speak," "standan" over "stand," "slep" over "sleep," "neah" over "near," imbuing their speech with an ancient cadence.

Distinct customs mold their social fabric, blurring the lines between familial roles and fostering a sense of unity. Fathers are addressed as uncles, uncles as fathers, elder sisters as elder brothers, and sisters-in-law as elder sisters, upholding ancestral traditions. Though the term *"baba"* [father] trickled in from Qianjiaping, it remains uncommon. So, regarding the tradition, he should rightfully call the man from Bingzai's lineage who vanishes beyond the mountains "uncle."

(Han Shaogong, *Bababa*)

Let us take another look at *White Deer Plain* and *Clumsy Flower*. For instance, *White Deer Plain* writes,

During the Song Dynasty, a provincial official from Henan was reassigned to Guanzhong. Crossing the majestic Qinling Mountains astride his mule, he arrived at Zishui County, where he switched to a sedan chair. Along the route, he paused by the Zishui River, entranced by the fluttering willow catkins and the verdant wheat sprouts carpeting the slopes. Suddenly, a snow-white deer leaped into view, vanishing swiftly amid the lush greenery. Startled yet captivated, the official commanded his sedan bearers to stop, alighted, and gazed intently, but the elusive deer had already vanished without a trace.

Filled with curiosity, he inquired anxiously of the sedan bearer about the name of the nearby plain. "White Deer Plain," came the swift reply. Nodding with understanding, the official resumed his journey by sedan chair.

Half a month later, he returned, decisively purchasing the land where he had witnessed the ethereal white deer. There, he erected a home and courtyard, resettling his family and even designating his own burial ground.

Similarly, in *Clumsy Flower*,

The inhabitants of Clumsy Flower Village cherish their history with a flair for dramatic storytelling, emphasizing their distinctiveness on the rugged Loess Plateau. They delight in recounting their origins in lofty, exaggerated terms, often referring to ancient times simply as "the old days." According to their narratives, in the old days, their roots trace back not to Clumsy Flower, but to Hongtong County in Shanxi. In a more vivid tone, it was under the expansive canopy of a venerable locust tree in Laoguawo Village, Hongtong County. Their life flourished in harmony. However, the narrative took a twist when, for reasons obscured by time, an imperial decree commanded their assembly under this sacred tree. From there, they were subsequently relocated to distant lands, notably Wozhou or Pingji. ... Despite historical accounts offering a structured account of this ancient migration, the people of Clumsy Flower Village uphold their folklore with unwavering conviction. They interpret these intricate details through their own lenses, perpetuating a legacy that blends historical fact with the enduring power of myth and belief.

Not only in the narrative of historical origins but also in recounting local experiences, these novels share a similar non-official, local perspective akin to root-seeking literature. Let us compare *Bababa* and *Clumsy Flower*.

During weddings, funerals, and festive gatherings in our village, a deeply rooted tradition unfolds where all voices unite in the solemn chant of "*jian*," honoring our past ancestors by singing. The ritual begins with fathers, then grandfathers and great-grandfathers, stretching back through the generations until we reach Jiang Liang, our revered forebear. Beyond Jiangliang lie the name of Fufang, but he was later than Huoniu who is later than Younai. As Younai was also born by his parents, who bore Younai's father? According to legend, that honor belongs to Xingtian—perhaps the figure celebrated for his "indomitable spirit" in Tao Qian's poetry. When Xingtian entered this world, the sky bore the hue of white clay and the earth the color of dense black mud, so tightly compressed that not even a mouse could slip through. With a sweeping arc of his mighty axe, he rent the sky from the earth. Yet, in his fervor, he accidentally decapitated himself. Thus, he used his nipples for eyes and his navel for a mouth. His laughter thundered across the land, reverberating with each colossal swing of his axe. For three years, he tirelessly hammered upward, lifting the heavens, and for another three years, he pounded downward, settling the earth beneath.

(Han Shaogong, *Bababa*)

In Clumsy Flower Village, the steadfast belief endures that Thunder God, the deity who hurls hailstones from the heavens, is aided by Huo Jijiao. While Thunder God resides in the celestial realm, Huo Jijiao inhabits the earthly domain. Only when summoned by Thunder God does Huo Jijiao ascend to fulfill his duties in the heavens, after which he returns to live a humble life on earth, much like any ordinary person. Huo Jijiao is regarded akin to a devoted attendant of Thunder God, faithfully carrying out his celestial responsibilities.

(Tie Ning, *Clumsy Flower*)

However, in contrast to the deliberate emphasis on the boundaries between nation and locality, normative and non-normative in root-seeking novels, the narrative of "feigned history" pays more attention to places within the national territory. Places are not foreign lands; they become places with localities. As mentioned earlier, the integration and grassroots transformation of contemporary national politics inevitably alter traditional forms of locality's existence. By examining the national and local timelines in novels such as *Manchukuo, Clumsy Flower, White Deer Plain, Saint Tianmenkou, Big Breasts and Wide Hips*, and *Empty Mountain*, we can observe this entanglement of nation and locality.

In *Clumsy Flower*, we can see instances of national timelines like "AD 1895, the twenty-first year of Guangxu," "AD 1902, the twenty-eighth year of Guangxu," "1911, autumn of the third year of Xuantong," "August 16, 1945 ..." Xiang Wencheng and Gan Ziming establish a new-style national elementary school in Clumsy Flower Village, "what is taking place in the village synchronizes with the new cultural movement of science and democracy." Yet, while the daily life in Clumsy Flower Village conforms to the rhythm of the times, it also maintains its local time at its own pace. "Thereafter, the people of Clumsy Flower Village collectively refer to events before the Japanese entered Zhaozhou as 'before the incident,' and those after as 'after the incident.'" "Before the incident, Swedish missionary Shan Muren spread Christianity to the village and opened a Sunday school there." "It was a dusk when the moon rose first. After the incident, the people of Clumsy Flower no longer noticed such a fine moon," "The twilight of Clumsy Flower Village changed." "The disappearance of Wanderer in the dusk seemed like the end of an era. Before the incident, it seemed like the beginning of an era." In *Empty Mountain* by A Lai, there exist similar dual timelines and histories: on one side, "Enbo became a monk in his youth, following his uncle Jiangcun Gongbu, a lama in Wanxiang Temple, and in the new calendar year 1950, they were forcibly secularized by the government"; on the other side, "the year Gela and her son returned to Ji Village was one of the most famous years in Ji Village's history. In the oral history of Ji Village, this year was called the "highway year." Some storytellers also referred to it as the 'car year.'" The partial overlap of "nation" and "locality" in "feigned history" narratives make it legitimate for local narratives to overthrow national narratives.

Here, we can see these novels carrying forward elements similar to *Red Sorghum* by Mo Yan from the 1980s—the state conquers and transforms localities, yet localities demonstrate strong capabilities for dissolution and self-sustenance. It is precisely because of this that the local narratives of "feigned history" becomes possible. For example, in *Clumsy Flower*, there is a performance of the rural performance of "Exodus with Moses," "Moses, scarcely taller than the tables and chairs that dotted the stage [to resemble mountains and hills], had cotton clinging to his mouth and chin. Leaning heavily on a millet straw stick, he was adorned in a regal purple robe that left his two arms exposed."

How does the "modern" enter and transform the "locality?" In *Clumsy Flower*, items such as vanishing cream, German medicine, Polar Bear bicycles, Gospel churches, baptisms, Western suits and ties, towels imprinted with "Good Morning" in red calligraphic style English letters, Japanese newspapers, night schools, Mao Zedong's *On New Democracy*, and rear-end hospitals are examples of "modern" elements entering "local" China. Among many "modern" interventions, the entry of "Christianity" and "modern revolution" into the "locality" becomes a common theme in the local narratives of "feigned history."

For instance, in *Saint Tianmenkou*, "Many years ago, three azure-eyed French missionaries arrived at Tianmenkou, funding the creation of a soaring steeple house they dubbed a church, earnestly making it their home. Despite years of unwavering evangelism by these azure-eyed French missionaries, they remained unable to sway the natives of Tianmenkou to embrace their beliefs or step foot inside their sanctuary." Later revolutionaries, however, were able to recognize that "the people of Tianmenkou, caught between the contradictions of the Xue and Hang families, urgently needed proper guidance." Fu Langxi and Dong Zhongli's revolutionary practices were built upon the discovery and understanding of local experiences.

Though similar to the religious practices of the French missionaries, the revolutionary ideas were also imported, they were perceived differently in Tianmenkou, just as Hang Jiufeng said: "It's not me but my body dying to rebel!"

In recent years, there has been considerable academic attention to the distinctions between macro and micro history. Similarly, both as late-modernizing countries, the study of Indian scholars is enlightening for us: "For genuine Indian historical compilation, nationalism alone is inadequate because it obstructs our dialogue with the past. It dictates to us with the imperious tone of the nation, unilaterally determining which events are of historical significance, thus preventing us from freely considering our relationship with the past. However, it is such choices that a proper historical narrative requires. In this regard, making choices means striving to establish connections with the past by listening to countless voices of civil society and converse with them. These are the subtle voices submerged in the clamor of nationalist imperatives."[22]

Returning to the Chinese context, when we contemplate what kind of history that local narratives of "feigned history" construct, we are examining it from a historiographical perspective: whether it is a history where the nation, literati, and written language overlap, or one of folk "oral history." The construction of local narratives of "feigned history" is more complex than we might imagine. They do not intentionally disregard the nation "unilateral determining which events are of historical significance." In their historical perspective, "the voice of the nation" and "the voice of the common people" are intertwined. In contemporary China, "the history where the nation, literati, and written language overlap" and "folk oral history," as well as traditions at micro and macro levels, often coexist and integrate

---

22   Ranajit Guha. "History at the Limit," in *Research on the Common People* selected and translated by Liu Jianzhi, Xu Zhaolin, et al., (Beijing: Central Compilation and Translation Press, 2005), 340.

with each other. Similar to local narratives of "feigned history," they never outright reject "the nation"; nor can they. The local narratives of "feigned history" are a polyphonic history of "the voice of the nation" and "the voice of the common people," of written and oral traditions, of shouts and whispers. Objectively, there exist political differences and confrontations in local narratives of "feigned history" vis-à-vis the grand national narratives. This is most evident in the novels like *White Deer Plain, Saint Tianmenkou, Big Breasts and Wide Hips,* which redraw the picture of China's modern revolution with different political forces. Notably, the deliberate attempt to "set straight the chaos" overly emphasizes the intentionality in these novels, often depicting positive characters in a negative light and negative characters positively, intentionally blurring the political stance, class, and connections between human nature. Once this writing experience becomes generalized, from the perspective of character portrayal in novels, it may lead to new conceptualizations and idealizations.

From the perspective of a new historical outlook, the literary narratives local history of "feigned history" holds significant constructive meaning. "Most of our existing history textbooks are incomplete. It means that this kind of historiography is essentially imperial history, political history, and document-based history, and lacks ecological history, social history, and cultural history. In other words, we have only upper-class history without lower-class history, especially a thorough understanding and comprehensive grasp of the living conditions of the majority of people in their interaction with nature and society."[23] The local narratives of "feigned history" commonly discover and affirm the significance of local daily ecology, life, and culture. In *Clumsy Flower,* villagers pinch flower buds, trim branches, pick flowers, and men admire flowers while women sneak into sheds. On winter nights, girls on the warm *kang* of the Plum Pavilion talk about every-

---

23   Han Shaogong and Wang Yao. *Dialogues between Han Shaogong and Wang Yao,* 190.

thing, "What attracted them most is the characters and stories in the Bible. They match characters from the Bible with people from Clumsy Flower Village." *Manchukuo* portrays the "humble and ordinary daily lives of the common people." About *A Dictionary of Maqiao*, Han Shaogong writes, "Before I began writing this book, I ambitiously attempted to write biographies for everything in Maqiao ... like focusing on a stone, emphasizing a star, studying a mundane rainy day, scrutinizing a seemingly insignificant silhouette that I neither knew nor would ever know. At the very least, I should write about a tree. In my imagination, Maqiao should not be without a big tree. I must let one tree, no, two trees, grow tall on my manuscript, standing on the back slope of the Luo family in Maqiao Village. I imagine them towering over seven or eight *zhang* tall, with the smaller one reaching five or six *zhang*. Anyone who comes to Maqiao should see their crowns from afar, expanding their field of vision."[24]

Intentionally obscuring the historical origin, emphasizing the local experiences, and focusing on daily life, the pathways of local narratives in "feigned history" have already become familiar to us. Novels, based on fiction and imagination, convincingly present themselves as historical truths. Unofficial writings are becoming official history. The question arises: is the literary task merely to provide a local history different from official national history? We must be wary that local narratives of "feigned history" are becoming a form of literary politics in opposition.

Certainly, literature does not necessarily have to "depoliticize" or "deculturize" itself to achieve autonomy, nor must it necessarily divorce itself from history. However, if literature stops at the making of history and merely exchanges literary writing for distinguishing between truth and falsehood, as historical narrative perspectives diversify, literature becomes tolerated

---

24   Han Shaogong, "Maple Ghost," in *A Dictionary of Maqiao*, (Beijing: Writers Publishing House, 1996), 68–69.

by political ideologies, the lack of focus on the transformations of human mentality, spirit, and consciousness amid the changes of time will lead to the question that, regardless of the scale of history, whether literature is the most adept way of narrating history is worth debating. From a quest for truth perspective, local narratives of "feigned truth" can only be an intelligentsia's imagination of the local others. Even in narratives like *Records of Women's Idle Talk* by Lin Bai, the truth of the locality becomes suspicious when Lin Bai organizes and arranges Mu Zhen's narrative. In *A Dictionary of Maqiao*, a "personal dictionary," Han Shaogong profoundly recognizes this ideological choice and selection process: "Editing and publishing a dictionary for the village is an experiment for me. If we acknowledge that understanding humanity always begins with specific individuals or specific groups, and if we understand that any specific life will always have specific language expressions, then perhaps such a dictionary means something."

"This is a summary of non-public or counter-public language."[25] "But who can be sure that those fleeting images quietly omitted in compromise will not accumulate into language manipulation events that can erupt at any time in the depths of consciousness?"[26] Furthermore, even if historical truth is obtained, "the relationship of novels with the world is not just a geographical novel world, but a novel world in terms of literary spirit, author's literary perspective, and worldview."[27] Therefore, for such novels, setting their significance solely on the distinction between historical truth and falsehood clearly contradicts literary knowledge. Moreover, writing about insignificant histories, ecological history, life history, cultural history, grassroots history, and everyday life of the common people does not necessarily

---

25   Han Shaogong, "Editor's Preface," in *A Dictionary of Maqiao*, 1.

26   Han Shaogong, "Afterword," in *A Dictionary of Maqiao*, 400.

27   Yan Lianke, "The Relationship between Novels and the World—Lecture at Shanghai University," *Shanghai Literature*, No. 8 (2004).

guarantee the path to literature. We must recognize that how a place is narrated and how it is narrated in literature are two entirely different issues. Therefore, we must revisit these novels to determine to what extent they achieve the literary qualities of local narratives.

— How Is Place Depicted in Literature? —

C ritic Wang Yao, in conversation with Mo Yan, discussed, "The regional and spatial dimensions in literature should transcend geographical meanings."[28] Therefore, Mo Yan's depiction of place presents a proposition "beyond homeland," as he said, "[I] created 'Gaomi Northeast Township' to enter a humanistic geographical environment closely linked to his childhood experiences, one without walls or even national boundaries. I once said, if 'Gaomi Northeast Township' is a literary kingdom, then as its founding monarch, I should continuously expand its territory. ... Homeland, in the literary sense, is the geography of literature. For instance, the 'Gaomi Northeast Township' I wrote about in *Red Sorghum* had some stories with prototypes. By *Big Breasts and Wide Hips*, it broke through the so-called reality, even on technical matters, such as descriptions of vegetation, animals, sand dunes, reeds—all of these things fundamentally do not exist in the real Gaomi Township. When the Japanese translator of *Big Breasts and Wide Hips* went to Gaomi, he drew a detailed map, searched for sand dunes, searched for swamps, but found nothing, only a plain, a desolate village. I think, if a writer can assimilate others' lives and incorporate the lives from all corners of the earth into their 'hometown,' they can write forever."[29]

Literature's depiction of place not only needs to transcend "geographical meanings." From Wang Zengqi's rediscovery of the significance of local

28 Mo Yan and Wang Yao, *Record of A Conversation between Mo Yan and Wang Yao*, (Suzhou: Suzhou University Press, 2003), 202.

29 Ibid.

narratives to the local narratives in the style of "narrative of oddity" around 1985, to the local narratives of "feigned history" around the turn of the century, the gains and losses of literature's depiction of place have shown us that in the past three decades, Chinese literature and place have been not only politically manipulated but also more insidiously infiltrated and appropriated by political culture and history. In the current era of globalization, "Chinese experiences" have become prominent once again, and we can foresee a new round of appropriation and encroachment of places in the "enclosure movement."

Objectively, over the past three decades, local narratives in Chinese literature have contributed numerous new experiences in terms of concepts, structures, rhetoric, and linguistic styles, such as the imaginations of places of Mo Yan, Su Tong, and Yan Lianke; the encyclopedic cultural histories of places constructed by Han Shaogong, Jia Pingwa, Bi Feiyu, A Lai, and Chi Zijian; the revelations on the mutual shaping of people and places by Wang Anyi; the stylistic explorations by Mo Yan, Su Tong, Liu Zhenyun, Han Shaogong, Lin Bai, and Liu Xinglong; and the linguistic practices of Mo Yan, Cao Naiqian, Li Rui, Han Shaogong, Yan Lianke, Liu Zhenyun, and Liu Xinglong.

However, it must be critically noted that over the past three decades, local narratives in literature have been frequently hijacked and appropriated by cultural, political, and historical forces. This pervasive trend has constrained contemporary Chinese literature, even in transcending the geographic sense. Instances like Mo Yan's Gaomi Northeast Township still remain relatively few. To run a tally, the number of meaningful "geographical labels" are only the few created by writers such as Su Tong, A Lai, Han Shaogong, Wang Anyi, Jia Pingwa, Liu Zhenyun, Yan Lianke, Chi Zijian, Li Rui, Bi Feiyu, and Liu Xinglong—including "Xiangchun Street and Fengyangshu Village," "Ji Village," "Maqiao," "Shanghai Alley," "Shangzhou," "Yanjing," "Balou Mountains," "Beiji Village," "Lüliang Mountains," "Wangjiazhuang," and "Tianmenkou."

In 1956, William Faulkner, in response to *The Paris Review*, said, "Beginning with *Sartoris* I discovered that my own little postage stamp of native soil was worth writing about ... It opened up a gold mine of other people, so I created a cosmos of my own."[30] Here, Faulkner reveals the relationship between place and people. Over the past three decades, local narratives in Chinese literature seem to have provided us with few diverse characters from places. Instead, when places are hijacked and appropriated by politics, culture, and history, the diverse characters are also stereotyped, conceptualized, symbolized, and masked. Ecological history, life history, cultural history, and history of the lower classes are all present, but history is seen without people, and people are seen without literary archetypes.

Reading local narratives in Chinese literature over the past three decades, we can see that our writers are largely indifferent to the diverse characters of places. Moreover, from the perspective of local narratives in Chinese literature over the past three decades, the writing of Chinese writers often does not stem from literary creativity and imagination, but rather from a direct confrontation with meanings of "repression and resistance" in politics, culture, history, and so on. Local narratives in literature are certainly linked to geography, culture, politics, history, and so on, but literature must also narrate fictional and imaginary places beyond geography, culture, politics, and history. It is about "demanding stories from oneself" as well as "demanding fiction and imagination."[31]

To a certain extent, the limitations of local narratives in Chinese literature are also the limitations of Chinese literature as a whole. It at least exposes the current non-self-sufficiency and lack of imagination in Chinese literature. Literature must rely on the opposition of politics, history, and cul-

---

30 *The Paris Review: Interviews with Writers*, Vol. 5, (Beijing: Peoples Literature Publishing House, 2020), 33.

31 Su Tong, "About or Not About Writing," *Yangtze Jiang Literary Review*, No. 3 (2009).

ture to define its boundaries and to activate its creativity. This reminds us of Gabriel García Márquez's Macondo: "Rather than being a specific place in the world, Macondo is more of a state of mind."[32]

So, how should literature narrate a place? Our writers should first honestly return to the place to "observe it, listen to it, and understand it," rather than allowing concepts and themes to take the lead. Su Tong compares the literary narrative of place to painting a postage stamp. "Spending so much time painting a stamp not only requires one's patience and confidence but also burdens and tests others." However, "the stamp-painting-style writing career is actually dangerous; that Faulkner succeeded does not mean every stamp-painting writer will necessarily achieve the same result."[33] Also, patience and confidence alone are not enough. As García Márquez put it, "Everyday life in Latin America reveals that reality brims with extraordinary wonders."[34] Whether one can capture the miracles of everyday life is clearly a test of a writer's ability to fictionalize and imagine.

Literary narrative of place points to real places but more so to imagined places. "A novel is a coded rendition of reality; it speculates on the world. The reality within a novel diverges from real life, even though it is grounded in it. It is akin to a dream."[35] Living in the new circumstances of the globalization era, places keep changing, so our literature is no longer narrating places in the same context as Faulkner or García Márquez. How should contemporary literature narrate a place? Whether the literary experiences of Faulkner and García Márquez are still applicable has become a question, especially when we are so years apart from Faulkner and García Márquez.

---

32 Gabriel García Márquez, "The Fragrance of Guava," in *The Theory of Iceberg: Dialogues and Sub-dialogues*, ed. Cui Daoyi, Zhu Wei, Wang Qingfeng, Wang Yongjun (Beijing: Workers' Publishing House), 198, 718.

33 Su Tong, "About or Not about Writing," *Yangtze Jiang Literary Review*, No. 3 (2009).

34 Gabriel García Márquez, *The Fragrance of Guava*, 711.

35 Ibid.

Two Essays on "Just Online Literature"

— Just Online Literature —

Initially, I contemplated titling this article: "If Online Literature Is Literature, Why Isn't *Stories*?"[1] My assessment does not originate from the apex of today's online celebrity writers—these prominent figures actually represent a small fraction compared to the immense output and capability of contemporary online literature. Furthermore, even if these writers, constituting a minority, have already been "canonized" as we envision, whom should we benchmark them against and the texts of online literature to evaluate their level of classicism and aesthetic worth? In reality, our assessments hinge on the internet's inherent selection mechanism.

---

1   *Stories* is a Chinese magzine focusing on publishing folktales and other kinds of popular stories.—Trans.

Of course, we cannot use impressions based on reading feelings or insufficient field investigations as the basis for evaluation; doing so would misjudge today's online literature. We cannot simply juxtapose texts to engage in high-level discussions about their merits and demerits, just as we cannot compare a traditional writer with an online celebrity writer, nor can we compare an online celebrity writer with a storyteller from *Stories*. However, what can be compared is how online literature's narrative techniques fundamentally tell an engaging "story." In this regard, apart from being able to tell longer stories, online literature has not made much progress compared to *Stories*; it is just that what used to be called "suspense" is now termed "pleasure points" in online literature.

Furthermore, perhaps more importantly, in a certain sense, the grassroots spirit emphasized by online literature is most akin to *Stories*. Since restoring its title in 1979, *Stories* has explicitly raised issues of the "writing for the people" of stories. This idea of "writing for the people" is also the foundational argument for many online writers who emphasize their moral superiority in writing. Almost in every discussion about online literature, online writers stand on the moral high ground of writing for the people, easily transforming criticism against them into the question of "Are you against writing for the people?" Well, under the almost unanimous premise today that "writing for the people is literature," I wonder if we can comprehensively solve issues left by history such as *Stories, Longmen Zhen, Ancient and Modern Legends*, and even *Zhiyin*? As we establish the identity of online literature, we also clarify the tradition of *Stories* in contemporary writing lineage. In my understanding, most of today's online literature should be in line with the tradition of *Stories*.

If you believe returning to the tradition of *Stories* diminishes online literature, then let us elevate it as everyone suggests. We can tentatively agree that we can categorize online literature as "online literature" or "genre fiction" for discussion. The next question, then, is how to identify online literature within a literary lineage. A widely accepted viewpoint is that online literature originates from the suppressed popular literature system of modern Chinese literature. If this viewpoint stands, Chinese online literature from the turn of the century onward should be traced back to the revival of mainland China's original popular literature driven by popular literature systems in Hong Kong and Taiwan since the 1980s; the discovery and recognition of modern popular literature; and extending further back to the "*shuobu*" (说部, ancient novels and notes) tradition in classical literature. The internet has activated and opened the literary potential of this traditional lineage.

Following this line of thought, a schematic of the integration and separation of highbrow and lowbrow literature is often used to explain online literature in contemporary Chinese literary studies. However, revisiting the beginning of modern Chinese literature, we find that what we now view as "sophisticated" literature did not necessarily exclude "popular" literature. Chen Duxiu proposed in his *Literary Revolution Theory* the "Three Principles," with the first advocating for "overturning the flattery of aristocratic literature and establishing straightforward lyrical national literature." Zhou Zuoren, on the other hand, argued that "popular literature should emphasize what is contrary to aristocratic literature, namely, content that is rich and sincere." (Zhou Zuoren, "Popular Literature") Their opposition was directed at the "bad taste of modern era" criticized by Mao Dun in "Are There Any Works That Represent Old Culture and Old Art?."

As of today, what online literature continues to be criticized for is still the "bad taste of modern era." This "bad taste of modern era" that disregards the enlightened achievements of the May Fourth Movement in today's online space is unprecedented in modern Chinese history. Observing the facts of modern Chinese literature, it is not just the narrated literary history; "popular" literature has not always been "suppressed." At times, "popular" literature has been appropriated by politics and capital, becoming the most prominent part of literary epochs, such as the popularization of literature in the 1930s and 1940s, and the New Heroic Legends of the Seventeen-Year Literature Movement.

Another point worth noting is that whether it is the Chinese *shuobu* tradition (which, if passed down today, has almost without exception been transformed by literati) or modern Chinese popular literature, both are essentially forms of literati writing. This raises the question: can the literary abilities of present online writers in China fully connect with the *shuobu* or popular literature lineage of literati writing?

The factual history of literature differs from its imagined and narrated history. Narration is an exercise of power. As a significant literary phenomenon over the past two decades, online literature is practical. It has challenged the singular paradigm of elite literary imagination and narrative, repaired, and expanded the broader literary ecology. With the accumulation of practical achievements, online literature is inevitably becoming the narrator of its own history.

Today, the entire literary perspective, the mode of literary production, literary institutions, and literary structures have diverged significantly from the canonization and the way literary history was constructed, which were established after the May Fourth Movement and centered around writers, professional critics, and editors. The revolutionary changes that came with the new media, as some researchers have pointed out, "have not only changed the ways of media production and consumption but also helped break down barriers to entering the media market. The internet has opened new spaces for public discussion of media content, and the Web has become an important display window for grassroots culture."[2]

The grassroots culture characteristics of online literature mean that the cultural enlightenment conveyed through literature is no longer dictated by a patronizing elite at the cultural forefront but rather emerges as a negotiated dialogue within a shared cultural space. An intriguing topic arises: now

---

2   Henry Jenkins, "Quentin Tarantino's *Star Wars*? Grassroots Creativity Meet the Media Industry," in *Convergence Culture: Where Old and New Media Collide*, 131–168, (New York: New York University Press), 2006.

that online literature has gained the power of self-narration, is it willing to be portrayed as a lower tier "popular" literature within traditional literary hierarchies? Is it willing to be described as a retaliation resulting from the suppression of modern Chinese popular literature? Or even, is it willing to set its own literary prospects as a "Chinese-type literature" that has developed within the global literary landscape?

In other words, in contemporary China, any description based on existing literary conventions cannot satisfy the ambition of online literature to establish its own naming rights, especially after the integration of online literature with capital.

I once pointed out that when online literature is narrowly understood as fiction on internet platforms, and "literature" is replaced with "IP" (intellectual properties), the consensus between traditional literature and online literature under the label of online literature has increasingly lost its connection to literature. If domestic internet platforms and celebrity writers did not fear literary power both within and outside the system, would they still hypocritically discuss "literature" at such conferences? The divide between traditional literature and "online literature" is no longer just a difference in literary concepts but a rupture between literature and non-literature. Traditional literature fears the grassroots capital power of internet platforms and celebrity writers, hoping they will act charitably, relinquish power, and foster some literary ideals and public spirit. But can the internet literature community really live up to these hopes?

The problem here is that online literature has entered an era dominated and defined by capital oligarchs. At some point, the pioneering and rebellious nature of online literature suddenly ceased to be emphasized. The "literature" of online literature has suddenly been defined as "online literature" akin to popular genre novels, while platforms like One, Douban Reading, Guoren Novels, which allow small-scale but free writing, are not considered literary platforms. It seems that online "literary behavior" is only associated with internet platforms controlled by big capital. In this era of online literature, literature has actually lost much of its relevance.

I think if traditional literature and "online literature" still seek literary consensus, it should not just be a one-sided endorsement of "online literature" by a few critics to argue its "literariness." Since we are discussing literature, not just IP, the capital-controlled internet platforms and celebrity writers should also convince us that everything they do is "literature," even if it is their own definition of literature. We can perhaps step back and admit that online writings are "online literature" akin to genre or popular novels. In that case, traditional literature should abandon using traditional literary theory and criticism to interpret online literature and fantasy that classic literature we imagine that may emerge online. It is crucial to reaffirm that online wrting is a different form of writing, a literary product consumed by the general public in contemporary China, adhering to the production, dissemination, and reading rules of "online literature." The "literariness" of online literature is not self-sufficient; extracting just "online literature" does not encompass all of online writings.

Online literature is just online literature, not what we typically discuss as "literature." We should respect the historical facts of Chinese online literary development and the entire media ecology it encompasses. If we focus solely on media changes, online literature corresponds to print media literature. In the context of the national planned economy, literature was taken as something that could be planned and organized. Under this national planned literature system, writers may have had some freedom in their writing, but literary journals and other publications were monopolized by quasi-governmental institutions like the Literary Federation, Writers Association, Publishing Houses, etc. These institutions appointed literary editors to manage extensive "literary plans" on behalf of the state, producing "required literature."

By the late twentieth century, traditional literary journals (including newspaper supplements) had almost vanished as the sole literary media.

However, we cannot conclude that traditional literary journals have completely exited the literary scene. Whether we acknowledge it or not, today's literary media landscape is still largely controlled by the national planned literature system through print media, while online literature, although regulated by industry authorities, is primarily under the control of capital. There are writers who traverse between print and online media, but this was more common in the early days of online literature, much like the explorations of literary innovation in online literature's early years. In fact, before the advent of the "IP era" in online literature, those writers who gained readership online still aspired to receive recognition from traditional literary journals. This recognition was crucial for their works to be canonized or acknowledged within the existing literary establishment. This helps explain why A Yi considered being published in *People's Literature* a significant milestone in his writing career, despite his novels already having garnered excellent reader reviews online.

Broadly speaking, if we pinpoint the birth of online literature to Pizi Cai's publication of *The First Intimate Contact* in 1998, Chinese online literature has gone through at least three phases to date. The first phase is essentially the migration of traditional literary natives to the Internet. During this phase, online literature actually represents a "reaction" against the rigid literary tastes of the print media. If print media literature opens to a certain degree, this part does not necessarily have to be realized on the internet. At the turn of the century, during the nascent period of online literature, the first writers to embrace the internet were attracted by its freedom of expression. At least until 2004, the online literary ecosystem was still in a "wild growth" period: poets were writing avant-garde poetry online, novelists were experimenting with various types of novels, and capitalists had not yet found a profitable model for quick and sustainable monetization. With platforms like Qidian introducing fee-based reading (which matured into a tipping system) and the strong entry of capital from companies like Shengda, online literature entered the stage of "genre literature." This era saw the rise of many prominent figures. Online literature unleashes the enormous potential of Chinese genre literature. Gradually, it began to diverge from print media literature, though certain literary perspectives could still respond to the literary realities unfolding online. Then came the third stage: the advent of the "IP era" in online literature. Writers of online literature no longer needed final literary validation through traditional print media. Online literature and its derivatives relied on metrics like clicks, ratings, followers, income, box office, etc., establishing a reader-centric aesthetic and evaluation mechanism that was self-sufficient. Such mechanisms are deeply rooted in the so-called grassroots. Online literature, considering China's current literary and artistic system, may participate in current literary dialogues, but this interaction fundamentally does not impact the ecology of online literature. Instead, it compromises and yields to gain larger capital and profit margins.

In such a literary ecosystem, we actually face a choice: either relinquish literary authority and expand the literary boundaries to accommodate online literature—returning to my initial point, since online literature is literature, why isn't *Stories*? But literature without boundaries is no literature at all; or simply sever ties with online literature and allow it to grow freely outside the realm of traditional literature. This severance does not mean rejection; migrants from online literature can freely enter the domain of traditional literature. Thus, online literature remains online literature, *Stories* remains stories, and "literature" remains "literature." We do not need our "literature" to absorb the sparse literary fragments of online literature or go to great lengths to prove that online literature fits our definition of "literature." Online literature can also choose not to bear the burden of literature but simply fill the reading time of non-literary needs in the name of "literature." As I say this, perhaps negatively, the responsibility of literary enlightenment has been abandoned, but this is the reality of online literature in China today. At least for now, online literature is just online literature, and the people need it.

— On "Just Online Literature" Again —

Last year, during a class at the Lu Xun Literature Institute for online writers, I raised a question: how does online literature differ from literary traditions before the advent of online platforms? Is it simply an extension of print media literature? Can all the problems surrounding online literature be answered and resolved using traditional literary conventions and criteria? In other words, is online literature new literature or old literature? Looking back now, given the industrialization push from online literature practitioners and various government departments, these questions are too narrow.

If we merely understand online literature as a shift from writing and publishing on paper to writing and disseminating online, we clearly fail to grasp the revolutionary changes that the "Net" has brought to literature. This transformation not only changes the medium of publication and dissemination but represents a type of literary creation that could only occur in the online environment, fundamentally different from previous forms of writing.

If we analyze the texts of online literature within the framework of traditional literature, we can roughly categorize them based on "aesthetic decline": novels (with "literary youth literature" exhibiting most literary qualities), long stories, "entertaining fiction," and scripts for film, online games, animation, and other productions. It is basic literary knowledge that novels and stories differ; when measured against the standards of "modern novels," these categories represent only a small portion of authors and works. As for the latter three categories, unless we expand the boundaries of literature, traditional literary studies generally do not consider them as literature.

However, they dominate today's online literature and are precisely where capital accumulation is most active, largely driving the heat surrounding online literature. Without expanding the boundaries of literature, these three categories amount to little more than a generalized form of online writing.

Online literature is not just a literary problem; but far more than a textual problem.

Before the advent of the internet, the medium of literary publication and dissemination had already undergone several changes, from oracle bones and tortoise shells to bamboo slips, silk, and paper. However, the literary environment, thinking, and various relational modes of literature remained relatively stable. It is the unprecedented internet environment, internet thinking, and relational modes that have formed the "communicative" field for the production and dissemination of online literature. The interaction between writers and readers, who both "attend" and "participate" should be considered the defining feature of online literature.

As a literary activity based on communicative fields, online literature cannot be the solitary contemplative literature of old. Its distinctiveness lies in its various fan culture attributes, ranging from lower-level immediacy such as instant reading, likes, comments, and tips, to fully developed forums, online communities, and offline activities with their own mobilization mechanisms. These attributes constitute new "writer-reader" relationship modes. This new relationship mode breaks through the relatively closed production and consumption of traditional literature. "Writing on the internet" unfolds within these relationship modes, naturally leading to the development of "communicative" internet thinking, writing habits, stylistic rhetoric, and language. In essence, online literature is a part of contemporary Chinese popular culture, especially youth culture. Therefore, explaining online literature should be seen as encompassing "culture" that is larger than "text" or "literature."

As a manifestation of popular culture, online literature still retains some traditional literary characteristics. While traditional literary interpretation methods can address issues like evaluating online novels, this does not mean online literature can simply assimilate into traditional literature. Using traditional close reading and canonical approaches can affirm the literary status of a few online celebrity writers. However, this tiny recognition contrasts sharply with the vast output of online literature, raising doubts about its significance. This is because a fundamental fact is that making comprehensive aesthetic judgments about the literature of an era through accumulated aesthetic experiences via close reading relies on obtaining sufficient and representative samples. Not to mention that literary production capacity and output were maintained at relatively low levels in classical times, even in modern times with the possibility of large-scale literary production, strict aesthetic admission systems and selection mechanisms still ensure that aesthetic judgments are made concerning the "entirety" of literature.

However, for online literature, relying on individual critics and literary researchers, it is nearly impossible to achieve comprehensive close reading of texts. Therefore, today, when we discuss online literature, we need to consider to what extent our judgments are facing the "entirety" thereof. Besides strongly individualistic aesthetic styles in online novels, considering the genre specificity and standardization of stories, "fun reads," scripts for movies, online games, animations, and similar products, can we imagine using statistics and advancing data processing technologies to cover a large sample or even the entirety of online literature?

It can be argued that contemporary research on Chinese online literature largely adheres to the established paradigms of traditional humanities. However, the unique nature of online literature demands the active involvement and support of disciplines such as cultural industries, popular culture psychology, statistics, communication studies, field investigations, and data technology.

Regarding online literature itself, on the surface, discussions often revolve around an era of celebrity writers, suggesting that these figures could serve as the pinnacle when evaluating literary merit. Yet, the question is, how many studies convincingly demonstrate how these celebrity writers challenge literary norms, expand the literary landscape, and explore new possibilities? What exactly does their prominence signify in the broader context? Frequently, assessments of celebrity writers are juxtaposed against the sheer volume of crude and unremarkable textual output in online literature—a case of "the tallest dwarf," nothing more.

However, if we consider the activating potential of online literature on animations, online games, films, and other industries related to literature, the conclusion may not be so. Simply put, online literature is fundamentally an economic activity, somewhat akin to what we often refer to today as "cultural and creative" endeavors. If there is a distinction, it may lie in scale: from small-scale workshops to large industries. Due to the combined influence of capital and policies, online literature focuses on the industrial illusion of arts and culture. To answer how literature can avoid merely endorsing industry, research on the significance of online literature in contemporary literature should focus on capturing the fragmented literary elements dispersed within economic activities. These elements not only serve as the driving force of industries but also activate the potential for literary creation itself.

Indeed, confined to the language-centric "literariness," online literature cannot be equated with the accumulated human literature of the past. However, the literariness of online literature may manifest through the proliferation and dissemination of texts structured around language. Therefore, when I say, "online literature is just online literature," it is not to diminish its value; rather, it seeks to shift away from a "text worship" that solely values literary texts structured around language. It emphasizes the "literary periphery" derived from online literary texts, fully respecting the fundamental attributes of online literature.

Looking at the history of online literature spanning over two decades, we must realize that similar to modern literature, online literature did not start out as the broad spectrum of online writing it is today. Its aesthetic value could sustain itself within the text itself—focusing on the text rather than its derivatives. Speaking of this, we can now address the question at the beginning: contemporary online literature boasts a rich "periphery," distinguishing itself from the "new literature" or "modern literature" traditions that began in the late nineteenth century, just as these traditions distinguished themselves from earlier "classical literature." Before the advent of the internet and online literature, new literature or modern literature had already established aesthetic norms, evaluation mechanisms, modes of production, and dissemination, legitimized itself through associated literary institutions, and continued its literary tradition through refinement. For a century now, modern literature has seen twists and turns, yet these twists and turns have not altered the fundamental fact that "modern literature is modern literature." Even before the internet, modern literature dominated, and during the nascent stage of online literature, it emerged as a variant of this "modern literature."

Initially, online literature did not foresee its current outcome; it rewrote its historical logic only after the emergence of tipping mechanisms and profit models. At least before 2004, online literature thinking mirrored modern literature thinking. What was then considered "online literature" was essentially a repair and transformation of the modern literary tradition, as seen in works like *The First Intimate Contact* and *Wukong*. Similarly, the profit model of online literature was primarily based on the offline publication of physical books. Almost simultaneously and subsequently, with the advent of the "IP era," influential online works began expanding from physical books to online games, mobile games, films, and animations. Consequently, the "literariness" of online literature also shifted and expanded. For extreme examples, *Jade Dynasty* and *Piaomiao Zhi Lü* were essentially modern literature in 2003. However, as their games were successively developed, their more complex derived literary aspects became prominent. If *Jade Dynasty* and *Piaomiao Zhi Lü* did not initially show this, by the time they progressed to the stage of scriptwriting for films, online games, and animations, the literary nature of their story scripts often thrived through parasitic prolif-eration. Modern literature, online novels, stories, and "fun reads," may also have derivatives, but their relationship with derivatives is not as deeply in-tertwined and symbiotic as the integrated and cohesive complex found in online literature's story scripts. The literary significance of the text itself can still sustain independently.

It is worth noting that even with the maturity of profit models in online literature, literary-youth-oriented writings and online novels by authors like Cangyue, Maoni, Xu Gongzi Shengzhi, Xiaoqi Xiao, Fenghuo Xi Zhuhou, and Jiutu maintain deep ties to modern literature, and their classicism can be recognized within the lineage of modern literary traditions. On the other hand, shallow texts by Tangjia Sanshao, Wo Chi Xihongshi, Tiancan Tudou, Meng Ru Shenji, and Chendong as well as stories with background of online games by authors like Hudielan, Kulou Jingling, and Wuzui, require read-ership as a crucial parameter to discuss their classicism, or must consider the combined aspects of "online gaming" and "stories." The concept of "com-posite" texts is crucial to understanding the uniqueness of online literature. Therefore, the new classics of online literature should not only emerge from online novels but also encompass long narratives, "fun reads" and scripts for films, online games, animations, among other productions, each with its own classicism. They should not be indiscriminately mixed under the aes-thetic standards of modern literature.

Furthermore, it should be recognized that the widespread availability of the internet inevitably results in the lowering of the literary entry barriers that modern literature finds difficult to maintain, leading to the possibility of "universal writing" and a more segmented readership. In the era of "uni-versal writing," deviating from existing literary conventions and creating "new literature" is just one aspect of writing motivation. However, within the vast sea of online literature, the results of such literary creation and the creation of literature itself are easily overshadowed. Moreover, as profitability becomes feasible, the literary aspirations of writing become increasingly diluted and less significant. "Literature" is only remembered and valued when there is potential for more capital support and a fanbase of readers. Essentially, literature in any era is the result of various forces grappling with each other. While I do not deny that modern literature is also the result of combined effects such as aesthetic logic, political logic, capital logic, and reader logic, the transition from modern literature to online literature shows that aesthetic logic is evidently no longer an absolute controlling force. Instead of solely focusing on the small portion of online novels that closely resemble modern literature, we should acknowledge that the largest share of online literature revolves around creating stories, "fun reads," scripts for films, online games, animations, among other productions centered on capital and ordinary readers. To assert "online literature is online literature" captures this reality to a significant extent. Shifting from modern literature centered around authors, texts, and professional readers to online literature centered around capital and the general readership is crucial when discussing the uniqueness and evaluation systems of online literature—it respects the manifestation of online literature's reality.

Over the past twenty years of online literature, from "online literature is modern literature" to "online literature is online literature," capital has been a significant driving force. Capital's transformation of online literature distinguishes it from modern literature, with the most notable change being the shifting status of readers. Modern literature revolves around an "oligopoly" of authors, editors, and professional readers, whereas online literature's essence lies in how ordinary readers shape its entire landscape. In the realm of communication, readers are potentially treated more equally. Capital's intervention dictates that it must heed the voices of ordinary readers rather than ignore them, with statistical and big data technologies ensuring that even the opinions of unknown individuals accumulate into significant outcomes. Therefore, in online literature, writing that disregard reader interests is almost unsustainable. This naturally leads to authors depending on capital, accommodating and complying with readers, and the one-sided prosperity of stories, "fun reads," and scripts for films, online games, animations, among other productions that match current reader interests.

Another related question is whether online literature continues the tradition of modern popular literature. My answer is negative. Those familiar with the history of modern literature should understand that if there truly exists a distinction between "high" and "low" literature, they both belong to the broader category of modern literature. There is no such thing as popular literature without the notion of elite and sophisticated literature, and vice versa. Today, just because online literature writers proclaim their grassroots and populist nature, and online critics observe it as such, does not automatically mean that online literature is a retaliatory rebound of suppressed popular literary energy.

I approach this notion with skepticism. The grassroots and populist nature of online literature does not inherently oppose an imagined elite and sophisticated literary enemy. Online literature is simply online literature in its entirety; it does not concern itself with what elite and sophisticated literature is, even within its creative aspects. Fantasy literature is an important trend in today's world literature. The "fantasy" aspect of online literature not only fills the gap in the modern literary tradition's "fantasy curriculum" but also reflects current literary trends, capital trends, and reader demands. Therefore, the study of online literature should not only look backward but also focus on its current nature, even if these attributes are dominated by capital and reader logic—they might still represent something "new." Examining fantasy-themed online novels through this lens, whether integrating resources from domestic and foreign fantasy literature or constructing imaginative worlds, reveals the influence of capital and ordinary readers. The contributions of fantasy-themed online literature to creating local fantasy novel genres and establishing complex epic novel structures are noteworthy. These aspects of online literature should inspire contemporary Chinese writing within the modern literary lineage, yet they are often overlooked by writers and their works in the tradition of modern literature.

The vibrant capability of creating and consuming diverse genres in online literature in China is unparalleled in literary history. Similar to modern popular literature, a celebrity writer in online literature pioneers specific genres. Yet, what sets online literature apart is not just the creation of personal styles but also the swift replication and dissemination catalyzed by capital, leading to ongoing aesthetic dilution and consumption of individual styles. Thus, studying online literature encompasses not only exploring aesthetic proliferation but also understanding aesthetic erosion, which, in a way, defines online literature. Given this, can future online literature rebuild its relationship with capital and readers? While I acknowledge the current "IP era" of online literature often conforms to capital and reader demands, I anticipate it will continue evolving along the path of "online literature is online literature," moving toward a phase of "recreating online literature."

"Recreating online literature" signifies a shift from an era dominated by capital and readers to an era where "celebrity writers" reign. Here, celebrity writers not only hold economic "voice" but also embody literary ideals through interactions with readers. They serve as exemplars of literary trends, styles, and principles, opening new avenues for the modern literary tradition.

It is crucial to emphasize that my assertion, "online literature is online literature," does not imply its ultimate replacement of modern literature. Just as classical literature persisted subtly during the era of modern literature, there will always be space and reasons for modern literature to coexist alongside online literature. Looking ahead, beyond online literature, there will certainly be challengers to its existence, much like how modern literature could not foresee online literature. However, as long as human writing practices endure, such challenges will inevitably emerge.

The Thoughts, Actions, and Writings of Youth

I t is inevitable to scrutinize modern Chinese literature through the lens of novels. In May 1918, Lu Xun, at the age of 37, published *Diary of a Madman* in Volume 4, Issue 5 of *New Youth*. By today's standards, Lu Xun, born in the 1880s, epitomizes a quintessential young writer. In 1923, at the age of 42, Lu Xun released his story collection *Call to Arms*. Three years later, at 45, he published *Wandering*. Even today, he remains a figure of youthful vigor in literature. Prior to *Diary of a Madman*, he had endured a decade-long hiatus. Setting aside this period, Lu Xun, making his literary debut in his twilight youth, bestowed upon modern Chinese literature the collections *Call to Arms* and *Wandering*. For writers today, continuing to be called youthful after 45 might be stretching it, wouldn't you agree? Thus, around age 40 emerges as a pivotal historic moment for writers to create their most significant works.

Writers today aged 45 were born in 1975. Considering 1978 as the dawn of the reform and opening up era, those born in 1975 were merely three years old. Hence, it is reasonable to classify writers under 45 today as part of the generation born during the reform and opening up era. This generation of young writers encompasses the well-known figures born in the 1970s, 1980s, and 1990s. If we measure them against Lu Xun's *Diary of a Madman, Call to Arms*, and *Wandering*, what sort of novels have they penned at comparable ages? Indeed, when using Lu Xun as a benchmark, I am prepared for dissent: how many Lu Xuns exist in the annals of modern Chinese literature? Without delving into Lu Xun's examples, let us instead cast a glance back at the forebears or fathers of today's young writers—the writers born in the 1950s and 1960s. What were they penning around age 40 or even earlier? Recently, I penned an essay for *Wenhui Daily*, meticulously detailing their writing, publishing endeavors, and contributions. Here is a partial directory:

(Note: Names are followed by birth year, and works are followed by the author's age at the time of the work's first release)

Zhang Chengzhi (1948)	*Black Steed* (33), *Rivers of the North* (36), *Golden Pastures* (39).
Lu Yao (1949)	*Life* (33), *Ordinary World*, Volume 1 (37), *Ordinary World*, Volume 2, Volume 3 (39).
A Cheng (1949)	*King of Chess* (35), *King of Trees, King of Children, Amorous Everywhere* (36).
Li Rui (1951)	*Thick Soil* (36).
Shi Tiesheng (1951)	*My Distant Qingping Bay* (32), *Life as a Zither String* (34), *Stories from the Countryside* (35), *Notes on Principles* (45).
Jia Pingwa (1952)	Shangzhou series (32), *Turbulence* (34), *Ruined City* (41).
Wang Xiaobo (1952)	*The Golden Age* (40).

Can Xue (1953)	*Cabin on the Mountain* (32), *Yellow Mud Street* (34), *Old Floating Cloud* (36).
Han Shaogong (1953)	*Bababa, Gui Qu Lai* (32), *Womanwomanwoman* (33), *A Dictionary of Maqiao* (43).
Ma Yuan (1953)	*Goddess of the Lhasa River* (31), *The Temptation of the Kailas Mountains* (32), *Fiction* (33).
Wang Anyi (1954)	*Bao Town* (31), *Love on the Barren Mountain, Love in a Small Town* (32), *Love in the Brocade Valley* (33), *Uncle's Stories, The Song of Everlasting Regret* (41).
Mo Yan (1955)	*Transparent Red Radish* (30), *Red Sorghum* (31), *Big Breasts and Wide Hips* (40).
Zhang Wei (1956)	*The Ancient Ship* (30), *September's Fable* (36).
Tie Ning (1957)	*Rose Gate* (32), *Big Bathing Woman* (43).
Ye Zhaoyan (1957)	Night Mooring on the Qinhuai series (29–30).
Wang Shuo (1958)	*The Troubleshooters* (29), *Wild Beast* (33), *Having the Time of Life* (34).
Yan Lianke (1958)	*Years, Months, Dates* (39), *The Passage of Time* (40).
Liu Zhenyun (1958)	*Ground Covered with Chicken Feathers* (33), *Hometown, Regime, and Blood* (33), *Daily Conventions in Hometown* (34), *Material and Spirit in Hometown* (40).
Lin Bai (1958)	*A War of One's Own* (40).
A Lai (1959)	*Red Poppies* (39).
Sun Ganlu (1959)	*Visit to the World of Dreams* (27), *The Messenger's Letters, Inviting Women for Riddles* (29), *I am a Young Drunk* (30).
Yu Hua (1960)	*1986* (27), *One Kind of Reality* (28), *Cries in the Drizzle* (31), *To Live* (33), *Chronicle of a Blood Merchant* (35), *Brothers* (45).
Han Dong (1961)	*Banished!* (43).
Chen Ran (1962)	*Private Life* (34).
Hong Ying (1962)	*Daughter of the River* (35).
Su Tong (1964)	*Escape in 1934* (24), *Wives and Concubines* (26), *Rice* (28), *My Emperor Life* (29), *The Embankment* (45).

Ge Fei (1964)	*Flock of Brown Birds, Qinghuang* (24), *Enemy* (26), *Peach Blossom Paradise* (40).
Chi Zijian (1964)	*Manchukuo* (36), *All Nights in the World, The Last Quarter of the Moon* (41).
Bi Feiyu (1964)	*Feed Me* (32), *Qingyi* (36), *Corn, Three Sisters* (37), *Yuyang* (38), *Plain* (41).
Bei Cun (1965)	*The Baptismal River* (28), *The Love Story of Mazhuo* (29).
Li Er (1966)	*Coloratura* (35), *A Cherry on a Pomegranate Tree* (38).
Dong Xi (1966)	*A Resounding Slap in the Face* (31), *Record of Regret* (39).
Ai Wei (1966)	*Cross-Country Race* (34).
...	

I have not undertaken a rigorous statistical analysis like this on the publishing and reception of writers born in the 1970s, 1980s, and 1990s. Should anyone be willing, they could undertake such an assessment based on the criteria above. Some may argue that the canonization of works from the 1950s and 1960s was established within the framework of the old literary system centered around journals—a product of collaboration among literary oligarchs including writers, editors, critics, university professors, and influenced by political ideologies. The recognition of literary classics in history necessitates time for consensus to form. Looking forward, perhaps in a decade, literary history could compile a catalog that includes today's young writers born in the 1970s, 1980s, and 1990s. How about that?

First, it is important to acknowledge that our literary criticism and research have not fully embraced their responsibility to canonize today's young writers compared to their predecessors. This contention makes sense to some extent. During the formative years of this generation of writers, contemporary young critics were not sufficiently present to serve as discoverers, advocates, and protectors of contemporary young writers.

Second, it is crucial to recognize that young writers from different generations find themselves within distinct literary epochs (the twentieth century being considered a golden age of literature prompts my skepticism, though this is not the focus here). The earliest appearances of today's young writers can be traced back to the mid-to-late 1990s. Factors such as the commercialization of literature, the revolution in media, the release of energy from the popularization of literary consumption, the diversification of literary life, and the demotion of aesthetics that comes with the redefinition of literature have collectively contributed to serious literature under discussion here from outshining others.

Third, one must consider that older generations of writers have monopolized a significant portion of literary resources due to their accumulated literary prestige, as evidenced by journal indices and recent literary awards and rankings. It is the literary world was previously criticized for pandering to young writers. However, considering the monopolistic control of literary resources, such pandering toward young writers, especially those at the outset of their careers, seems more akin to charitable support. In contrast, the practice of flattering older and established writers appears to be a normalized convention. Taking journals as an example, while traditional youth literary magazines like *Mengya*, *Young Writers*, *Youth Literature*, *West Lake*, and *Youth* have dedicated sections and columns for new literary voices, established literary journals such as *October*, *People's Literature*, *Harvest*, *Flower City*, *Zhongshan*, *Shanghai Literature*, *Lotus*, *Works*, and *Mountain Flowers* also feature these. However, compared to the space allocated to renowned writers, the effort to foster new talent can be seen as a conventional adherence to aesthetic correctness.

Regarding considerations on various variables, the hope is to solidify this final point: the writing of the young writers today is an ongoing and unfinished reality. At least in terms of physiological age, it seems there is promising potential.

Speaking of literary institutions, the tradition established since the May Fourth New Literature to nurture and promote young writers has never been interrupted. Of course, specific to any era, there are different aims and methods for nurturing and promoting young writers. Let us start with before 1949. What was the concept before 1949? Looking at the birth years of these individuals—Xia Yan in 1900, Shen Congwen and Hu Feng in 1902, Ba Jin and Ding Ling in 1904, Zhou Yang in 1908, and Jin Yi in 1909—their writings before 1949 are all considered youthful writing, not to mention writers younger than them. Even writers born in the late nineteenth century belonged to youth literature in the 1920s and 1930s. Incidentally, nearly all famous writers before 1949 stopped writing in their youth. Therefore, almost everyone before 1949 was a young writer, focused on journals and publications, discovering literary amateurs who were younger, newer, and less familiar, that is, nurturing and introducing young writers.

In contrast, the People's Republic of China established a comprehensive system of literary successors cultivation, aligned with political imaginations for national literature. This system is reflected not only in publication and distribution but permeates every minor aspect of literary production. For quite some time, nearly all emerging young writers have been integrated into the literary successors cultivation system. In recent years in Jiangsu, besides national talent policies, local initiatives such as Jiangsu New Literature Vanguard, Youth Literary Talent Development Program and Mentorship Program by Renowned Authors are also in place.

In terms of literary journals, starting in the 1980s, some began to cultivate their own literary visions and micro traditions, exemplified by publications like *Harvest, People's Literature, Beijing Literature* and *Shanghai Literature*, which were notably open to avant-garde youth literature at the time. However, this landscape underwent revolutionary changes after the late 1990s. On the one hand, traditional literary journals faced decline due to reduced government funding and dwindling readership (recently, there has been increased government investment in literary journals such as *Harvest, Shanghai Literature, Beijing Literature, Flower City, Yuhua, Yangtze Poetry*, and *Works*, significantly boosting operational funds and author compensation). On the other hand, each publication's unique mini traditions expanded their respective boundaries.

Moreover, the advent of new online spaces provided novel avenues for literary production and author development. If we view online writing not merely as online literature, particularly notable is the generation of writers from the 1970s to the 1990s, many of whom, especially those born after 1985, had significant prior experience in online writing before gaining recognition through traditional journals. Platforms like One and Douban have undeniably become breeding grounds for emerging literary talents. These various online new media not only continuously supply fresh literary talents to traditional journals but have also independently established literary spaces with distinct aesthetic differences from traditional platforms.

From the perspective of traditional publishing, while journal issues remain a state-controlled resource, book publishing offers greater freedom. Notably, publishers such as Republic, Hinabook, and Wenjing predominantly focus on original works by young writers, serving as pivotal forces in nurturing their growth. For instance, among the recently released and upcoming books, there is the Documentary Pavilion series edited by Luo Dani, featuring *My Ninety-Nine Deaths* (Yuan Ling), *Going Home* (Sun Zhonglun), *Loved Ones on Earth* (Huang Deng), *Northern Boulevard* and *Died in Yesterday's World* (Li Jingrui), *Pilot* and *Hunter* (Shuang Xuetao), *Something Out of Nothing* (Liu Tianzhao), *Winter Swimming* and *Wandering* (Ban Yu), *Submarine at Night* (Chen Chuncheng), *Land of Freedom and Love* (Yun Yetui), etc.; and also the Youth Arts and Literature Pavilion series edited by Li Hengjia and Zhang Shiyang, featuring *Jiama* (Mo Yin), *Outing* (Qiao Mai), *Zhaoqiao Village* (Gu Xiang), and *An Asteroid Falls in the Afternoon* (Shen Dacheng), etc.

It is noticeable that among them, it is the first literature book published for writers like Sun Zhonglun, Ban Yu, Chen Chuncheng, and Huang Deng

Meanwhile, Hinabook has seen a strong surge in mainland Chinese original literature by young authors, alongside contributions from Hong Kong and Taiwan, including several titles in the Shuobu series, such as *Flanders Mirror* by Dome, *Goose* by Zhang Xiu, *Typhoon Day* by Lu Yinyin, *Deep River* by Dong Lai, *Ancestor's Love*, and *Bowling Alley Stream of Consciousness* by Lu Yuan, *Idle Theorizing* by Li Yao, *The Tiger and the City That Never Sleeps* by Chen Zhiwei, *Gaps of Migration* by Dong Jie, *Night Notes on a Mist Island* by Bu Liu, *Imitation Life* by Chen Sian, *Hidden Songbird* by Bu You, and *New Millennium Fantasy* by Wang Moshu.

Wenjing, on the other hand, has published works such as *Willing to Tremble* by Guo Shuang, *Please Don't Leave the Car Accident Scene* by Ye Yang, *Childhood Beast* by Lu Yuan, *Fulfillment* by Dan Bao, and *Fat Man at Peace* by Wen Zhen. Additionally, Chuchen Culture's publication of Zhou Kai's debut novel *Moss* in 2019 has sparked significant attention.

These publishing entities range from departments within established publishing houses to independent studios and book companies, maintaining loose cooperative relationships with traditional publishers. For instance, Hinabook has established numerous collaborations with the Sichuan People's Publishing House. Notably, while some do not operate as separate entities, they have internal sections devoted to original literature by young authors, such as the Young Writer Originals series at Shanghai Literature and Art Publishing House, overseen by Lin Weike, which has released titles like *When All Things Stop Growing* by Zhao Zhiming, *The Ferocious Rabbit* by Zhang Dun, *Eighteen Ways for the Melancholy Youth of a Small Town to Die* by Wei Sixiao, *The Song of the Golden Chain Man* by Cao Kou, *Heartbreak Stories from Zhumadian* by Zheng Zaihuan, *Awkward Era* by Man San, *People Who See Cetus* by Tangfei, *Firing Random Shots into the Sky* by Li Liuyang, *Stars of Water Margin Shine* by Li Li, *The Beggar Family* by Chuizi, *Jealousy* by Zhang Lingling, etc.

Equally noteworthy are the new literary publications of the new century, such as *Dandu, NEWRITING*, the revamped *Fictional World*, and discontinued journals like *ZUI Found, Dafang*, and *Chutzpah!*. These publications differ from traditional literary journals. Additionally, there are publishing brands like Fuben Production, Lianbang Zouma, Hei Lan, Pulsasir, and Paul's Pocket, which facilitate exchanges among literary enthusiasts, particularly the latter, who retain a rich exploration and provocative young writing spirit. However, economically speaking, these brands facilitating exchanges among peers are far less resilient than any established publishing house or magazine, and indeed face challenging circumstances.

Why do we patiently analyze the literary system of the past two decades, particularly the publishing system and its relationship with the growth of young writers? It is because the contemporary literary system, once comprised of universities, literary organizations, critics, and journals, was not conducive to young writers' provocative or creative writing. Overemphasis on literary tradition often evolved into literary dogma, making it difficult to encourage young writers to produce particularly bold or provocative works. Yet, if not confined to literary domains centered around traditional journals, the expanding literary spaces have actually provided young writers with far greater possibilities than their predecessors. However, in reality, the expansion of literary boundaries has not significantly increased the potential for youth literature.

Take my experience overseeing Flower City Interest of *Flower City* as an example. The envisioned potential of literary works by authors did not materialize as expected. I discussed this sentiment with novelist Zhu Yue, who handles literary publications at Hinabook, and he shares a similar view. Furthermore, it is concerning that with the recent inventory unloading, whether publishing institutions outside traditional literary realms can consistently find the authors they seek remains a question.

At the 2019 Shanghai-Nanjing Dual Cities Literary Workshop (the Third Session) convened by Jin Li and me, critic Huang Dehai vehemently questioned our literary maturation system, suggesting that it makes it too easy for young authors' immature works to be published. He believes,

Can we introduce a concept alongside youth writing called "mature writing?" Let us evaluate works based on their maturity rather than the age of the author. The constant encouragement of the youth has posed a problem: contrived and affected styles often come into view because they are different. In contrast, mature writing deliberately addresses this issue. Over the years, we have excessively encouraged uniqueness in young writers, making publication too accessible for them. Consequently, their writing faces no obstacles, lacks progression, and fails to engage in deep reflection; instead, it conforms to magazine requirements, following a prescribed formula. This inadvertently contributes to a homogenization process that we vehemently oppose. While we consistently decry homogenization and assert the diversity of young writers, our methods of encouragement often paradoxically push them toward conformity under the guise of seeking innovation and change.

(Adapted from the meeting script without speaker's review.)

So, what about those so-called mature young writers? Just glance at the numerous figures in literature and mainstream media today, upheld as exemplary by the literary establishment. Their works are unanimously praised by a comprehensive array of literary institutions for embodying a mature and stylistic approach, reminiscent of earlier declarations likening someone to China's Kafka, China's García Márquez, or China's Carver, reflecting a consistent literary mindset.

On my desk lies a copy of *Zhongshan* magazine's curated publication *Literature: My Advocacy*. Since 2014, *Zhongshan* has annually hosted gatherings for young writers, each session featuring dialogues and debates. The culmination of these exchanges is encapsulated in this anthology *Literature: My Advocacy*. Apart from a select few born in the 1970s who did not articulate their advocacy, nearly all influential writers in contemporary Chinese literature born in the 1980s and 1990s are represented here. Yet, reading through these advocacies, one 'cannot help but feel a sense of discontent. While these advocacies are undoubtedly personal, discussing literature, literary readings, mentorship, techniques, and aesthetic ideals, they lack the fresh perspectives and vitality that one would expect from younger writers, when compared those born in the 1950s and 1960s. There is a noticeable absence of avant-garde spirit. It seems that only a handful, such as Fu Yuehui and Wen Zhen, touch upon their contemporaries and the shared experiences, knowledge, and especially the spiritual void between "me" and "my peers." Many of these numerous fragmented "me" consciously or unconsciously detach themselves from historical and contemporary relevance, becoming isolated individuals in their own time.

Even from a narrow literary and aesthetic standpoint, they seem to lack self-awareness and fail to awaken to and reflect upon the connections between "me" and "us" as part of a "community of shared destiny in literature." Let alone consider the broader connections between "me" and "our" larger community of shared destiny beyond literature. Thus, literature continues to proliferate like a viral contagion across networks and mobile platforms, akin to writing.

Furthermore, it is crucial to acknowledge that the challenges in youth literature extend beyond merely literary concerns—they are inherently tied to broader youth issues. I previously cited two recent artistic projects by Jiang Fangzhou as examples, proposing the concept of literary expansionism. This approach aims to use literature as a catalyst to ignite young people's awareness and intellectual capabilities in questioning and expressing contemporary Chinese issues. Within the expansive realms of big literature and big art, the collaboration and dialogue among youth ultimately push the boundaries of thought.

In the two projects Jiang Fangzhou took part in, *A Perfect Result* touches the Republican-era industrial sites, factory life, urban memories, and familial experiences, that are also the literary resources of her contemporaries such as Sun Pin, Shuang Xuetao, Ban Yu, Qi Jinnian, and earlier authors like

Lu Min. Their novels—*Dinner for Six, Shark in the Center of the Water, Moses on the Plains, Wandering,* and *Lifelong Joy*—reflect various degrees of entanglement with memories of the Republic's industrial past. *A Perfect Result* marks just the beginning of reconstructing and weaving the fabric of these historical industrial memories. It moves forward along the path envisioned by Jiang Fangzhou, aiming not only to be a novel for general readers but also a medium for architectural designs, stage settings, graphic arts, multimedia productions, and photography. In this collective endeavor to forge memories, literature assumes a role as a guiding force, a wellspring of inspiration, and the soul of the narrative.

Reflecting on history, a pivotal aspect of the emergence of May Fourth Movement of New Literature was its role in providing a platform for young intellectuals to become new writers. The tradition initiated by May Fourth New Literature, focusing on the entity of "new youth" and "new writers," still struggles with limited inheritance among the older generations of young writers today. When comparing the youthful state of today's young writers to their predecessors, it becomes evident that they have benefited from superior university education, including robust literary training, within a more globally interconnected context. Despite these advantages, young writers have not naturally assumed the mantle of leading youth thought and action in our time.

It is closely followed platforms such as 706 Youth Space, Dinghai Bridge, Pulsasir, and publications like *Dandu*, observing the thoughts and actions of these young communities. These platforms provide a microcosm of the disparity between today's young writers and their predecessors, let alone the wider youth community. Many young writers today neither actively pursue independent thinking nor translate their ideas into actionable efforts. In the extreme, their literary pursuits often serve as receptacles for abundant information, piecing together fragments into novels that paint a landscape both eccentric and superficially barren in our contemporary milieu.

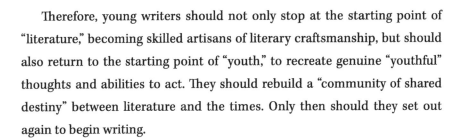

Therefore, young writers should not only stop at the starting point of "literature," becoming skilled artisans of literary craftsmanship, but should also return to the starting point of "youth," to recreate genuine "youthful" thoughts and abilities to act. They should rebuild a "community of shared destiny" between literature and the times. Only then should they set out again to begin writing.

Whispering, and the Possibility of Literature

At the sixth review meeting of the Yu Dafu Novel Award, Professor Wang Yao proposed the necessity for another revolution in novels, suggesting that a new "novel revolution" is quietly underway. It has been too long since literature last talked about revolution. Professor Wang Yao's remarks naturally sparked interest in the literary community and mass media. Fu Xiaoping of *Literature Press* invited nearly twenty writers and critics for a talk, while *Jiangnan* magazine initiated more extensive discussions, and Professor Zhang Li was organizing related activities.

I second Professor Wang Yao's assertion of a "new revolution," as well as his assessment that it is happening quietly. Over the past five years, I have hosted the Flower City Interest column in *Flower City* magazine.

Tasked with expanding literary boundaries and exploring the possibilities of aesthetics, it is impossible not to yearn for the "literary revolution" that might happen. However, when benchmarked against the paradigm of the literary revolution in modern Chinese literature of the past century, I believe we are in an era of "literary non-revolution"—an era where "literary non-revolution" signifies the impossibility of a revolutionary rupture similar to the early days of modern Chinese literature. "Non-revolution" is present and even future literature's norm.

First, the "literary revolution" in modern China, whether during the May Fourth Movement or the reform and opening up era, was a fusion of the New Culture Movement and intellectual enlightenment, a natural outcome of mutual support. The logic during these periods, as articulated by *On the Construction of Literary Revolution* by Hu Shi, *On Literary Revolution* by Chen Duxiu, and *Ideological Revolution* by Zhou Zuoren, is quite clear. Zhou Zuoren concluded that "in literary revolution, reforming language is the first step, but the second step of reforming thought is even more crucial. We must not be overly optimistic about linguistic reforms and neglect this major challenge." Thus, in the 1980s at the onset of reform and opening up, the literary revolution similarly evolved through mutual stimulation with intellectual liberation and cultural enlightenment. Therefore, to address whether a literary revolution is possible today, one must consider whether we can continue the deepening of intellectual liberation and cultural enlightenment within the historical lineage of the May Fourth Movement and reform and opening up.

Literature does not have an isolated fate; even other art forms related to literature face the issue of mutual support and stimulation. We can adopt many indicators to measure the so-called avant-garde literary revolution era of the 1980s. When I speak of the avant-garde upheaval, it is not just the era of avant-garde literature, nor merely the era of avant-garde novels. Avant-garde art, from the "Star Art Exhibition" to the "85 New Wave to the China," then to the "Avant-Garde Contemporary Art" in 1989, represents the most powerful and fruitful aspects of avant-garde art in China during the 1980s. Similarly, avant-garde music and drama may have had a global influence far surpassing contemporary avant-garde literature.

Furthermore, although figures like Liang Qichao began using "revolution" in a modern sense, from earlier Chinese linguistic origins and modern practices, revolution has always been intense, disruptive, and transformative. In this regard, modern literary revolution is no exception; the mindset of struggle and violent means have always been infused into literary revolution. Even present literary revolution aims for the most peaceful meaning of discarding the old and embracing the new, it still raises two questions: who can lead this literary revolution? Whose fate does literary revolution change?

Regarding the first question, Lu Xun wrote in *Literature & Art and Revolution*: "First there must be armies before there can be revolution. Everywhere revolution has already occurred, it was the army that arrived first: these are the pioneers." "Before the revolutionary armies arose in foreign lands, there was Jean-Jacques Rousseau who was forced to leave his country and Vladimir Korolenko exiled to the farthest borders ..." So today, who in Chinese literature can be our Rousseau or Korolenko of literary revolution? If we delve deeper, our belief in literary revolution to some extent presupposes modern time and the theory of literary evolution. In modern time, human civilization exists with hierarchies and differentials. In the spectrum of traditional/modern, backward/advanced civilizations, we have experienced major shocks, as well as considerable psychological anxieties. Regardless of smaller literary revolutions, two major literary revolutions have occurred in the era of transitioning from repression to openness, both during the May Fourth period and the beginning of the reform opening up.

Young people are on the evolutionary chain, new, future-oriented, progressive—this is often the premise upon which we entrust literary revolution to the youth. Observing the various literary revolutions in modern Chinese history, young people have always been pioneers. However, for youth growing up in peaceful years, as Su Qiqi, one of the editors of *The Clock Suddenly Speeds Up: Born in the 1970s*, remarked: "Poverty is our common background. As children, we stood on the ruins just after a storm passed through, lacking in material goods and equally lacking in spiritual wealth." Similar sentiments are also recognized by author Liang Hong, who articulates more specifically: "Perhaps it is not just me. Individuals born in the 1970s in the present cultural (or literary) space seem to be a silent, indistinct group. You can hardly find figures who can be analyzed as representatives. There has been no sensation, no creation of fresh and bold texts, no unique avant-garde thoughts, and of course, no particularly exaggerated or exceptional actions. They almost all wear a look of heavy-heartedness, doubt, and premature aging" (Liang Hong, "Moments between History and I"). If the generation born in the 1970s is considered "impoverished," then the subsequent generations born in the 1980s and 1990s are even more likely to be so. The world has been flattened, discrepancies narrowed; as a result, it is difficult to find provocateurs and challengers like Han Dong, Lu Yang, and Zhu Wen, who engage in "rupture."

Stepping back, even if there are so-called youthful pioneers, the revolution still requires a mobilizable base of literary masses, among whom the largest share should be young artists. According to statistics from *Shenzhen Youth Daily* and *Anhui Poetry Press* on the "1986 Modern Poetry Group Exhibition in China": "In this so-called irresistible age in 1986, there were over 2,000 poetry societies nationwide and ten times that number of self-proclaimed poets, with thousands of poetry collections, poetry newspapers, and poetry journals practicing rupture in traditional forms." Not all literary youth can become avant-garde writers and artists; they may just be "literary" without being "avant-garde," or they may eventually give up literature over time. However, challenging established norms and systems with avant-garde, rebellious, resistant, and creative actions is the most valuable part of being a literary youth. If there truly was a golden age of avant-garde literature, it should also be the golden age of literary youth. I have stated on multiple occasions that if the data of 470 million readers of online literature is reliable, while proving the prosperity of online literature, it also indicates that the overall literary aesthetic of the nation is worrisome. It is almost certain that these readers are unlikely to become fellow travelers of the literary revolution we imagine. In stark contrast, after literature ceases to revolutionize, literary youth also become a form of "group mockery."

Moreover, the implementation of literary revolution at the practical level urgently requires insightful editors, publishers, and critics. Today, nearly all literary histories discuss that the avant-garde literature of 1980s China was formed by a "shared community of imagination" consisting of individuals like Can Xue, Ma Yuan, Yu Hua, Su Tong, Ge Fei, Sun Ganlu, Hong Feng, and others, each with their own starting points in writing. One question I have always pondered is how these individuals, with their distinct approaches to writing, were summoned together. In 1986, Wu Liang and Cheng Depei edited and published two anthologies: *The New Novel in 1985* and *Exploration Novel Collection*. It was these two anthologies that allowed scattered avant-garde writers across various literary journals to come together. This assemble was done under the auspices of "new" and "exploration," with a deliberate intent of "editing" and "design." Wu Liang and Cheng Depei explicitly stated: "1985 was both the result and summary of the changes in novelistic concepts in the preceding years, as well as the beginning of further development toward the future." In the preface of *New Novel in 1985*, which had a "tendentious selection" approach, Wu further emphasized the significance of the year 1985: "The fiction created in 1985 shattered my theoretical dreams with its extraordinary achievements, foretelling to me the quiet arrival of a literary modern movement, which would shake all the theoretical fantasies confined within."

In addition to this meaningful fiction anthology in 1986, there was also a "Modernist Poetry Group Exhibition" in the poetry community, organized by *Poetry Press* and *Shenzhen Youth Daily*. In April 1988, Yu Hua mentioned in a letter to Cheng Yongxin, editor of *Harvest*, about an "extremist novel collection": "I have always hoped for such a collection, an extremist novel collection. It seems that all the quality novel collections in China now cater to various aspects, even in terms of themes. I feel that yours will be different. It will not consider the so-called objective and comprehensive display of contemporary novel-writing, but will display a kind of power, a heretical power. Just like the fifth issue you edited for Harvest last year." This letter refers to the *New Wave Novel in China* edited by Cheng Yongxin.

In the literary revolution of the 1980s, the journal *Harvest*, edited by Ba Jin, was the least concerned with conservatism and peace. Its character was abnormal, revolutionary, and destructive, as mentioned in Yu Hua's letter referring to Issue No. 5 in 1987 and Issue No. 6 in 1988, both of which were almost entirely composed of writers representing the most radical creations of that time, such as Ma Yuan, Yu Hua, Ge Fei, Su Tong, and Sun Ganlu.

Looking back years later, Cheng Yongxin who was a young editor at that time recalled, "With the support of the new head of *Harvest*, Li Xiaolin, I assembled some young writers to appear like picking potential stocks, time and again. They eventually became influential writers in China, such as Yu Hua, Su Tong, Ma Yuan, Ge Fei, Wang Shuo, Beicun, Sun Ganlu, Pipi, among others, who were regarded as representatives of avant-garde novel in China." The strongly pre-designed avant-garde posture of *Harvest* gave the writers within it the illusion that a new literary era was dawning. In a letter to Cheng Yongxin on October 7, 1987, Su Tong wrote, "I have read *Harvest*, and besides Hong Feng and Yu Hua, Sun Ganlu and Se Bo are also impressive. This issue feels like the new era has begun, doesn't it?" Speaking of transformation, if everything is in place today, we inevitably confront the question of "whose life are we revolutionizing" in this literary renaissance: whom do we critique, and which aspects of literature have become outdated? The May Fourth Movement condemned old literature, while the reform and opening up era refused Bei Dao and heralding the emergence of new literary ideals. Therefore, if we are unable to honestly assess which works are stale and which are innovative, where can a literary revolution truly find its foundation? It is essential to deeply reflect on whether this shortcoming lies in our aesthetic judgment or a lack of courage.

Interestingly, 1998, the year when Han Dong, Lu Yang, and Zhu Wen incited "rupture," happened to be shortly after the debut of the writers born in the 1970s. This marked a historical divide, and since then, it seems there has been no literary revolution. Unlike the proactive "rupture" by elder figures like Han Dong, Lu Yang, and Zhu Wen, the initial rebelliousness of those born in the 1970s was cultivated and manufactured by mass media. Subsequently, those born in the 1980s quickly adopted this mode of entry. The emergence of new literary youth was not a result of self-renewal in literature. As we see in today's literature, the growth and fame of young writers increasingly depend on their mastery and manipulation of media resources. Moreover, in conjunction with the media, young writers also align with beneficial literary systems. Thus, literary communication, activities, and promotion occupy a significant portion of a writer's career. The parasitic nature of young writers within the entire literary system and literary lineage results in their inability to declare middle-aged and older writers as old literature in an intergenerational sense.

Therefore, my pessimism about today's literary revolution is based on the fact that we have so much groundwork to do, or that we simply cannot complete it. So much so, we dare not talk about literary revolution. Han Dong once said that their "rupture" was spatial. "There are two incompatible types of writing in the same space." (Han Dong, "Memorandum: Answers to Questions about 'Rupture' Behavior") Based on my observations of Chinese literature for more than 20 years, this spatial relationship of incompatible writing orders still exists. Last year, Interface Culture published a book titled *Wild Writers Interviews*, subtitled *We Are Writing On-Site*. These writers labeled as "wild" include Zhao Song, Zhu Yue, Liu Tianzhao, Yu Shi, Duyan, Yuan Ling, Sheng Wenqiang, Chang Qing, Yang Dian, Shi Jiepeng, Kang He, Hu Lingyun, and Gu Qian. The label "wild" is roughly equivalent to what

Han Dong described as "a small number, marginal, non-mainstream, folk, excluded, and ignored."

According to my understanding of contemporary Chinese writers or directly referring to the original publication list by Hinabook in recent years, this list could be longer and younger. By comparing this extensive list with the authors of the shortlisted works for the Sixth Yu Dafu Novel Award, which prompted Professor Wang Yao's call for "another revolution," we find very little overlap. I have not discussed this with Professor Wang, but does the heterogeneity of these "wild writers" align with what he refers to as "quietly"? One thing is certain: although they share the same spatial position in time as Han Dong and others in their "rupture," interviews reveal that they do not aim to instigate another spatial "rupture" between "in the wild" and "in the system" thus positioning themselves as initiators of a literary revolution. Not only do they not seek this, but they also overlook or are unaware of the existence of alternative spaces. Their writing has become self-referential and adaptive, a deeply personal endeavor. Even if we can identify the heterogeneity in their texts, they have lost the extreme posture characteristic of avant-garde literary practitioners from the 1980s, and naturally, they do not choose the passionate stance of the avant-garde.

Indeed, the imagination of the current literary landscape has shifted from linear, hierarchical relationships to parallel, equivalent relationships. For instance, authors such as Jinhezai, Maoni, Jiangnan, Tianxia Bachang, Xuehong, Cangyue, Wuzui, Dangnian Mingyue, Xuanyu, Tonghua, Xinyiwu, Tangjia Sanshao, Nansansan, Hudielan, Meng Ru Shenji, Liulianzi, Fenghuo Xi Zhuhou, and Wochi Xihongshi are engaged in capital-defined online literature. Even though traditional so-called pure literature (elite literature or refined literature) may identify them as popular literary figures, they cannot be excluded from the contemporary Chinese literary landscape through vertical hierarchical relationships.

Today, this kind of vertical aesthetic superiority and inferiority is purely imaginary. From the perspective of online literature, they perceive themselves as part of the same literary tribe as pure literature, on an equal footing, but they do not seek dialogue. A similar situation exists in science fiction literature, including Liu Cixin, Jiang Bo, Tangfei, Baoshu, Chen Qiufan, Chihui, Hao Jingfang, Xia Jia, Wang Kanyu, and Feidao. Science fiction literature has its own publications, circles, dissemination pathways, and evaluation mechanisms. However, in recent years, with Liu Cixin and Hao Jingfang winning awards as a landmark, this professional yet narrow circle has been broken, and the geographical map of science fiction literature has expanded.

If we delve further, there are many smaller literary tribes than traditional journal literature, wild literature, online literature, and science fiction literature. Even individuals can become a literary tribe. They use journals, books, and other print media, as well as online communities, public accounts, and groups to define boundaries and territories. The relationship between tribes, between tribes and individuals, is no longer confrontational, conquering, or assimilating, but rather pacified and peaceful, which can be external or internal.

Therefore, we have entered an era of whispered literature, which I call the "literature non-revolution" era. In this "literature non-revolution" era of writing, the sacred literary career has been reduced to the everyday literary life where everybody writes. Literature can be related to the inner self, the system, and business. When we really want a literary revolution, we cannot form a group, become an army, or deploy a formation. In essence, our longing for literary revolution is nothing more than the grandeur of historical narrative. So, let us imagine the possibility of literary revolution together. If writers themselves cannot be relied upon, should we rely on journal planning? Or on the imagination and construction of researchers and critics? What kind of insight and ability to control time and space are needed to piece together literary fragments collected from various sources into a richly historical yet future-oriented literary map? Or, in the "literature non-revolution" era today, is every participant at most just a collector and possessor of literary fragments?

Contemporary Multi-Ethnic Chinese Literature as a "Literary Entity"

The Literary Entity Series: Library of Multi-Ethnic Classic by Contemporary Chinese Writers (Volume One) includes classic works by contemporary novelists and poets from five ethnic groups: Mongolian, Tibetan, Uyghur, Kazakh, and Yi, with writers such as Ayanga, Mo Hasbagan, Akbar Majid, Alat Asem, Tashi Dawa, Erkesh Kurmanbekovyna, Jidi Majia, Tsering Norbu, and Pema Tseden. These nine novelists and poets are not only the most outstanding and influential representatives in the development of their respective ethnic literatures but are also significant figures in the history of contemporary Chinese literature as a whole.

Based on the characteristics and attributes of the current Chinese literary ecological field, these writers should be examined, recognized, and named within the framework of the richness of "diversity" in contemporary multi-ethnic Chinese literature. Contemporary multi-ethnic Chinese literature embodies a unique and self-sufficient ethnic identity, which includes corresponding ethnic cultures and literary traditions. Against this backdrop, we need to consider whether the literature of the Mongolian, Tibetan, Uyghur, Kazakh, Yi, and other ethnic groups has been fully recognized and understood in today's context of contemporary Chinese literature. How can we more deeply and accurately identify the ethnic nature of literature?

Literary Landscape of Wanderers in Different Cultural Spaces

The landscape of contemporary Chinese literature is shaped by writers from various ethnic groups. In today's fluid world, writers naturally become wanderers across diverse cultural spaces, and these journeys lead to the integration, folding, dialogue, and fusion of diverse cultures. This ongoing process of engagement and transformation involves continuous choices and reinventions. Therefore, the writings of China's ethnic authors capture the rich nuances of a dynamic world.

Mongolian writer Ayanga wrote six novels in *No Barbed Wire in the Sky* in the twenty-first century. They were directly translated from Mongolian by Hasen, who wears multiple hats as a poet, novelist, and translator. Ayanga's narratives often unfold at the intersection of tradition and modernity. In these moments, the hesitations, confusions, and progress inherent in the modernization process become central themes in his literature. As a result, profound cultural reflections are the backdrop of his novels.

In a sense, Ayanga is not only a thinker and spokesperson rooted in his ethnic culture but also a custodian of contemporary Chinese literary heritage. His writing continues the exploration of the relationship between tradition and modernity, a cultural theme pondered by generations of Chinese writers since the modern era. Reading his works reveals stories of the humble herder leaving his family searching for lost homelands; marksman troubled by melancholy empathizing with wolf packs; the monstrous vehicle disrupting the ancient, stable lives of pastoral communities; unruly women retaining her own principles in her turbulent life; young life married to a declining noble family dying for her choice of love and freedom; and the dual nature of a stranger's deception cloaked in admiration and ambiguity. Ayanga excavates the thoughts, values, and religious beliefs of nomadic peoples from their history, customs, and daily lives. His novels serve as both ethnic fables and elegies for the changing nomadic culture increasingly eroded by industrial civilization.

Mo Hasbagen's three short-to-medium-length novels from *The Homeland of Wolves and Songs* have also been translated by Hasen. Born in 1950 on the Ordos grassland of Inner Mongolia, Hasbagen has spent his entire life there. Unlike the sense of loss and longing seen in Ayanga's works, Mo Hasbagen writes about the constants amid historical changes. These "constants" exist in the bonds between family, fellow beings, and all living things: whether it is the old man's family deep in the desert in *The Homeland of Wolves and Songs*, the wise yet simple Baorihu in *Deep in the Heilongui Desert*, or the clever Captain Taolimu in *Reeducation*, they all steadfastly uphold their original intentions, embodying love and inclusivity. His novels reveal not only the local significance of Mongolian grassland customs but also the enduring spirit of Mongolian grassland culture and its unique aesthetic values.

Pearls and Agates includes two distinctive short stories by Alat Asem: *Pearls and Agates* and *Malik Milk Tea*. The former affirms the moral principle that "gold is not the true measurement of justice; the enduring scale of this world is the moral nature." Following the unexpected death of their newly remarried father, the sons find themselves hesitating between gold and moral nature. The latter begins with the idea that "a man's unseen face is his true enemy." After the celebrated and revered former mayor passes away, his family receives a bank card and land deed from a mysterious woman, leading to a web of mysteries that unravels Malik's vibrant life before the world.

The bilingual nature of Alat Asem's writing enhances the literary possibilities of "mutual observation" between languages, making the language of his novels particularly distinctive. His Chinese works exhibit the word formation and syntactic characteristics influenced by Uyghur thought, with word choice, morphological variations, and syntax differing from standard Chinese expressions. For instance, the novels frequently transform the abstract into concrete metaphors, utilize inverted predicates, and include numerous parallel structures. His novels belong to the realism tradition but are also imbued with fables, stories, and myths, depicting animals and plants as sentient beings capable of communication, thus creating a magical realism style.

In the era of globalization, how to navigate the balance of preserving ethnic traditional culture, maintaining distinctiveness, and avoiding homogenization is a great challenge. In this regard, Alat Asem makes an enlightening example.

The Kazakh people are a nature-loving nomadic ethnicity. Before the mid-twentieth century, they primarily lived in pastoral and mountainous areas, migrating seasonally in search of water and grass. However, their way of life began to change, with many herders settling down. This shift not only altered their lifestyle but also transformed the reasons for living and the foundation of their spirit. *My Suleiman is Missing* includes fifteen short and medium-length stories by Kazakh novelist Akbar Majid. As a representative contemporary Kazakh writer, his novels depict grand peaks, vast wilderness, bright sun in cloudless sky, and freely grazing cattle and sheep, resembling an "elegant and beautiful paradise outside the Central Plain." His themes explore the courage of men on the grasslands, battling bears with short swords, as well as the tenderness of discovering secrets of springs with girls. There are Kyrgyz musician playing his last tune in four-cornered yurts, flying blue doves reflecting the dreams and hopes of youth, and distant snow-capped mountains symbolizing a longing for home. In works such as *Lame Wild Horse, Blue Dove, Blue Dove, Red Calf, Patrolling the Mountains*, and *My Suleiman is Missing*, Akbar Majid's words transcend the earthly realm, seamlessly blending the poetic life of the Kazakh people, the sacred beings of the grasslands, and the vibrant land itself.

The Home of a Village is a new short story collection by another prominent Kazakh writer, Erkesh Kurmanbekovyna. Located on the China-Mon-
golia border, Beita Mountain is her hometown, a remote area with limited
access to modern civilization. She spent a brief childhood on a pasture
before moving to the city for education and work, but those childhood experiences remain most unforgettable. She writes about an ordinary family
in the village, the canola flowers in strong gales, the horses discovered on
rock walls while haymaking with her father, and the village brides. Writer
Liu Liangcheng remarked, "This Kazakh shepherd girl, who left her yurt
and pasture in childhood, traveled the world and eventually returned to
her birthplace—Beita Mountain pasture. Her returning is so absolute, completely forgetting the city, forgetting the influence imposed by Han culture,
and even fogetting the passage of time, simply back to the essence of life."
In her novels, each family, each story reflects the observations, understand-
ings, and confusions people face amid the impact of new things and ideas,
as well as the hopes and struggles of nomadic peoples during cultural transformation. Through this, she deeply explores themes of life, reproduction,
love, and death. Thus, *The Home of a Village* represents countless ordinary
days and nights of the Kazakh people, embodying the essence of life and
conveying the light of faith.

Erkesh's bilingual background enables her to navigate effortlessly between two cultures and lifestyles, showcasing a unique cross-cultural advan-
tage. Moreover, her works reveal a Xinjiang beyond the familiar Gobi Desert
or local customs, undoubtedly enriching its literary landscape. Broadening
our perspective, the literary ecology of Xinjiang is diverse and vibrant, making Xinjiang literature one of the most colorful parts of contemporary Chinese literature.

The Delayed Elegy is a poetry collection by contemporary renowned poet
Jidi Majia, featuring several long poems and a variety of proses, including
speeches, prefaces, comments, and dialogues, along with dozens of illustrations. In his poetry, Jidi Majia expresses elegies for his father, hymns to his

ethnic group, as well as reflections on his own existence and thoughts on the fate of humanity. In his prose, he discusses cultural similarities and differences, the significance of poetry, and the power of literature. The unique illustrations filled with Yi ethnic elements expand his identity as the "singer of the Yi people." His works encompass poetry, prose, and art, intertwining self, ethnicity, and the world—each aspect transcending its own boundaries. As a poet translated into multiple languages, Jidi Majia truly possesses the potential to converse with the world.

— Same Ethnicity yet Distinct Aesthetics —

The Literary Entity Series: Library of Multi-Ethnic Classic by Contemporary Chinese Writers includes three Tibetan authors: Tashi Dawa, Tsering Norbu, and Pema Tseden.

Tashi Dawa is a "writer engaged in the literary history," with several of his ethnically prominent novels woven into the fabric of contemporary Chinese literary history, representing the mystique and splendor of Chinese literature in the 1980s. Born in Xizang, he also studied, worked, and lived there. His novels serve as a literary ethnography of the Tibetans. The expansive and desolate roof of the world, the mountains and rivers of southern Xizang, colorful Buddhist flags fluttering from rooftops, the nomadic tents of the Kham people, the young lounging in sweet tea houses, and the old women bargaining with pinching fingers—these all populate his narratives. "We Tibetans have lived this way for generations: sitting and chatting, sitting and doing business, sitting and reciting scriptures, sitting and soaking up the sun, sitting and drinking, sitting and doing handicrafts, lamas sitting and attaining enlightenment." The daily scenes in Tashi Dawa's novels come from his understanding of his homeland, rooted in blood and faith. From the late 1970s to the early 1980s, during a time of transition, the remote ancient cities of the plateau inevitably faced impacts from modernization. Modern material life began influencing Tibetan youth, subtly altering their religious beliefs, philosophies, and moral concepts. As a result, Tashi Dawa focused on various young people from the lower strata of urban life—police officers, homeless individuals, nurses, students, and salesmen—each displaying a range of emotions: some are uplifted, others contemplative; some are passive, others are infatuated with trendy jeans and disco culture ... They have departed from old paths but are struggling to find their rightful places in life.

The historical recognition of Tashi Dawa's novels in magical realism may overshadow his richness and groundedness as a contemporary chronicler of the ordinary Tibetan people's fate. Nevertheless, his most impactful significance within contemporary Chinese literature undoubtedly lies in the multidimensional space and surreal narratives marked by the publication of *Xizang, a Soul Knotted on a Leather Thong* in early 1985. In these novels, the story, plot, and characters become less important; he uses magical realism to explore the survival history and cultural psyche of his own people, becoming a paradigm for entering the literary mainstream from the borderlands.

Tsering Norbu's *The Robber Tavern* includes eight short stories published between 2009 and 2018, making this the first collected edition. In *Mercy in Dirt*, the Tibetan girl named Amu with eyes like Guanyin harbors unspoken desires throughout her life. The souls left behind by war meet the sculptor in a roadside room in *Qumixinguo* every night. The two wives of *Veterinarian Norbu* go to the Ganden Temple in Lhasa together to pray for his swift reincarnation, accompanying each other like sisters. In *Mourning*, the Tibetan mother and the Han father met as the fate would have it, whereas their differences in regional identities lead to their separation and a tragic legacy for their descendants. On the golden grass slopes lies *The Heart Full of Caterpillar Fungus*. It is easy to imagine Tsering Norbu's worldview and literary resources based on his ethnic identity, which is understandable. However, when discussing the relationship between ethnic identity and literature for this "individual" writer, we must specify which part of his ethnicity influences his literature and how it does so. For literary criticism, Tsering Norbu is a "practical" example.

Balloon by Pema Tseden features ten short stories, with the first and last being *Temptation* (1995) and *Balloon* (2017), spanning over twenty years. He once said, "I yearn to tell the stories of my hometown in my own way, a more authentic hometown the wind blows by." This collection includes stories like *The Silent Holy Stones*, which discusses the impact of traditional Tibetan culture on daily life, as well as *Tharlo* and *Balloon*, which depict the peaceful life in Tibetan areas affected by external changes. Notably, *Tharlo* and *Balloon* have been adapted into films, both of which have competed in the Horizons section of the Venice Film Festival. In China, *Tharlo* won the Best Adapted Screenplay at the Golden Horse Awards and Best Low-Budget Feature at the Golden Rooster Awards. Pema Tseden himself won the Most Media Attention Director and Screenwriter Awards for *Balloon* at the Shanghai International Film Festival and the Golden Coconut Award at the Hainan International Film Festival.

Characters such as the deceased stone carver in *The Silent Holy Stones*, the reincarnated lama in *Wujin's Teeth*, the veiled girl in *Soul Searching*, and the shepherd Tharlo in *Tharlo* are all vividly alive. While the ethnic and regional aspects of scenery, customs, and cultures undeniably influence one another, the current literary and artistic portrayals of Xizang often exaggerate these elements, which can hinder deeper and higher reflections on humanity and artistic exploration. Pema Tseden's novels and films, in a sense, serve as epics of ordinary Tibetan lives.

Pema Tseden has acknowledged in interviews that literature has greatly aided his later film creations. From a contemporary dissemination perspective, film can be more powerful than literature. His films also showcase the skies, rivers, and temples of Xizang, but these elements transcend mere "landscapes." In *Old Dog*, *The Silent Holy Stones*, and even in his earliest work, *Grassland*, his landscapes are psychological. The settings resonate with the inner silence of Tibetans, often unspoken, with the elderly characters in *Old Dog*, and *The Silent Holy Stones*, as well as Tharlo's silence in *Tharlo*, embodying a poignant strength.

Furthermore, Pema Tseden's films, particularly *Old Dog*, *Soul Searching*, and *Tharlo*, feature towns that are still under construction. Notably, these films include spaces such as bars, KTVs, police stations, photo studios, and salons, with construction sites recurring as a scene, alongside streets filled with dust from passing tractors and motorcycles and dirty puddles. These landscapes and spaces are crucial structural elements of Pema Tseden's vision of Xizang. He is more concerned with the everyday lives and evolving changes in Xizang, where even the "sacred" is related to ordinary people, as seen in the temples and young lamas in *The Silent Holy Stones*.

I have always looked forward to someone seriously studying the differences in writing among writers from the same ethnic group. For instance, when it comes to worlds where deities still exist, the works of Tsering Norbu, along with fellow Tibetan novelists like Tashi Dawa, A Lai, and Pema Tseden, are completely different. Tsering Norbu's novels transform the "divinity" of ethnic religions into human "spirituality." Despite their Chinese terms showing one Chinese character difference, "spirituality" more often refers to the religious sentiment in daily life. Therefore, Tsering Norbu's novels infuse a sense of "spirituality" into human life, rather than merely existing as "divinity."

The Vastness of Diversity, Coexistence,
and Abundance of a "Literary Entity"

E thnicity is not an abstract label. When reading the novels and poems of these writers, the most direct manifestations of ethnicity are in the natural scenery, customs, and daily life, as well as in modes of thinking, cultural traditions, and aesthetic spirits. These writers and poets from different ethnic groups often start from a specific place in vast China—this place is what we commonly refer to as "hometown," which is also a point of constant reflection in their writing journeys. Their novels typically feature a structure of physical departure from home and spiritual return, and they are invariably cultural transgressors themselves. It is noteworthy that regardless of their ethnic background or where they live, they are all inevitably situated in the transformative era from the mid-twentieth century to the present. Thus, themes of change and permanence, transience and eternity, fear and doubt, as well as profound contemplation, naturally become common literary motifs among them. Consequently, their writings are a part of contemporary Chinese literature amid the modernization of their times, as well as part of the broader literary history of modern China. From the May Fourth New Literature to today, these sensitive novelists and poets resonate with the secret voices of different ethnicities. The so-called "literary entity" emerges from rich and diverse voices while maintaining ethnic distinctiveness. Such richness and diversity are indeed a hallmark of contemporary Chinese literature. Of course, this does not prevent us from recognizing the temporal, global, or human aspects within these writers' texts. However, I believe that "entity" should not serve as a simplistic excuse to erase differences. From the perspective of pursuing literary ecological diversity, it is essential to fully respect and achieve the different voices and sounds that converge in this multi-ethnic "literary entity."

Regardless of how literary historians emphasize the objectivity of writing in their compilations, literary history inevitably retains the unique emotional attitudes and value positions of the compiler, which certainly influences the discourse on multi-ethnic literature. Many contemporary Chinese literary histories often reveal such limitations: relevant writers only gain entry into the framework of contemporary Chinese literary history if they write in Chinese, or if their works in their mother tongues are continually translated into Chinese texts. In fact, ethnic groups such as the Mongols, Tibetans, Uyghurs, Kazakhs, and Yi all possess their own languages and rich cultural and literary traditions, showcasing a dual construction of language and literature to this day. Of course, it is unrealistic to expect all compilers of contemporary Chinese literary history to master the languages of various ethnic groups. Furthermore, translators and researchers like Bahtiyar, Hasen, Su Yongcheng, Hadachi Gang, Jin Lianlan, and Long Renqing, who have rich bilingual experiences, could have been involved in compiling contemporary Chinese literary history. However, in reality, they are seldom included. This raises a question: How can literary works written in Mongolian, Tibetan, Uyghur, Kazakh, and other ethnic languages, which have not been translated into Chinese, enter the discourse of contemporary Chinese literary history?

It should be noted that in the landscape of contemporary Chinese literature, there are quite a few bilingual writers, such as Ayanga from the Mongol ethnic group, Pema Tseden from the Tibetan ethnic group, and Alat Asem from the Uyghur ethnic group, all of whom engage in bilingual writing. Bilingual writers typically fall into two categories: one whose influence may arise from within their own ethnic community, and the other whose writing, mediated by Chinese, receives more widespread dissemination. Thus, the discourse on multi-ethnic literature in contemporary Chinese literary history essentially focuses on the works of ethnic writers who write in Chinese.

The compilation of literary history and contemporary literary criticism face similar challenges. If the narrative of contemporary Chinese literary history cannot encompass minority writers and their works that use languages other than Chinese across the entire country, the landscape of contemporary Chinese literature remains incomplete.

The so-called "golden age of literature" in the 1980s is often a "hot topic" when discussing contemporary Chinese literature: Why do we need to return to the 1980s? What inspiring elements did the 1980s provide for contemporary Chinese literature? However, even during this "imaginary golden age," the literatures of the Mongol, Uyghur, Kazakh, Yi, and other ethnic groups did not receive adequate recognition and visibility. Perhaps the only literature that gained attention during this period was Tibetan literature, as Tashi Dawa's novels profoundly influenced the Chinese literary imagination of reality in the 1980s. Based on his capabilities demonstrated in his 1980s works, he has the potential to enter the ranks of world-class writers. Ewenk writer Ureltu also brought a brand-new literary experience to the domestic literary scene in the 1980s, impacting the emergence of the root-seeking literary movement.

In contrast, we must ask: How many writers today can transform the current literary imagination and influence the literary landscape like Tashi Dawa and Ureltu did in the 1980s? Often overlooked but deserving of attention is the increasing number of bilingual writers in the country who are shifting from writing in their mother tongues to writing in Chinese, becoming literary creators in a "foreign" language. Chinese writers, long constrained by a single-language environment, often fall into linguistic inertia, while "cross-border travel" between languages or different ethnic cultures can foster writers' experiences, reflections, and insights.

When we bring together writers such as Ayanga, Mo Hasbagan, Akbar Majid, Alat Asem, Tashi Dawa, Erkesh Kurmanbekovyna, Jidi Majia, Tsering Norbu, and Pema Tseden, it is clear how they use their unique ethnic experiences, language, cultural resources, and aesthetic insights as starting points to weave their literary "whispers" into the "voices" of contemporary Chinese literature. As a unified multi-ethnic country, the true charm of China's cultural landscape (including its literary landscape) largely lies in its richness and diversity, rooted in its harmonious coexistence of differences. This profound and diverse coexistence is a cultural treasure that the nation takes pride in. At the same time, multi-ethnic literature in China, through its processes of inheritance and development, has gradually become an essential part of Chinese literature and even world literature. Ethnic writers, through their ethnic identities, exhibit a recognition and belonging to their respective ethnic traditions, allowing their writings to reflect the living conditions and life scenes of their communities deeply and concretely, thus providing an important paradigm for contemporary multi-ethnic literature.

It is important to recognize that multi-ethnic literature, with its unique spiritual creativity, cultural expression, and aesthetic presentation, offers rich aesthetic experiences and broad interpretative spaces for contemporary Chinese literature, particularly for socialist literature since the reform and opening up. Thereafter, the rapid modernization has transformed the customs, lifestyles, and cultural concepts of various ethnic groups, leading to increased social mobility and a quiet erosion of traditional ethnic characteristics and their foundational roots. The once-solid ethnic bonds are loosened. Correspondingly, many ethnic languages are endangered, traditional customs are being lost or distorted, and ethnic spiritual values are being warped, posing significant challenges to the outstanding cultural traditions within these groups. This shared cultural anxiety exists among all ethnicities.

The "literary entity" seeks a deep understanding of ethnic values, and these ethnic writers break through superficial ethnic traits to further explore the spiritual sentiments, psychological characteristics, emotional attitudes, and thought structures of their own ethnicities. This deeper ethnic psychology reflects the unique attributes of its members under shared values. In this sense, multi-ethnic literature aims to explore profound ethnic values, gain insights into the complex psychological activities of ethnic groups, and reveal their unique psychological patterns.

There is a popular saying: "The more ethnic it is, the more universal it gets." However, if ethnic identity is replaced by a narrow, parochial localism, what is more ethnic further drifts from getting universal. Thus, moving toward a "literary community" signifies a journey toward a contemporary multi-ethnic Chinese literature within a conversational, rich, and vast landscape of world literature.

PART II

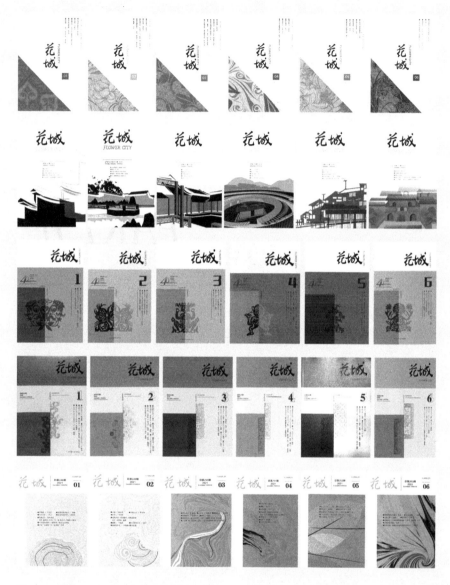

Flower City magazine (2017–2021)

Flower City Interest
(2017-2021)[1]:

A Private Archive of the Chinese Literary Scenes

_ Let's Talk About Their Novels Too _
(Issue I, 2017)

Pema Tseden has directed a remarkable series of films, including *The Silent Holy Stones*, *Old Dog*, *Soul Searching*, and *Tharlo*. Like Tang Di, both writers have also helmed their own projects, such as

---

[1] "Flower City Interest" is a column that I have proudly hosted in *Flower City* magazine since its inaugural issue in 2017. Each edition presents a distinct thematic interest, exploring a new topic through a mix of keywords, texts, dialogues, and comprehensive evaluations. Below, you will find a collection of comprehensive evaluations from Flower City Interest over the past five years.— Author.

Four Ways to Die of My Hometown and *A Man from Manchuria*. While they are undeniably filmmakers actively involved in the industry, their dual roles as directors and novelists do not inherently justify bringing them together for discussion. Of course, one could opportunistically label their work as "crossing boundaries" or "transcending fields." However, these terms have become somewhat clichéd, often used by those who have only superficially crossed over and are not universally embraced.

Imagine a carpenter who is merely average within the carpentry community, yet occasionally learns to construct walls or chicken coops. Suddenly, he is regarded as the best bricklayer among carpenters and the finest carpenter among masons. Is this so-called "crossing boundaries" truly a genuine compliment to a dedicated craftsman? In today's world, we often see individuals navigating various fields, yet all they seem to achieve is crossing different boundaries, becoming dual-career or multi-talented figures in an ever-evolving landscape.

Therefore, we must evaluate their films using cinematic standards while assessing their novels through the lens of literature. Reflecting on their novels and individual writing journeys, it becomes clear that they did not turn to "experimenting with novels" merely because of the acclaim their films have garnered. For instance, while Pema Tseden's films are steadily gaining international recognition, the mainstream media's pursuit of fame has rendered his identity as a novelist relatively hidden. In fact, the uniqueness of his films can be partially attributed to his literary background.

It is noteworthy that nearly all of Pema Tseden's films are based on independently created novels. Before directing his first film, *Grassland*, he was already an accomplished short story writer. He infuses his films with a distinctive "personal style," crafting clean and concise narratives that reflect not only geographical nuances but also the artistic portrayal of a humble person's inner epic. Additionally, as one of China's finest short story writers, he has cultivated a recognizable identity. This recognition is not derived from ethnic identity or exotic landscapes in "extreme" themes; even when discussing Pema Tseden's films and novels through the lens of ethnicity, he presents new possibilities. The author of *The Man Who Raises Leopards* is perhaps more renowned as a former photojournalist and traveler than as a filmmaker. His keen sensitivity to landscapes and people enables his book *Four Ways to Die of My Hometown* to blend various elements of prose, scripts, and imagery, preserving the fading essence of "hometown."

Meanwhile, Tang Di was a "secret novelist" long before emerging as a "young director." His novels circulated within a limited sphere, with their "secret" nature stemming from a lack of acceptance by mainstream literary journals. Therefore, when exploring their identities as travelers between film and literature, it appears that literature offers greater possibilities for film.

As a product of modern industrial society, film stands as a distinctly contemporary art form. Among various artistic categories, it is one of the most commercialized. Interestingly, the "craftsmanship" inherent in this medium allows it to preserve the "artisan spirit," which our contemporary era is currently grappling with. The few exceptional films throughout history consistently demonstrate meticulous attention to texture and detail. In terms of cinematic styles, Pema Tseden and Tang Di exhibit significant differences, yet they share a common dedication to narrative depth and selectivity. Pema Tseden often employs minimalism to its fullest extent, while in *A Man from Manchuria*, Tang Di embraces complexity, intricately weaving a sense of order.

This divergence also reflects their distinct approaches to novel-writing. In Pema Tseden's novels, the ever-changing world bears down on individual lives, with the grandeur of the era resonating through each character, much like nerve endings that convey the pain of a nation embodied in humble, nameless individuals. In this light, I recognize that "the pain Pema Tseden endures in history and real life may be something I can never fully grasp." Consequently, while reading his novels, the aspects we believe we can understand might be the most superficial, while those that remain "incomprehensible" could hold the very essence we should cherish. In an age dominated by verbose and overwhelming language, there is a pressing need for measured silence, for the unspoken, or for words that resonate with absence. Literature should "leave blank spaces" in our world, creating room for contemplation and solitary sorrow.

I have not closely examined how Tang Di has evolved into the agnostic voice of contemporary literature. Our literary evaluations, tired of "gigantism," are increasingly shifting toward an extreme opposite—highlighting the failures, small-town youths, gray crowds, and marginalized individuals in today's literary landscape without a clear value stance. The challenge arises when literature portrays the mundane realities of these individuals, often dragging narratives to the ground. This creates a dangerous tendency, leading to some of Tang Di's writings being positioned within this limiting framework for recognition.

However, much like the title of Tang Di's novel *Watermelons Grow in the Sky*, the "boredom" present in his works contains elements that soar, reminiscent of the constantly shaking camera in his films. His sense of "boredom" and "nihilism" carries a faith-based significance, rooted in his agnostic worldview. He inherits the avant-garde literary spirit of the 1980s and continues to be an unwavering stylistic experimenter. Although his experimental writing currently enjoys limited public exposure, if we assume a generation of "1980s writers" truly exists, then, much like Tang Di's films being labeled "a kind of noise," his experimental novels would similarly be considered "a kind of noise" among his contemporaries.

Since the 1990s, the rise of popular and online literature has led our writing and reading to become increasingly "emotional" yet "superficial." The grassroots foundation for novelistic stylistic experimentation is far less robust than it was in the 1980s. Regardless of how far Tang Di's novel experiments can progress or whether they can address the formalism issues left unresolved by avant-garde predecessors; our literature must first embrace certain "extreme" writings. In my conversations with young writers, I find that many, like Tang Di, view literature as a "faith."

Foreign Lands, or the Art of Literary Escape
(Issue 2, 2017)

Four writers belong to distinct generations: Wenren Yueyue and Duan Aisong, born in the 1970s; Li Yao, born in the 1980s; and San San, born in the 1990s. Residing in Hong Kong, Kunming, Beijing, and Shanghai respectively, these cities, from their unique perspectives in contemporary China, are "foreign lands" for one another. Placing these four cities side by side reveals the diverse wonders of a "developing country" at various stages of progress. The fact that these four writers can convene to discuss the concept of "foreign lands" resembles encounters during travel, each with different starting points. This special topic serves as their "hostel," where they pause momentarily before embarking on new journeys, uncertain of their ultimate destinations.

Before the modernization on a global scale, different nations cultivated their own imaginations of foreign lands, reflected in Eastern concepts such as Utopia, Peach Blossom Spring, and the Flowers in the Mirror. However, in the modern era, the East naturally became a site of fascination for the West, evident in Fan Liuyuan's romanticized views of Eastern women in Eileen Chang's *Love in a Fallen City*, or in Zhang Yimou's films navigating Western cultural landscapes. The internal "foreign lands" of the East and how the East becomes the "East" for the West are not the primary focus of our discussion. Instead, we are interested in how writers, through their creative practices, envision their worlds and how the effects of "foreign lands" manifest within "this" text, and what specific realities are they based on.

In this light, it is not just the four texts by these four writers that matter; each completed work in the grand tapestry of literary history should be seen as an independent "foreign land." Yet, this ideal is often not realized, as the current lack of imaginative depth in Chinese literature relegates independent literary creation to a mere production line in an age of consumption.

I anticipated that Wenren Yueyue would provide the urban literary experience of the bustling metropolis of Hong Kong, introducing it to my field of observation. My initial thought was simple: I always believed that Chinese literature lacked precise imagination and detailed writing from within the city's fabric. Much of modern Chinese literature's depiction of cities is nostalgic, lyrical, vague, and lacks clear definition. The urban writings of the 1930s "new sensationists" did not develop into a robust tradition in modern literature. In literature, the city only gains significance when contrasted with the countryside.

Wenren Yueyue's *Monkey Cool Cat* fit my envisioned concept of "urban literature" perfectly—a narrative about a city undergoing significant transformation, with people drifting, wandering, and distorting within it. Crucially, she did not presuppose an idyllic countryside from which to critique the city. Instead, she first immersed herself as a truly modern urban person in both body and mind, and then she observed and contemplated the city. In my imagination, Wenren Yueyue, along with the young natives of contemporary Chinese cities like Beijing, Shanghai, and Guangzhou, would have experiences distinct from those of urban migrants. This, I believe, will form the foundation of future Chinese literature.

However, another set of short stories derived from her longer novel-writing, the "Urban Foreign Land series," temporarily shifted my focus away from urban literature about the new tribes of urban newcomers. Unlike her *Monkey Cool Cat* and *A Gold-Digging Story*, which write about cities from within, these stories of the Urban Foreign Land series are set in cities spanning from the 1930s and 40s to the 1970s and 1980s—New York, Paris, Moscow, Hong Kong, and Vienna. These "foreign land" cities in her novels represent the prehistory or fringes of today's global metropolises. I am still not clear on what kind of long novel Wenren Yueyue is constructing, but just by examining these "small cities" with a length of about 20,000–30,000 Chinese characters, it is evident that she sincerely intends to be a voyeur of the city's secrets. The urban pasts accidentally revealed in these stories might lead to a city's unpredictable darkness. Wenren Yueyue says her writing is in the style of *Strange Tales from a Chinese Studio*. What if it were even more bizarre and enchanting? Indeed, "urban literature" delves into a city's darkness, like Orhan Pamuk's depiction of Istanbul. I still hope that one day Wenren Yueyue will lead us to peek into "her city"—Hong Kong or New York.

Duan Aisong believes that *Ximen Inn* returns to traditional forms out of pure nostalgia and expectations for this real-life inn, as well as a final glance at the travelers who have come and gone over the past thirty years. It is also a recollection and lamentation of the fate of the protagonist thereof. However, I see Ximen Inn as emerging from a small town, as the "foreign land" Duan Aisong constructed within it. A novel shouldn't provide a replicated "second-hand reality" but rather create a "reality," a literary "foreign land." Good novelists are adept at the art of escaping reality. Based on this understanding, I align with Li Yao's perspective on novels: "The conception of this novel is based on the idea that the entire world is a vast intertextual system, a complex network of meanings. Human life experiences are intertextual; one person's life contains all lives. The relationship between books and the world is the same. A book is the world; a book is all books. Everything is intertwined and inseparable. Even reality and fiction are one and the same. What we call reality is fictional reality, and what we call fiction is real fiction. If we can accept that spiritual phenomena and material phenomena have equal reality, then since I have this idea, it already exists in literature." Li Yao's *Fragmented Stories of Mountain Trolls* is a "feigned history" yet represents a real world.

Finally, let us discuss San San's *White Tower*. San San is a novelist who has yet to establish a definitive style. Despite being at an age where the desire for fame is strong, San San remains unusually calm, writing sparingly and slowly. San San has an accurate ability to recreate and replicate experiences and emotions, capturing subtle feelings and encounters, and depicting the "slight pains" of growing up in "micro-eras." Most young novelists start their literary apprenticeship here; some even prolong this period, developing this "crude literature" into a personal or imagined generational style, as seen with the youth literature by those born in the 1980s. The media-driven writing trends by those born in the 90s goes this direction as well.

We should pay attention to young writers' works like *White Tower* but avoid categorizing such writing under the buzzword "creative writing." *White Tower* consists of two parts: one is the familiar "micro-era experiences" of young people growing up in Chinese cities since the 1990s, the "something from something" part. For example, *White Tower* describes the protagonist's sense of isolation and loneliness from ten years ago. However, I value more the "something from nothing" part of *White Tower,* the imagined part—the protagonist's dark experience of being taken hostage in a bank. This traumatic memory responds to the "white tower" mentioned at the beginning of the novel. San San wants to tell us: "When the snow falls heavily, the world is white, and the capped buildings resemble white towers. The towers themselves have a sense of superiority over people, an oppressive feeling on a spiritual level, which can be surveillance or oppression, a kind of psychological fear." Yes, "white towers" are piling up in our everyday world.

White towers, inns, urban foreign lands, and their submerged tribes—the theme here is "foreign lands."

Creating the "Post-85": A Parodic Literary Naming
(Issue 3, 2017)

I am skeptical of the generational literary labels coined by literary journals and other media. The "post-85" (born between 1985 and 1990), a subgroup within the broader category of "post-80s" (born in the 1980s) writers, seems to be a parody at best.

I don't wish to genuinely create a "post-85" to reshape the "post-80s," akin to how *Lotus* magazine aimed to redefine the "writers born in the 1970s" in the late 1990s. I don't wish to criticize either, as criticizing it further seems almost pointless, as Tong Mo put it. Adding or replacing a few individuals won't change the essence of a dubious label. It is the same mindset, doing the same thing.

In fact, if there truly is a group of post-80s writers, recent years have seen significant changes in their work. Not only have the writings of Di An, Zhang Yueran, Zhou Jianing, and Yan Ge evolved, but authors emerging from traditional literary journals like Sun Pin, Zheng Xiaolü, Shuang Xuetao, Fu Yuehui, and Cai Dong have also risen to replace Han Han and Guo Jingming as the mainstays of post-80s writers. These latecomers are "writers," not "cultural icons." Today, the concept of post-80s writers has already shifted.

For example, regarding the writers born in the 1970s and 1980s, generational literary labels often obscure more contemporaries than they represent. To put it bluntly, they disregard literature as an individual creative endeavor. Yet, we seem to relish this. On the one hand, we recognize the absurdity of defining literary generations by decades. On the other, those born in the 1990s are becoming buzzwords and driving forces in contemporary literary journals and criticism. "Pandering to the young" seems to be the only way to stay at the forefront of contemporary literature, and literary labeling is more like trademark registration—first come, first served.

For nearly forty years, contemporary Chinese literary trends have been characterized by a relentless pursuit of the "new." The easiest way to achieve this "new" is through generational production and labeling, much like the first fresh crop of chives in spring. However, the individual growth of writers and the uniformity imposed by generational labels can never align. If we reflect, literary journals in the 1980s did not rely solely on generational labels to create topics. Whether it was root-seeking, avant-garde, or new realism, these trends were not merely about "young." You could argue that the literary concepts coined in the 1980s were flawed, but they still possessed a genuine literary essence.

Instead of seriously pointing out the absurdity of something that is ludicrous to the point of being dull, why not play along with equal seriousness? Now, I am going to earnestly create the "post-85." Tong Mo, Chen Si'an, and Yang Biwei, all born after 1985, are the "post-85" writers I am making. Being "serious" always has its justifications. As I explained to Tong Mo the other day: Between the media-created post-80s and post-90s, there indeed exists a "post-85," a gray area of late-blooming post-80s. Born in 1985, their "life matters" coincided with the launch of full-scale marketization and the "rise of China." Taking 1985 as the starting point, they would have begun elementary education around 1992, and more importantly, completed their high school and university education in the twenty-first century.

By highlighting their educational and developmental backgrounds, I am not suggesting that they became a homogeneous "generation" due to a common era. This special issue precisely demonstrates that they only share a common "time" of growth and some ambiguous historical moments. Their writings, however, vary. Even though Chen Si'an and Tong Mo's literary lives intersect significantly, it hasn't prevented them from becoming distinct writers.

Yang Biwei writes poetry because she has much to express. Her poems cover both "public matters" and "private affairs," particularly those that possess a "public" quality. It is gratifying that no one has labeled her as an "intellectual" because she has too many personal hobbies and a richly varied daily life. We should recognize the connection between "rock music" and her poetry—both in terms of poetic form and spirit—but we shouldn't naively assume that the critical nature of "rock music" is what we often refer to as "critical realism."

Tong Mo's output is astoundingly small. Over the past decade, we have seen only a small collection of fairy tales and fewer than ten novels. She is an anthropological researcher, and her achievements in criticism are significant enough to call her an anthropologist. However, I hesitate to label her as one. I recognize the connection between her writing and anthropology, which is certainly not in the sense of "material" for general writers. Still, anthropology is a distinct field, and what I can relate to is the illuminating depiction of human "inner life" in her work *La Wu Huo Liu*. Her stories are melancholic.

Chen Si'an is an experimenter in the short story genre. I believe that, thanks to the efforts of countless writers throughout human history, "short story" is not just a literary form but a way of imagining the world, an ideology. This is particularly evident in Chen's short stories.

Creating the "post-85" should not be limited to their texts alone; it should also consider their "literary lives." They are "anti-professional writers." The term "professional writer" turns the free and spontaneous act of writing into a ritualistic "profession." Often, when one is a "professional writer," the impulse to write is not driven by an inner desire but by the need to demonstrate "professionalism" through "writing." While "professional writers" do not necessarily produce mediocre works, or "safe writing" as Chen Si'an calls it, the non-professional writings of Tong Mo, Chen Si'an, and Yang Biwei have a wild, thriving vitality.

Allow me to conclude with a quote from Chen Si'an:

Today, a creator's attempt to achieve greater development solely by improving the skills required in their field is already a delusion. This applies not only to writers but to creators in all fields. In the not-so-distant past, writers could focus solely on reading and writing, artists on painting, musicians on music. But now, creators lacking comprehensive skills and vision will only become handicapped creators. The times have changed; it is that simple. The concept of crossing boundaries is gradually disappearing because future-oriented creation requires broad knowledge and openness, abandoning confinement by boundaries. I love theater work; becoming a theater director forces one to understand and learn many things—literary, artistic, design, sound, light, performance, management ... I harbor multiple voices and identities in my mind. They occasionally clash, but more often they support each other.

Creating the "post-85" is not just a parodic literary label but a discovery of those solitary literary islands. Perhaps solitude is only our presumption; these islands have their own lives and landscapes.

Exiled from Literature: Plays and Playwrights
(Issue 4, 2017)

W hen we decided to focus on plays for this special topic, the first problem we encountered was that a script is not the entirety of a complete drama. We often say that theater is a composite art form, integrating literature, music, dance, visual arts, and other forms of art. Zhu Yi mentioned in an interview with my graduate student, Li Han:

> I believe a script needs to be performed. The ultimate purpose of writing a script is for it to be acted out. Wang Anyi once said, 'Every story has a form that suits it best,' which is its optimal mode of presentation. Some stories are suited for novels, some for movies, and some for songs. So, if I choose to write a story as a script, it is because I believe it fits this form best; it should be performed. If it remains merely on the level of reading, it lacks the richer layers of expression

Indeed, "a script needs to be performed," and the "literature" we can "read" from a script is only a small part of its entirety. Contemporary literary histories do include plays, but we often judge them solely based on their scripts. Are scripts suitable for "reading" also suitable for "performance"? We cannot dismiss the fact that plays are ultimately meant to be "performed," despite the existence of many scripts that can be "read," such as the classics *Thunderstorm*, *Teahouse*, *The Bus Stop*, and *The Savage*, as well as more recent works by Zhang Xian, Guo Shixing, Tian Qinxin, Meng Jinghui, and Liao Yimei. These are all outstanding literary texts, but to deny that plays are ultimately meant to be "performed" would be a mistake. Pointing this out might serve as a small defense for the tradition of literary journals not publishing scripts. Plays and playwrights have been exiled from literature, but literary journals should not bear the entire responsibility for this.

Should literary journals be kind to plays and playwrights? A few years ago, before winning the Nobel Prize in Literature, Mo Yan received the Chunshen Literary Award in Shanghai. It was the final year of the Chunshen Literary Award, and it was given to Mo Yan's *Frog*. In his acceptance speech, he humorously mentioned the "play" section in *Frog*, joking that he had always dreamed of publishing a play script in *Harvest*. But since *Harvest* didn't publish scripts, he had to sneak the script into a novel to get it published there. In fact, Mo Yan might have forgotten that *Harvest* used to publish play scripts. It wasn't just *Harvest*; many major literary journals in the 1980s didn't reject scripts. Early issues of *Flower City* even published many film scripts.

After plays and playwrights were exiled from literature, the first noticeable change was that today's literary journals rarely feature scripts. The near rules of literary journals rejecting scripts have created clear biases and gaps in our literature. In contemporary Chinese literature, particularly in theater, its pioneering nature far exceeds other literary forms and has persistently maintained its avant-garde exploration. Theater is also the part of Chinese literature most involved in the global literary scene.

In an essay discussing avant-garde literature around 1985, I posed a question: when did our contemporary Chinese literary history become centered around novels and poetry? What if it weren't centered on novels and poetry? For example, in the so-called new period literature, the first to arrive on the "avant-garde" scene, even more thoroughly than novels and poetry, and still persisting today, is theater—if we understand "avant-garde" as a rebellion against literary norms. Therefore, our narrative of the new period's "avant-garde literature" would certainly look different if we included theater, even if it wasn't the focus. Before avant-garde novels gained momentum, avant-garde theater led the revolution in contemporary Chinese literature. Even after the retreat of the avant-garde in the 1990s, plays like *Sifan, I Love XXX, Zero File, The Death of an Anarchist*, and *Rhinoceros in Love* continued to keep the avant-garde spirit alive.

Zhu Yi was introduced to me by Chen Si'an. She is a playwright known for several performed plays such as *I Am the Moon* and *Telemachus*. Both of these plays possess a readable literary quality. Through this introduction, we hope to draw attention to drama as literature and encourage the reintegration of plays and film scripts into literary journals.

It is also worth noting that although Zhu Yi is currently developing her career in the United States, she completed her undergraduate education in drama at Nanjing University. In recent years, it seems that *The Face of Chiang Kai-shek* has brought significant attention to Nanjing University's drama program. The undergraduate program in Drama and Film Studies at Nanjing University began in 2006, and in just a decade, it has produced a number of outstanding playwrights, including Zhu Yi, Wen Fangyi, and Liu Tianya. If it weren't for space constraints, we would have discussed Liu Tianya's *Sisters* in this special topic as well.

In many ways, the most vibrant part of contemporary campus literature is "youth drama performance." In my city, Nanjing, it is not only Nanjing University that has become a hub for drama; Nanjing Normal University's Nanguo Drama Society also has significant influence beyond the campus. What has been exiled must return. It is time for contemporary Chinese literature to fully recognize the value of drama—not just as something to be read, but as complete works to be performed. Literary research should extend beyond reading newspapers, journals, and books. Events such as the Wuzhen Theater Festival, the Lin Zhaohua Theater Festival, the Beijing Youth Theater Festival, and venues like Beijing's Capital Theater, Penghao Theater, the Hive Theater, and Hangzhou's West Theater, as well as Meng Jinghui's Theater Studio, Nanjing University's Drama and Film Studies Department should also be considered a key part of our observation of the scenes of contemporary Chinese literature.

As I write this, I am reminded of a line from Meng Jinghui's *Sifan*: "With a pact we made in the previous life and the heavy snow today, let's go down the mountain together." Yes, let us go down the mountain together.

Beyond "Heartbreaking Stories,"
— How Do Young Writers Imagine "Hometown"? —
(Issue 5, 2017)

O
n May 1, 1921, *New Youth* magazine published Lu Xun's short story *Hometown*. Even without considering the broader context of modern Chinese literature, his discovery of "hometown" holds significant importance. Although "hometown" has long been a dimension of Chinese literary emotion and lyricism, dating back to the era of *The Book of Songs*, it was in *Hometown* by Lu Xun that it first expanded so compellingly into a space of imaginative possibility. From him onward, "hometown" became a starting point for rediscovering and generating various meanings, and one of the archetypal structures of modern Chinese novels. It could lead to vast worlds and fulfill grand literary ambitions. Countless literary works have since proven that Lu Xun's *Hometown* serves as a foundational point in modern Chinese literature, with many writers inheriting its legacy in the mere century since.

Today, let us not dwell on the "hometown" in modern Chinese novels, but rather focus on how young contemporary writers depict "hometown." Young writer Zhao Zhiming wrote the preface to Zhen Zaihuan's short story collection *Heartbreaking Stories from Zhumadian*, titled "Coming from Hometown, You Should Know All About It." Hometown stories are also a significant starting point for young writers, just as they were for their predecessors. At certain stages in their writing careers, many young writers today dedicate their most important works to their hometowns. This includes active young Chinese writers like Xu Zechen, Ge Liang, A Yi, Cao Kou, Sun Pin,

Fu Yuehui, Zheng Xiaolü, Yan Ge, and more. If we were willing, this list could be even longer.

In 2015, *Heartbreaking Stories from Pingle Town* by Yan Ge was published. Her previous novels, *Queen of May* and *Our Family*, were also set in "Pingle Town," her hometown of Pitong Town of Pi County. She said, "I finally realized that I am fascinated by the dirtiness, ugliness, and vulgarity of our town. I want to use all the poetry and beauty in the world to describe it, to tell everyone that this is the world I see and I deeply admire and love it." Just two years later, novelist Zhen Zaihuan, born in the 1990s, published his collection, *Heartbreaking Stories from Zhumadian*, boldly incorporating "heartbreaking stories" in the title as well. This time, the setting was his hometown, "Zhumadian." Reading these two collections, I believe Zhen's claim that "these stories are not just novels but lived experiences." This honesty and sincerity are what make Yan Ge and Zhen Zaihuan's "heartbreaking stories" dedicated to their hometowns a variant of early twenty-first-century "youth literature." The "heartbreak" comes from the fact that the hometown is an inseparable part of their lives and writing about "hometown stories" is a way of mourning their past. This variant might also include the media-dubbed "small-town youth writers."

On the eighth of this month, the 109th Sinan Reading Club event had the theme "Small-Town Youth and Hidden Villages—The Era We Write" About featured young writers Zhao Zhiming, Zhang Dun, Wei Sixiao, and Zhen Zaihuan, collectively labeled as "small-town youth" representing a specific social stratum. In a subsequent report, *Jiemian News* explicitly stated, "There is now a group of writers called 'small-town youth,' who unabashedly write about the hidden scenes between rural and urban areas." The term "rural-urban fringe" might be a more familiar to describe such a place, and Yan Ge once said, "This rural-urban fringe is my Eden, and I joyfully dig for poetry here." I do have a few doubts, though. When we label a group of writers as "small-town youth," are we referring to their writing themes, their identities, or a specific literary temperament?

The fixed image of "small-town youth" owes much to Jia Zhangke's films *Xiao Wu*, *Platform*, and *Unknown Pleasures*. The urban-rural mixed spectacle and hormonally charged idle youth clearly define "small town" and "youth." However, the contemporary media narrative's "small-town youth" writers might not relate to this. The only similarity they might share with real "small-town youth" is their birthplace. Unlike true "small-town youth," they are often uprooted and taken to faraway cities before their "youth" is complete.

For instance, in a GQ feature on writer A Yi titled "A Yi: Writer, Patient, Father's Funeral," it is noted that writers labeled as "small-town youth" often end up in provincial capitals or major cities like Beijing, Shanghai, and Guangzhou, or even abroad in New York. Even if they return to their hometowns, their hearts and ambitions belong to the big cities. Therefore, just as "heartbreaking stories" of hometowns are variants of "youth literature," the "small-town youth" label for young writers is more of a fashionable literary tag.

If these writers are aware that "small-town youth" has been sung in a superficial and vulgar manner by pop groups like Top Combine, would they still identify themselves with it? An old article on Tencent Dajia titled "Don't Scold Small-town Youth, There Are None in Small Towns" captures this irony. "There are no more youths in small towns," yet a group of writers in cities are identified as so, reflecting the quirks of our era. If "small-town youth" writers can only write "heartbreaking stories" about their hometowns, portraying the hidden rural scenes and the pettiness and boredom of life and humanity as just a variant of "youth literature," it merely offers city readers "spectacle" and "novelty," which are forms of urban entertainment that dilute literary creativity and imagination.

Therefore, if there are truly "small-town youth" writers, they might need to learn from their predecessors and seniors like Su Tong, Zhu Wen, A Yi, Cao Kou, and others on how to write about "hometown stories," not just the heartbreaking ones.

Of course, more importantly, "hometown stories" are certainly not just "heartbreaking stories." Beyond that, how do young writers imagine and write about "hometown"? The three young writers featured in our special section—Yuan Ling, Xiao Chang, and Zhou Kai—offer entirely different perspectives on "hometown stories." While writers born in the 1970s are now considered veterans, Yuan Ling remains a young novelist with an ideal akin to the *Airs of the States* in *The Book of Songs*. In his work *Snow Falling on the Mountains and Frost on the Hollows*, we should note the tangibility of his language, which allows him to focus on documenting the upheavals and transformations of rural China. This documentation is not rooted in concepts or ideologies but in the symbiotic relationship between words, people, and the physical world. Each sentence, and every word reaches its intended place solidly. This tangibility and precision in language can effectively correct the overly emotional "sadness" often found in young writers' "hometown stories."

Xiao Chang, on the other hand, is less honest than Yuan Ling. His *The Bat Is Singing* and *Snow Falling on the Mountains and Frost on the Hollows* share similarities, telling stories of the elderly returning to their decaying hometowns. However, Xiao Chang's narrative is intertwined with the story of "me" bringing my lover Xiaojing back to my hometown. How do the urban and rural realms influence each other? Can "the countryside," as a literary tradition's counterpoint and critique of "the city," still hold its ground today?

Zhou Kai's *The Unforgivable Tsavo Lion* depicts a drifter moving from the countryside to the city. This drifter is not alone but represents a group in every Chinese city today. They embody the city's darkness and secrets, an unknown world. Even from a thematic standpoint, Zhou Kai's portrayal of rural people in the city is not of familiar laborers in factories, construction sites, restaurants, or entertainment venues but of the invisible people in the city's hidden corners. These rural migrants, for various reasons, are often seen as the city's underlying anxiety and potential malevolence. What kind of world do they inhabit, and how do they connect to the rural history they left behind? I hope Zhou Kai is more than just a pioneer of a new theme. And even when focusing solely on the theme of hidden rural areas, Zhou Kai's published novels reveal a world where dialect and rural life are brutal and murky with palpable intensity.

It is okay to write young "heartbreaking stories" if, like Yan Ge, we do not deliberately prune away the "dirtiness, ugliness, and vulgarity" of "our town," or if, like Zhen Zaihuan, we "live out" these stories with genuine life experiences. What we fear is the "forced sorrow," mere rhetorical "heartbreaking stories." Worse still, under the din of mass media and publishing marketing, the literary assembly line for "heartbreaking stories" might quickly take off, turning "heartbreaking stories" into mere displays of performative pain.

Today is my daughter's twenty-second birthday. She has spent a decade growing up in a small town. Will she one day write her "heartbreaking stories" about her hometown? Will she identify as a "small-town youth?"

Science Fiction and Literature on
— the Eve of the "Singularity Era" —
(Issue 6, 2017)

T he other day, I had an intriguing conversation with Fei Dao, and
he said that we are living on the eve of the "Singularity Era." The
term piqued my curiosity, as it seemed to aptly describe our times
from various perspectives. To gain a deeper understanding, I asked him to
explain what he meant by the "Singularity Era." My impression was that the
term had previously been used to describe the boundless aftermath of the
Big Bang. Fei Dao provided a thoughtful written explanation:

> Today, we might be living on the eve of what is called the "Singularity
> Era." This means that due to breakthroughs in artificial intelligence and oth-
> er technologies, a day might come when human society takes on an entirely
> different form, akin to a physical "singularity" beyond our comprehension
> and imagination. Consequently, all our predictions and reasoning about
> such an era may become completely invalid. The future "human/post-hu-
> man" might be a being vastly different from us in both physiology and psy-
> chology.

Since our discussion centered around "science fiction," Fei Dao's "Singularity Era" primarily refers to the impact that the increasingly popular "artificial intelligence" (AI) might have on humanity. According to the news, AI
has already become a national strategy, complete with a timeline. Beyond
national strategy, it is a reality that AI robots capable of playing chess and
writing poetry have already surpassed the majority of people in these activ-

ities. Personally, I find the "post-human" era of AI quite terrifying. Although I don't know if I will live to see it, my fear has already arrived. For instance, when teaching students today, I cannot imagine a classroom where the "people" are a mix of natural humans and AI "humanoids." I certainly don't want to share the benefits of the AI era while bearing the fear of coexisting with AI "humanoids." I wish those of us who harbor this fear could pass away before the dawn of this "Singularity Era."

Coincidentally, the novels in this collection all touch on AI, each exploring the various possibilities that the "Singularity Era" might bring, thus fulfilling the so-called "science fiction" aspect of these works. It should be noted that I did not deliberately design this "AI" theme to cater to the current excitement around the grand daydream of AI. I did not simply ask everyone to write "science fiction"; I wanted them to write with a "literary" approach. I am not fixated on whether the science fiction is "hard" or "soft"; I care about the literary quality of the science fiction, and how it realistically influences our current literary imagination and expression of the world. In other words, I hope science fiction can expand the entire realm of our literature. Therefore, when creating the *Harvest* annual literature rankings last year, I suggested to Chief Editor Cheng Yongxin that science fiction could be included as potential candidates, which is why *With the Dragon* by Baoshu made the cut.

Of course, I do not oppose science fiction fans who prefer "unliterary" but "scientific" science fiction. However, that is not the type of science fiction I envision or am willing to accept, even if it adheres more strictly to the science fiction genre. Thus, during my conversation with Chen Qiufan, I mentioned that in global science fiction literature, my personal preference leans toward Stanisław Lem from Poland. In my view, his novels are both science fiction and literature. However, many contemporary Chinese science fiction novels often appear as semi-baked "science" under the guise of "fiction," lacking true novelistic qualities. I believe that to establish science fiction as "literature," we should not overly emphasize its uniqueness as a genre. Instead, we should affirm its literary qualities in terms of humanity, history, reality, the fate of humankind, narrative form, and language. In our current context, alongside emphasizing the scientific nature of science fiction, it is equally important to recognize that science fiction is also literature.

The resulting interest in AI is perhaps intriguing—why is everyone concerned about it? Among the four novels, Chen Qiufan's *Orphans of a Beautiful New World* tells the story of an individual whose life is extended, yet who becomes an old relic in the new world. To some extent, this encapsulates my fear. Upon reflection, my fear might stem from being seen as an oddity in a beautiful new world as an old relic. Zhao Song's *Limits* touches on the important science fiction theme of "interstellar travel," but at its core, the novel deals with the universal human longing for immortality. It explores the love story between a person stubbornly insisting on remaining natural and another who, weary of immortality, reverts to a natural state. In a sense, Chen Qiufan and Zhao Song's two novels could be seen as two parts of a single story.

Zhao Song said: "I just wanted to explore the issue of life and death in a different way. If we could live for two or three hundred years, what changes would occur in our lives? How would our thinking and emotions change? Are humans inherently greedy for life and fearful of death? Between life and death, what truly troubles and unsettles us? After writing it, I still have no answer. I just vaguely feel that people don't always yearn for new beginnings; sometimes they long for an end."

Two writers are both contemplating a shared proposition. However, within our current literary classification, they belong to distinct realms: science fiction and traditional literature. Each approaches the question from their unique perspective, pondering whether humans are inherently "natural" or recklessly striving for "immortality." Humanity has always dreamed of eternal life; but when that day finally arrives, can we truly be joyful? Or will we celebrate eternal life momentarily, only to grow weary? If so, what do we do then? Hence, the interest of many writers in the eve of the AI "Singularity Era" may stem from our fear, loneliness, and helplessness in this dark night? Literature aptly carries this fear and confusion.

Young writer Du Li's *The World's Best Lover* is commendable for its focus on young people. Despite her potential immaturity, as she states: "It's rather idealistic. How could there be such a perfectly obedient android? Even the most perfect lover would become tiresome over a lifetime and eventually be discarded. Many people believe it's mutual torment, but I think the novel reflects dissatisfaction with real-life relationships. When you have to face the messiness of relationships, who can say they're blameless? I think that android is a comfort to the loss of youth."

Her writing reminds young writers to be honest and recognize their limitations. Fei Dao's series in this collection, in my opinion, leans more toward "fantasy literature." One could argue that "science fiction" is a subset of fantasy literature, but science fiction does maintain a distinction between "hard" and "soft." Fei Dao's "fantasy literature" doesn't have to be hard and can even disregard science to indulge in fantasy. In the context of contemporary Chinese literature, where fantasy literature is weak, Fei Dao's work is significant. Our culture has a tradition of discussing supernatural folklore, and Fei Dao's There is a Man series retains a kinship with that tradition.

Science fiction should ignite the imagination within Chinese literature. I hope today's "science fiction fever" is not merely a genre revival, but the dawn of a "Singularity Era" for contemporary literature. Can science fiction usher in a "Singularity Era" for literature? I recently discussed this collection of stories with the editor of a newspaper's literary section. He suggested that, aside from realistically capturing the world, we can also grasp it through the absurd and the magical. Today, is science fiction a means to understand our future world? If so, we might easily appreciate the worlds crafted by Liu Cixin, Han Song, Hao Jingfang, and the four authors themselves in this collection.

Their novels sometimes depict distant futures and grand human narratives, but more often, their works resemble a poet's verse, expressing sentiments like, "Tonight I do not care about humanity; I only think of you." This "you" in this collection of stories may not, but often in their other works, it refers to the contemporary China of the "Singularity Era" eve. In this sense, merely debating whether science fiction is "soft" or "hard" doesn't truly capture the essence of their novels.

Writing on the "Borderline"
(Issue I, 2018)

This special topic focuses on novelists Tsering Norbu, Alat Asem, and Hei He. From this special feature emerged The Literary Entity Series: Library of Multi-Ethnic Classic by Contemporary Chinese Writers (Volume One), which received funding from the National Publishing Foundation in 2019 and was published by Yilin Press in 2020. The series includes classic works by contemporary Chinese novelists and poets from five ethnic groups: Mongolian, Tibetan, Uyghur, Kazakh, and Yi. Featured authors include Ayanga, Mo Hasbagan, Akbar Majid, Alat Asem, Tashi Dawa, Erkesh Kurmanbekovyna, Jidi Majia, Tsering Norbu, and Pema Tseden. The essay "Multi-Ethnic Chinese Contemporary Literature as a 'Literary Entity'" in this book expands on "Writing on the "Borderline."

Spring: The Moment When Poetry Comes
(Issue 2, 2018)

"I heard that Chang'an is brimmed with poets," says the monk Kukai to Bai Juyi in the film *Legend of the Demon Cat*. There have been many interpretations of this film, and in the WeChat era, everyone can become a chatterbox critic, making China undeniably a "nation of speakers." The film can also be seen as a gossip, history of how Bai Juyi became "Bai Juyi the Poet." As a later-developing art form, film may go further than novels in terms of "novelistic discourse," as seen in *Legend of the Demon Cat*, which blends fantastical "wild imaginings" with "novelistic nonsense." Without delving into the rise and fall of the Tang Dynasty (AD 618–907) in *Legend of the Demon Cat*, the statement "Chang'an is brimming with poets" could be even more fitting for today. Gathered at various poetry events, WeChat public accounts, and group chats, people labeled as "poets" and "famous poets" create the impression of an era where "everyone is a poet." This is the shared context for poets writing today and Bai Juyi writing in the Tang Dynasty.

"Chang'an is brimming with poets" made Bai Juyi anxious. What about today's poets? One difference is that, in an era full of poets, Bai Juyi had Li Bai from thirty years prior to look up to as a benchmark. What about today? If we acknowledge that those labeled as "famous poets" are the current era's Bai Juyi or potential "Bai Juyi," then we can look back thirty years to the so-called "golden age" of literature in the 1980s. This golden age is documented in various literary histories and its poets are the predecessors of today's "everybody is a poet" era. However, these predecessors from thirty years ago rarely produce grand works now. They are only "predecessors" in terms of their seating arrangements at poetry events. More importantly, even during the so-called golden age thirty years ago, did these predecessors become the Li Bai of their era?

In other words, in that seemingly grand era, no one became the Li Bai of their time, so there is still a need to import voices from abroad to bolster our literary landscape. Writing within the world has been a cornerstone of modern Chinese literature since its inception. Importing foreign works may be better than "when the cat's away, the mice will play," but ultimately, as Lu Xun said, "We must combine the present with the past to establish a new tradition." In recent years, various places have commemorated the centenary of Chinese new poetry. In one hundred years, how many such grand poetry eras have there been like the 1980s? If we do not have our own Li Bai, can these grand eras still stand proudly? Of course, we can confidently say that our new poetry is only a hundred years old, while Li Bai was the fruit of a long development from *The Book of Songs* to the flourishing Tang Dynasty.

The achievements and lessons of a century of new poetry need to be reevaluated. Celebrating the complete triumph of new poetry over the old might still be premature. Even thirty years ago, and earlier, despite the absence of our own "Li Bai," the "Bai Juyis" of the time continued their writing.

Now, let us consider today's "Bai Juyis." In the film *Legend of the Demon Cat*, Bai Juyi becomes the poet Bai Juyi because he is haunted by his *Song of Everlasting Regret*. In creating this poem, Li Bai becomes an artistic rival for Bai Juyi, but primarily, *Song of Everlasting Regret* is Bai Juyi's own statement about his identity as a poet. If he lived in an era where "Chang'an is brimming with poets" but had no Li Bai to look up to and no ambition like writing *Song of Everlasting Regret*, then the notion of "everybody is a poet" is merely an illusion of a flourishing poetic era.

Regarding the origins of Chinese poetry, "*siwuxie*" should be considered one. This is the starting point I hoped for in this poetry feature and the reason I chose Bing Yi, Yu Zhen, Sun Qiuchen, Kang Xue, and Zhou Xinqi. In their work, there is a preserved sense of innocence, sincerity, and honesty toward the world and aesthetics. Having our own "Li Bai" is important, but if young poets today merely turn "Li Bai" into rigid "literary knowledge," making their writing an indigestible mix of imitation, translation, and showing off, it's better to open their hearts, like the poets in this feature, embrace the world, love and be loved, hurt and be hurt, and carefully wipe clean each Chinese character and place it where it belongs, thus composing a poem.

Spring is the moment when poetry comes.

Prose in the Wild
(Issue 3, 2018)

I am not entirely sure if "field" is meant to contrast with "indoor work," but one thing is certain: field must be done "in the wild." Thus, it seemed interesting to appropriate "field" as the keyword for this prose feature. It is both a verb, indicating the act of writing, suggesting that literature is not confined to "indoor" endeavors, and a noun, referring to the completed "field" by Mao Chenyu and Liu Guoxin. Their literary outcomes accumulate as their "workbooks."

"Wild" encompasses the geographical and everyday spaces of fields, countryside, and wilderness, but more importantly, it signifies an unrestrained "wild heart" in a spiritual or aesthetic sense—a wild, untamed, and raw literary temperament. Contemporary literature is increasingly "domesticated," disciplined, constrained, and often self-indulgent and decorative, with prose being particularly affected. Despite this deviation, many writers still revel in it. Hence, I propose the concept of prose in the "wild," hoping to correct this deviation by turning toward, rooting in, and embracing the "wild." This can involve traveling between different geographies or a shift in the writer's mind, replenishing and nurturing it.

For field, writers must first be active doers, or practitioners. With instant information and convenient transportation, one can quickly learn about distant events and travel to any corner of the earth, even beyond. However, our knowledge and arrival are often second-hand experiences and landscapes, making it hard to convert them into unique personal feelings and experiences, thereby failing to create an "imaginary foreign land" for individuals. As a result, emphasizing action and practice aims to regain physical and mental health, liberation, and freedom, transforming passive knowledge and arrival into proactive exploration and discovery.

Liu Guoxin, as an outsider and intruder, maintains a sense of humility, awe, taboo, and anxious curiosity toward Xinjiang and the unfamiliar world. A prose writer should not arrange their journey based on travel guides and literary conferences but should restore the freedom of a wanderer on the earth. Liu Guoxin's "wandering" in the border inns' markets and "ambling" in southern Xinjiang villages exemplify this. It is through this "wandering" and "ambling" that he saw the camels of Turpan, the bazaar of Urumqi, the pigeons of Kashgar, the bread of the campus, the market of the border inns, the donkeys of the countryside, the invisible breaths, the children stepping on yellow leaves, and the deserted Erdaoqiao ... all these mundane scenes and events are brightened, becoming personal firsthand feelings and experiences.

Prose deeply relies on personal sensations and experiences. The current impoverished state of prose can largely be attributed to the lack of firsthand, authentic personal sensations and experiences. In her collection *Westward Notes*, Liu Guoxin repeatedly acknowledges her "shallowness" as a passerby and temporary resident. Many contemporary prose works attempt to disguise this "shallowness" with borrowed knowledge and literary cosmetic surgery designed to impress readers. When reading these works, one might encounter a wealth of obscure facts, giving the illusion that China is a land of unofficial scholars. However, this so-called knowledge often turns out to be "excessive redundancy," with the shallowness remaining just as shallow, and the inserted content feeling like prosthetics, disconnected and wandering.

There are also some deceptive tricks used in writing, such as linguistic showmanship that dazzles without conveying any real meaning. Some writers rely on insincere emotions to create forced climaxes or exaggerate their own minor pains and falsely portray them as representative of the entire nation, making it seem as if they are always on the verge of tears, showcasing their supposed suffering. Meanwhile, other writers avoid confronting the darker and more evil aspects of reality, instead creating harmless, pain-free, and pleasantly refreshing illusions of peace on paper. Proses are becoming increasingly trivial and constrained, turning into mere desktop ornaments and sentimental "chicken soup for the soul." Additionally, some employ cheap charity to pose as profound humanism and realism, among other tactics.

However, Liu Guoxin's "shallowness" is precisely the sincerity needed in prose, where the writer acknowledges the limitations of their journey—possessing an unrestrained "wild" heart, full of ambition, yet aware of their shame, anxiety, confusion, and weakness. This consciousness nurtures her genuine restraint. As she says, "During my nearly three months in Xinjiang, I transitioned from romanticism to reality, from night to day or day to night ... Writing this now, I feel my life in Xinjiang was like paradise, especially at the border inn, where ordinary days turned legendary. Here, I felt closer to my body and soul, carrying them with me every day, caring for them like a baby." Her *Westward Notes* leaves an invisible darkness and a temporarily unreachable secret land for herself and her readers. If she revisits these places in the future, what will her *Westward Notes* be like?

"Field" is more than going to the "border regions." For Mao Chenyu, the "wild" refers to his hometown, to which he frequently returns from his current life in Shanghai. Many dedicated prose writers have written about their hometowns, but how many have done so after truly rooting themselves there like Mao Chenyu? The feigned "nostalgia" is a common ailment in prose.

"The village is increasingly full of bad things." On April 26, 2012, Mao Chenyu wrote in an article titled "I Am Going to Dongting Lake This Afternoon" on his personal website, "For nearly a month, there has been massive construction in Ximaojia. Internal management is in disarray, and the villagers' group cannot effectively govern their affairs, nor can the clans coordinate public matters." The website's home page features a detailed peaceful natural ecological map with birds, fish, frogs, snakes, deer, rice, and camphor trees, contrasting sharply with the perceived disarray and decay of the village. Mao Chenyu, an idealist, easily becomes a pessimist in the present.

While the novelist's "stamp-sized place" is often a rhetorical device, Ximaojia area is real and specific to Mao Chenyu. He has meticulously detailed the contemporary historical evolution of this place by the Dongting Lake in Hunan:

> In 1958, during the People's Commune Movement, two natural villages from the Ximaojia area were relocated. The Ren and Liu families' villages merged with the Chen and Mao villages, forming the Third Production Team. In the 1970s, due to the construction of the Tieshan Reservoir in the county's highlands, the Third Production Team relocated and absorbed two large Liu family households, commonly referred to as "Tieshan's." When the land was redistributed to individual households, the Third Production Team split into the Fourth and Fifth Villager Groups.
>
> As a result, Ximaojia now comprises four clans: the Mao, Ren, Liu, and Tieshan's Liu families. Regardless of political reforms, the Mao clan has always considered others as tenants in their village, thus maintaining control over village affairs. The Mao lineage, tracing back twelve generations to a single ancestor, has seen many branches die out over time, leaving two main branches that have further divided into two sub-branches—one with four households and the other with five, totaling nine households. Currently, three households have moved to the city, two have members working away from home year-round, leaving only four households residing in the village.

Mao Chenyu doesn't fit the typical mold of a writer aware of his literary identity. For him, writing is just one facet of his intricate relationship with his hometown. His pursuits extend beyond the written word to include documentary filmmaking with projects like "Rice Movies" and other artistic endeavors. Mao Chenyu is a profound excavator of his hometown. He delves into the local history and customs from an archaeological perspective, though this kind of knowledge archaeology is not his strongest suit. He is a sincere ecologist, a naturalist, an ethnography student, a rural philosopher, an art practitioner, and an ardent traditional winemaker ... Despite the variety, these identities harmoniously coexist, making him difficult to categorize within conventional academic disciplines. He is, without a doubt, not an expert in the strictest sense.

His public account includes a segment titled Shamanic Art, featuring entries like "The Magpie's Image Event" and "The Story of 'Seventh Sister' and Young Witches." Mao Chenyu, in many ways, embodies the primal shamans of early human civilizations, assuming numerous roles. This feature includes his writings not to confine him to the role of a "prose writer," but to recognize how his organically grown words, sprouting from the countryside and earth, can inspire contemporary prose. These texts naturally branch into philosophy, ethnography, anthropology, and art, yet their roots remain firmly planted in the earth. As Mao Chenyu says, "The earth thinks." Thus, the earth should be considered the world's deepest and most expansive thinker.

As writers, Liu Guoxin and Mao Chenyu share a common trait: they investigate to gain knowledge and then infuse their works with appropriate emotions and thoughts. However, their prose "field" still appears overly precise and tidy. If Liu Guoxin, aware of her limitations, could become a forceful dismantler of constraints and barriers, and if Mao Chenyu could grow like wild grass spreading to the edges of the fields, stubbornly remaining as resilient barnyard grass even in the rice paddies, we might restore prose as the freest literary form. Independent in character and healthy in mind, they would start by "wilding" themselves and "wilding" prose, becoming true fielders in the genuine sense of prose writing. Let us imagine such prose and imagine such an atmosphere.

The Overlap of Multiple Subjects
(Issue 4, 2018)

When I stumbled upon Sugiura Kohei's *Multi-subject Asia* in a bookstore, I was immediately drawn to the title. The concept of "multi-subject Asia" is explored in depth in the final section of the book's first theme, "Thoughts on Asian Design," specifically within "Asia's Multi-Subject Phenomena." Sugiura explains: "In the mythical space of Asia, countless 'small subjects,' or even 'subtle presences' not deemed as subjects, populate the universe's myriad phenomena." His idea of "multi-subject" counters the Western perspective where the designer is always the central subject. He believes good design satisfies clients, designers, and users alike, embodying a "multi-subject" approach.

I appropriate the concept of "multi-subject" to describe the contemporary literary landscape as an "overlap of multiple subjects." This emphasizes that the literature of any era is coauthored by countless different subjects, creating an interwoven or cacophonous narrative. In modern Chinese, "overlap" means "to superimpose, making one thing occupy the same position and coexist with another."

This involves continuously replacing the "who" in "who is writing" with "multiple or countless small subjects.'" These "small subjects" are not the uniform "I" that branches out from the rigid literary dogma of a communal "we." Instead, they encompass countless diverse others beyond the "I." A healthy literary ecosystem should tolerate "multiple or countless small subjects," or even "subtle presences" not deemed as subjects. In other words, an organic and vibrant literary era should be one where multiple subject overlap and intertwine.

It is undeniable that even before the internet, writing could be "multi-subject," but published and disseminated works often ended up as "single-subject." At best, they could achieve "few-subject" or "limited-subject" status. This was the reality of contemporary Chinese literature before online writing became feasible. Literary production centered on published newspapers, journals, and books effectively ensured a "few-subject" or "limited-subject" scenario. However, the development of the internet, particularly in the era of Weibo and WeChat, has provided the necessary technical support for "multi-subject" literary expression. While literary expression certainly involves more than just technical support, it is undeniable that bypassing traditional publishing platforms and directly writing online, presenting a complete personal writing history from the apprentice stage, is an experience shared by Shen Shuzhi, Datou Ma, and Li Ruo.

For instance, Shen Shuzhi writes:

> I started writing diaries (the way an article is published is called "Diary Writing") on my Douban home page in 2010, influenced by friends I followed who wrote about rural landscapes and people. Their writings awakened something in me, especially Fengxing Shuishang, who wrote wonderfully about the countryside in southern Anhui. Reading his work resonated deeply with me, prompting me to start writing. At that time, I had a lot to write about, being a student with plenty of time. I often wrote day and night, immediately publishing my work online, receiving encouragement and comments, which made me feel less alone, and motivated me to continue.

Similarly, Datou Ma reflects:

> I live on Douban. I registered an account during high school when there were few users. Before that, I was active on Tianya Forum. When some friends moved from Tianya to Douban, I followed. I started on Tianya at

around twelve, writing posts, following threads, making friends, and becoming a moderator. Later, I used Douban similarly.

Li Ruo shares her experience:

In late 2015, an editor from NetEase's The Livings column reached out to me for submissions, and my articles were published. I always thought getting paid for writing was out of my reach, something reserved for sophisticated writing. I used to think my writing was not good enough. But my stories about migrant work and rural life got published! From then on, I fell in love with writing.

Thus, it is the online realm that has truly ushered in the era of "multi-subject overlap" in literature and made it a tangible reality. Without the internet, beyond occasional literary enclaves like Folk Language and Literature in *Tianya* and Flower City Interest in *Flower City*, I wonder how many literary journals would have embraced Li Ruo's writing—not out of charitable literary egalitarianism or as mere sociological field samples, but as literature deserving genuine respect. It is not just Li Ruo's narrative essays chronicling "observations and experiences," or even Datou Ma's professional "travelogue," which, diverging from traditional travelogues, might encounter publication hurdles. Not to suggest they couldn't be published in newspapers or magazines, but considering someone like Fan Yusu, whose "I Am Fan Yusu" was only released on the WeChat public account NoonStory, one can conservatively estimate that within existing literary journals—an objective hierarchy or stifling order exists—Li Ruo's work would most likely appear in local newspaper supplements, while Datou Ma's travel narratives might find space in non-literary periodicals. Therefore, literary journals still have a long way to go in embracing and accommodating the overlapping and competitive writing of "multiple subjects."

Perhaps "multi-subject overlap" can only truly flourish in the online sphere. On the internet, NetEase's Li Ruo and Douban's Shen Shuzhi, and Shen Shuzhi and Datou Ma both on Douban, can coexist. Whether Shen Shuzhi and Datou Ma, both from Anhui, have any intersection on Douban is beside the point—they exist independently on the internet, writing individually and cultivating their own readerships. Just as they may or may not intersect, their readerships are similarly diverse. Moreover, the internet serves as a breeding ground for new literary forms, such as Datou Ma's novels and travelogues.

"Multi-subject overlap" is not merely about "who is writing." Although "the death of the author" was proposed as early as the 1960s, it is worth considering whether we can hastily declare the "death of the author" when trying to fully grasp the significance of these "records" or "non-fiction" writings by Shen Shuzhi, Datou Ma, and Li Ruo. I believe their writing is distinct from fiction—authors are inherently part of "records" or "non-fiction" texts. How could these "records" or "non-fiction" not be connected to the "subjects" writing them?

Consider Shen Shuzhi, Datou Ma, and Li Ruo—they arrived in Beijing in the new millennium, each pursuing different professions, possessing unique life aspirations and lifestyles, navigating distinct urban landscapes, and consequently, viewing the world through different lenses. Indeed, sharing the same city, these writing "subjects" each have their own "identities." These "identities" serve as their starting points and backgrounds, setting the limits for their detailed exploration of urban life and shaping their imagination and narratives. The "writings" of these diverse "subjects" overlap, intersect, or compete with one another. Are they engaging in dialogue or confrontation? Are they offending or absorbing, converging, or flowing, as they do in the current internet landscape, where they coexist without necessarily interacting? Let us avoid imposing hierarchical structures or creating literary "pecking orders," and instead, allow them the freedom to speak, illuminating all "subtle presences."

From "Old Tales Retold" to "Fan Fiction"
(Issue 5, 2018)

G enerational differences are objectively real, regardless of physiological age. In May 2018, *Break the Wall: Keywords about Network
Culture*, edited by Professor Shao Yanjun of Peking University, was
published. Its foundational premise acknowledges the existence of "walls"
between various cultural communities. Because these "walls" exist, the
idea of "breaking the wall" exists. The book, presented through keywords,
unveils a "community" of youth subculture, which, to many of us, remains
an "unfamiliar community." Reading it reveals that the differences between
various groups in our world are far greater than we might have imagined.
This serves as the context for our column—"From 'Old Tales Retold' to 'Fan
Fiction.'"

From a certain perspective, both *Seven and a Quarter* by Huang Chongkai and *The Tiger and the City That Never Sleeps* by Chen Zhiwei are results of
textual reconstruction. Huang Chongkai repositions Taiwan filmmaker Edward Yang and his films, along with the cinematic era, in terms of time and
space, retelling Edward Yang's stories under the promise of new technology.
Chen Zhiwei's novel "poaches" and re-encodes various textual resources.
Their work seems akin to the familiar practice of "old tales retold" in literary
history, but it is not exactly the same. Their writing background is rooted in
new artificial intelligence technology, and the vibrant new world of youth
cultures like cinephile culture and fan culture.

"Old tales retold" is a noteworthy phenomenon in contemporary literature, though not an entirely new one. Within modern Chinese literature as
an example, a tradition of "old tales retold" can be traced. While Lu Xun was

not the first to experiment with this tradition, his *Old Tales Retold* stands as a classic example. Lu Xun described *Old Tales Retold* as "sometimes based on old books, sometimes purely made up, and often showing a lack of reverence for ancient figures compared to contemporary ones, leading to occasional flippancy." However, he also emphasized that he was "first of all, very serious" about it. To Lu Xun, there is a traceable path "from seriousness to flippancy." While Lu Xun scholars might defend the flippancy in *Old Tales Retold,* Lu Xun himself distinguished and reflected on it. Broadly speaking, seriousness and flippancy are two ends of the "old tales retold" spectrum. A good novelist can subtly balance between these two ends. Lu Xun's *Old Tales Retold* is serious overall, with flippancy in parts. Drawing a line from "seriousness" to "flippancy," *Oneness* by Feng Tang approaches the flippant end, while the rewriting of "Stories of the Tang Dynasty" by Wang Xiaobo balances well between seriousness and flippancy. Moreover, considering the new aesthetics of "nonsensical," humorous, and even "spoof" styles represented by Hong Kong filmmaker Stephen Chow in the early twenty-first century, the boundary between seriousness and flippancy becomes increasingly ambiguous.

Although infused with cinephile culture, Huang Chongkai's *Seven and a Quarter* can still be considered "old tales retold." By crafting a narrative around the popular entertainment of Edward Yang's films, Huang's work looks back to Edward Yang of another era, recalling Lu Xun's *The Flight to the Moon*, which portrays the downfall of a hero.

The Tiger and the City That Never Sleeps by Chen Zhiwei exemplifies "emergent literature." While Chen Zhiwei repeatedly assures me that the "knowledge" embedded in his novels is not essential for understanding them, it is undeniable that the experience differs with or without that background knowledge. I asked Chen Zhiwei to unveil the underlying themes of his novel and also exchanged thoughts on *The Tiger and the City That Never Sleeps* with his contemporary, the novelist San San. They both possess a similar depth of "knowledge." Born in the late 1960s, I find myself significantly distanced from their cultural references, recognizing only a few universally acknowledged classic elements. Thus, without delving into Chen Zhiwei's knowledge, *The Tiger and the City That Never Sleeps* might be perceived as avant-garde literature at its most flashy.

The Tiger and the City That Never Sleeps diverges from the traditional "old tales retold." Take a look at this exchange between Chen Zhiwei and me:

Q: Taking *The Tiger and the City That Never Sleeps* as an example, having knowledge of contemporary anime and its memes undoubtedly alters one's understanding of references in the novel. Once those references are recognized, what seems negative might actually be quite positive. The main storyline of *The Tiger and the City That Never Sleeps* is derived from Toriyama Akira's *Dragon Ball*, making it a retelling of the anime, or in other words, a piece of "fan fiction." While "old tales retold" isn't new in traditional literary creation, is there a difference between the "second creation" in contemporary fan fiction and traditional "old tales retold?" Where do these differences lie? Actually, even without looking to the younger generation of writers, Wang Xiaobo's "old tales retold" and similar literary practices from before already show significant differences.

A: The lyrics from He Yong's "Pretty Girl" in 1994 go: "Sun Wukong threw away his golden staff and crossed the ocean/Sha Wujing sails to fish everything out/Zhu Bajie returned to Gao Village stay with a female masseuse/Tang Sanzang chews on instant noodles, becoming a fortuneteller on the street." I am not sure if this Sun Wukong is the same as the one from *Dragon Ball*, although it aligns well. In *Dragon Ball*, Sun Wukong does abandon his staff and travel to Japan, even becoming an alien (a *Saiyan*). Toriyama began *Dragon Ball* in 1984, completing its serialization by 1995. I finished reading the manga around 2000. This work sold billions of copies and holds the Guinness World Record for the most game adaptations of a manga. Yet, it took twenty years post-serialization for someone to write a serious piece of related "fan fiction." It is quite late in fact. And it is an outdated question,

"Have you watched *Naruto*?" since it began serialization in 1999. My taste in anime is quite retro, favoring works from ten to twenty years ago, like *Serial Experiments Lain* (1998) and *Revolutionary Girl Utena* (1997). Even among the recently popular Masaaki Yuasa's works, I prefer older ones like *Kemonozume* (2006) and *Kaiba* (2008).

This brings me to my first point: the inherent lag in literary creation and the literary circle's resistance to progress. Literature is not news; it is vague and significantly delayed. I am actually indulging in nostalgia, yet many readers perceive it as "new knowledge." The second point addresses the differences between young people's "fan fiction" and traditional "old tales retold." The primary distinction lies in the arbitrariness of the original text selection. Even an author like James Joyce used Homer's *Odyssey* as a reference for *Ulysses* because it was a classic. Young fan fiction writers, however, can jump off from any point. My use of *Dragon Ball* is quite selective and intentional compared to most fan fiction authors who lack a strong authorial consciousness. They might start writing immediately upon inspiration from reading anything without questioning why simply because they want to. For example, both *Ghost Blows Out the Light* by Tianxia Bachang and *Grave Robbers' Chronicles* by Nanpai Sanshu share a tomb-raiding theme. Initially, the latter intended to use characters from the former directly, writing it as fan fiction before modifying it into a stand-alone story. Online novels can even become fan fiction based on other online novels.

Another difference is the insignificance of intertextual references. With a weaker authorial consciousness, intertextuality becomes irrelevant. A popular type of fan fiction in the fan community is HP fan fiction, or Harry Potter fan fiction, widely written and read across different cultures. I know a friend who writes it but admits to never having read *Harry Potter* and even believes "the original novels are probably not well-written." Their joy lies in "pairing characters," with anyone forming a "CP" (couple). Ever heard of the pairing of Dumbledore and his phoenix?

Third, my works differ from typical online fan fiction, a distinction that is easily felt. Few would classify my novels as "fan fiction" without my own admission. My authorial consciousness is strong, perhaps even more so than other serious novelists. Unlike traditional serious novelists, though, I also experience the thrill of "pairing characters."

I argue that the shift from "old tales retold" to "fan fiction" reflects more than just a trend. *The Tiger and the City That Never Sleeps* by Chen Zhiwei may not strictly fall under the category of popular "fan fiction," but it exemplifies how parts of our literary era are now being expressed in the manner of fan fiction. This literary phenomenon, which is occurring online, has already begun to influence the literary creations of the younger generation, yet it has not received the attention it deserves.

Whether it is anime and cosplay that attract niche communities, or fan fiction such as "CP literature" that has become a distinct genre, new media platforms are fostering a more diverse and abundant literary production. Most researchers, as I understand it, do not regard this as a literary phenomenon; at most, they see it as a "cultural entertainment" phenomenon. Participants in "fan fiction" may also view it as a form of play, a grand carnival among like-minded individuals, diligently creating for their own enjoyment.

With such youthful creativity and passion poured into such text production, whether in the early days of "CP literature" focused on football star fandoms or the later phenomenon of Harry Potter fan fiction, what the producers of these "quasi-literature," "sub-literature," and "marginal literature" are doing, participating in, or hoping to gain are all worthy of field research. The goal of studying such writing is not to discipline it into existing literary genealogies, but to recognize that if youth writing in this field has sustained rich productivity, it is at least worthy of attention. Furthermore, these writings may reveal the past and future of youth literature. Gaming behavior is the starting point, but reflection on and mastery of this behavior can lead to true creation.

Huang Chongkai, with his broad vision and ambition, attempts to rewrite and rethink Taiwan's literary history in a literary form. In his review of film history, he chooses Edward Yang, who adeptly presents Taiwan's changing landscapes through singular perspectives (a murder case, a child's observation). Similarly, Chen Zhiwei uses *Dragon Ball* as a framework, boldly creating anew on the foundation of Akira Toriyama's imaginative second-creation work. His text, with unrestrained imagination, unfolds like a continuously expanding maze. From *Journey to the West* to *Dragon Ball* and then to Chen Zhiwei's *The Tiger and the City That Never Sleeps*, the shells of characters from Sun Wukong to Super *Saiyan* Wukong to the Tiger come off, revealing a unique literary presence through free growth and proliferation. What remains constant is the soul of creation.

Chen Zhiwei's writing highlights the aspects I am concerned with the trend of contemporary popular "fan fiction," that is, the literary potential of characters separated from their original stories. This process of stripping and recreating characters can be random for the author, essentially a form of play. I believe that the "authorial consciousness" Chen Zhiwei proposes is important. From the starting point (respecting originality and paying homage to the classics without random replication) to the production process (reflective recreation process), Chen Zhiwei's writing differs from the popular "fan fiction" in cyberspace. These differences, subtle in the vast homogeneous creations, bring inspiration and a sense of renewal and possibility to literary experiments outside the internet.

Perhaps it can be expected that among the young writers who indulge in the carnival of "fan fiction," there may be future pioneers of new literature. Of course, the attention we give should not be about encouraging everyone to write "fan fiction" online. In fact, if you are not a fan, it is difficult to participate in the creation of "fan literature" that consumes popular culture. We should consider the relationship between the popular culture of the younger generation—such as film and television, anime, online games, online literature, and live streaming—and their writing. The literature of the younger generation should not merely inherit literary traditions; with an open literary view, youth popular culture can also become a new source of energy for new literature.

Literary "Journey to the West"
— Might Be More Than a Novel's Geography —
(Issue 6, 2018)

The concept of "West" in Chinese civilization has not been static. During the Han (202 BC–AD 220) and Tang dynasties, the term "Western Regions" referred to lands beyond the Yumen Pass and Yang Pass (in Gansu Province). Earlier still, the Zhou (1046–256 BC) territories around the capitals of the Han and Tang dynasties, Chang'an, were considered the westernmost lands. The well-known *Journey to the West* is about traveling westward to India to retrieve Buddhist scriptures. In modern discourse, "the west" specifically refers to the cultural divide between East and West, which differs significantly from the ancient geographical concept. My aim is not to trace the long historical evolution of "the west" in the Chinese context—a task beyond my expertise—but to acknowledge that regardless of its geographical changes, the Buddhist Paradise (India), Western Regions, the westernmost lands and the west possess a fascinating and strange allure that comes with the exotic geography, appearing distant and foreign as the center imagines the border—the other and the foreign.

In literary terms, moving westward, or going a journey to the west, involves examining how the exotic, the strange, and the heterogeneous can invigorate literature's potential. From this perspective, Chinese modern literature has been energized by two formidable forces from the "West": one from the Western world in Europe and America and the other from the vast internal regions of the western part of China. Each has injected new cultural and literary elements, shaping the flesh and bones of Chinese modern literature. Intriguingly, the latter has sometimes been mobilized to counter the former, using the wild and ancient remnants of Chinese western civilization to contend with the modern West, transforming time into space to establish national and local values. Thus, a literary journey to the West can lead to different outcomes depending on which "West" is explored.

China does not have a clear distinction like between Paris and the provinces. *Wu Ding's Journey to the West* by Tangfei was originally titled *West of Beijing*. In this novel of hers, using "Dadu" (the Grand Capital) instead of "Beijing" might enhance the novel's spatial imagination. However, from a literary geography and aesthetic perspective, "West of Beijing" offers a view of the vast interior of the continent. The areas "East of Beijing," or those slightly north or south, have been economically advanced at different stages of China's development. The Northeast is an old industrial region, while the eastern coastal areas to the south are results of reform and opening up. The central transitional zone between East and West often prefers to identify as "central leaning East."

This special topic, first of all, does not talk about the "West" of the "Eastward Spread of Western Learning," but considers the "West" in terms of the Chinese geographical map, "West of Beijing." Then, a literary journey westward should first explore, in the sense of literary geography, the geographical and cultural landscapes that shape literature. Before 1949, literary contributions, based on writers' origins, beside Sichuan in Southwest China, primarily came from "East of Beijing," including northern, southern, and parts of central regions. Even writers from central and Sichuan regions became prominent after moving eastward, such as Guo Moruo, Ba Jin, and Shen Congwen, who did not achieve fame in Sichuan and Hunan. The temporary literary prosperity in Xi'an, Guilin, Kunming, Chongqing, and Yan'an in the West and Southwest was due to specific war situations and geopolitical factors. Therefore, extremely, until the mid-1970s, Chinese modern literature was essentially Eastern literature in terms of literary geography. Most literary histories are written this way, and the facts are basically so.

This does not mean that the writing of "localized" writer of western literature was entirely absent during this historical period. Recently published regional literary histories of provinces or of even smaller geographical space have unearthed many "localized" western writers, particularly among various ethnic groups in the west, each with its own "small traditions." Literary histories have recognized poets like Chang Yao, but the inclusion of western "local" writers as an indispensable part of Chinese literature is a development of the last 30–40 years.

Three or four decades ago, it was rare for writers "localized" in the western regions of China to achieve classic status. Yet, this did not diminish the profound impact of western regional culture on the development of modern Chinese literature. As early as the 1980s, numerous studies explored the relationship between Sichuan culture, Hunan culture, and modern Chinese literature. In fact, regarding the relationship between regions and literature, Lu Xun, when editing the *Compendium of Chinese New Literature*, did not limit himself to the eastern regions. Thus, he said, "Jian Xian'ai described Guizhou, and Pei Wen focused on Yuguan." The romanticism, eccentricity, and wildness of writers like Shen Congwen and Ai Wu contributed more evidently to the heterogeneity of modern Chinese literature. Similarly, if we consider heterogeneity, northern and northeastern writers are also noteworthy. Although in terms of novels, contemporary Northeastern literature is in significant decline, with only a few mentioned authors such as Chi Zijian, Diaodou, Liu Qing, Sun Huifen, Jin Renshun, Shuang Xuetao, and Ban Yu, in the 1930s and 1940s, modern Chinese literature experienced a strong "northeast wind," much like the "northwest wind" in Chinese literature and art in the 1980s.

Whether in literature, film, or music and art, the great geographical discoveries of the western regions since the 1980s have significantly impacted the ecosystem, tastes, and landscape of Chinese arts and literature, such as the Southwestern avant-garde artists and poets, and the "northwest wind" in film and music. Writing this, I still vividly recall the phrase "My home is on the Loess Plateau," as well as Chen Kaige, Zhang Yimou's film *Yellow Earth*, and Yang Liping's dance, all of which are popular symbols of the western region. In terms of the revolution in novels, the western region of the 1980s reminds us primarily of Xizang enlightening Tashi Dawa and Ma Yuan's "experimental novels."

However, it does not stop there. The novels of Wang Meng, Zhang Chengzhi, and Zhang Xianliang all have their own western backgrounds, though we rarely discuss their "western" literary and poetic significance of the 1980s independently. Broadening our view from the west to the central region, in fact, Han Shaogong and the "Shaanxi Army's Eastward Expedition," for example, whether in literary temperament or self-identity, both belong to the geographical concept of "west of Beijing" in Chinese literary geography.

Mr. Man and Ding Yan's novels depict merely the landscapes and people of northwestern China. Mr. Man once lived there, but from the beginning, he does not identify as a "localized" writer. Ding Yan remains a "localized" writer but will soon move to Beijing to pursue a master's degree in anthropology. Even so, unlike before the 1970s, in the literary westward journey, we now see the rise of many "localized" writers from Gansu, Qinghai, Ningxia to Inner Mongolia, and Xinjiang. For instance, in Xinjiang, there are writers like Liu Liangcheng, Li Juan, Dong Libo, Wang Zu, Shen Wei, Alat Asem, and Erkesh Kurmanbekovyna. The situation is similar in the Southwest. After three or four decades of effort, the literature of "localized" writers in the western regions has become a significant part of Chinese literature. Thus, this special topic, in my imagination, extends far beyond just the three novelists Ding Yan, Mr. Man, and Tangfei. Even from a geographical perspective, there should be more writers included, not just from the Northwest but also from Yunnan, Guizhou, Sichuan, Xizang, etc.

Ding Yan has extensively traveled the vast western regions. She writes, "The various ethnic groups in the Northwest live together in a serene atmosphere, an unforgettable image. Daily life includes taboos and the tensions of living, talks, and unspeakable things, releasing a comfortable vitality between taboos and freedom. The bustling markets and shops are vibrant, with the distant mosque domes glistening with golden crescents. Everything is harmonious and comforting." I have seen photos she took during her travels in the west—vast, deep blue skies, quiet mountains, buildings, and people leading a peaceful life. In a sense, Ding Yan, through literature, reconstructs an encyclopedic folk history of the multi-ethnic settlements in the west, without falling into exotic spectacle or sensationalism. Her work *Dadongxiang* presents the cycles of life and death with a sense of ritual, order, and the religious solemnity of everyday life. Different generations' spirits quietly reflect the light of human nature in the mundane world.

Mr. Man spent his childhood in Xining because his father moved from the south of Yangtze to Qinghai Province in the 1960s and 1970s, settling down there. The dual life experience of Suzhou and Xining created a contrast between eastern and western literary landscapes for him. His work *The Devil* is dedicated to his father and the Northwest of his memory. He believes the Northwest is a broader stage for storytelling, where the distance between people is closer, and conflicts and contradictions are more intense. Therefore, unlike Ding Yan, he rarely writes about people against the backdrop of western ethnography. Instead, he draws from the stylistic and rhetorical significance of "going west for enlightenment" to capture the grand and open spirit of the west.

More importantly, the west is both spatial and temporal. If Ding Yan is immersed in the "constancy" and "unchanging" aspects of the west, Mr. Man perceives "rewriting" and "change." The traditions initiated by Wang Meng's *In Ili* and *This Side of the Landscape*, Zhang Xianliang's *My Bodhi Tree* and *Half of Man is Woman*, A Lai's *Red Poppies* and *Empty Mountain*, and Tsering Norbu's *Prayers in the Wind* that directly confront contemporary western realities and trauma memories are continued by Mr. Man's *The Devil*. This allows the broad sense of "scar literature" to be remembered, written, and passed on in the current generation of young writers.

It is worth mentioning that I was initially unsure whether *Wu Ding's Journey to the West* of Tangfei could be included in this special topic, because this novel breaks through the narrow literary geographical boundaries I set at the beginning. The westward journey of Wu Ding reaches St. Petersburg, but as Tangfei said, "The West has always existed in the imagination of Eastern civilization as a foreign world. As the origin of Buddhist culture, or the world of European civilization, and also the realm of the dead. The West that Wu Ding goes to is Europe, but in this story with the 'reverse entropy' setting, the Eastern world is more modern. Moreover, Wu Ding's group do not go there to 'obtain' something. The goal is clear, just to pass through, then return. Whether building the road succeeds ultimately returns to themselves. The geographical significance of the 'West' is dissolved, and unlike other stories, it is not a spiritual symbol encouraging the traveler to move forward. The 'West' is just a midpoint, a station. The westward journey is the endpoint of the story."

Tangfei's *Wu Ding's Journey to the West* opens the possibility of imagining and rethinking the "West" beyond ethnography, historical reflection, and novel rhetoric. To some extent, the sense of loneliness in *Wu Ding's Journey to the West* is not given by specific geography and culture but is a worldview that may be rooted in the more ancient human imagination of the "West." Therefore, Tangfei's "entropy" regarding the West means that in Chinese literature, the "West" can be greater than a geographical concept, and in this aspect, Liu Liangcheng's recent novel *Message Delivery* is another worth detailed discussion.

Let's Explore the World Together
(Issue I, 2019)

T
he writers featured in this special topic are those who have ventured to various corners of the globe since the turn of the century. They are the newbies, the new youth in the globalization era. Their writing is genuinely "new," yet their placement under the banner of contemporary overseas Chinese literature is due to their current lives, studies, or work abroad. Without this label, they would still write; even if they weren't writing, their lives would unfold just as they do.

Recently, there has been a call within literary research circles for contemporary Chinese literature to encompass "overseas Chinese literature." I have a modest question: If "contemporary Chinese literature" were to include Hong Kong, Macao, Taiwan, and "overseas Chinese literature" within a unified Chinese framework, the imaginative construction of a literary community between the mainland and these regions would naturally be seamless. But what about "overseas" beyond China's borders? Can we integrate "overseas Chinese literature" into the realm of contemporary Chinese literature solely based on the recent "Sinicization" of a few North American Chinese writers? It is crucial to recognize that this "Sinicization" and the robust literary market in mainland China have a nuanced relationship—these writers cater to mainland readers, inevitably shaping their aesthetics and needs. Indeed, their writing increasingly mirrors that of mainland Chinese authors. However, "overseas Chinese literature" is not synonymous with "North American Chinese literature," and "North American Chinese literature" does not equate to these few prominent novelists in mainland China. It also extends beyond the scope of novels.

My graduate students conducted a survey of North American Chinese writers, and the findings show that since the 1990s, over 50 Chinese writers have published novels, and more than 20 Chinese poets are featured in the anthology *Poetry Across Oceans*, edited by Mi Jialu. Incorporating such a broad and diverse range of North American Chinese literature into contemporary Chinese literature would require substantial conceptual and structural changes. Moreover, writers like Huang Jinshu and Li Zishu, who are part of the Malaysian Chinese literary tradition, have already become integral to their national literatures, and their aesthetic similarity might make integration into contemporary Chinese literature challenging.

Whether in literary perspective or practice, some overseas Chinese writers seem more entangled with the Cold War context. I believe there is an earlier factor at play: the "weak nation" mentality revealed by the May Fourth generation of writers. Indeed, terms like "Cold War," "foreign land," "diaspora," "marginality," and "loneliness" are frequently used to interpret overseas Chinese writers. Although the Cold War's global political landscape ended in the 1990s, the Cold War mindset and its associated aesthetic psychology have not entirely faded. I have noticed that recent media reports on visits by overseas Chinese writers still use terms like "foreign land," "diaspora," "marginality," and "loneliness" as starting points and keywords. I admit that the inherent loneliness of being in a foreign land is a universal human experience, not confined to any specific era, nation, or generation. The question is, how has this sense of loneliness evolved as China's perception of the world and the world's perception of China has changed?

I observe that many overseas Chinese writers visiting China are increasingly attuned to what "contemporary China" wants to hear and are able to express it effortlessly. They are shaped by the literary concepts valued by "contemporary China," which, in turn, imagines them according to preconceived notions. Some overseas Chinese writers seem to cater directly to these familiar literary perspectives and rhetoric, subtly shifting from "exploring" the world to "exploring" China. This shift can cause certain aspects of overseas Chinese writing to obscure more complex elements, thus hindering our understanding of its richness.

It is undeniable that writers who grew up during the Cold War naturally experience shifts in their thinking, aesthetics, and literary views with the arrival of globalization in the 1990s. For instance, the literary works of overseas Chinese writers such as Yan Geling, Zhang Ling, and Chen He, which significantly impact contemporary China, require further exploration in terms of their relationship with the Cold War era, the marginalization of Chinese writing in North America, and the Chinese reading market. We also need to figure out why their recent works tend to converge on "specific" themes.

These writers, born in the 1950s, now share similar themes and topics with mainland Chinese writers of the same generation. Does "overseas" offer any differentiation for them? Similarly, sharing the North American "overseas" experience, why are they so different from writers like Fan Qian, born in China in the 1950s, or Ha Jin, a Chinese-born writer in the 1950s writing in a non-native language? Regarding the English writing of Chinese, what about the differences between Chinese American writers like Amy Tan, born in the 1950s in the United States, and Ha Jin, born in China? Although I haven't conducted specialized research on "overseas Chinese literature," both in terms of expanding the field of modern and contemporary Chinese literature and my editorial strategy for this column, I hope to introduce younger overseas Chinese writers beyond Yan Geling, Zhang Ling, Chen He, and Fan Qian, even younger Chen Qian, Zeng Haowen, and Yuan Jinmei, who arrived in North America in the 1980s and 1990s.

The evolution of modern Chinese literature since the 1950s has witnessed numerous generational shifts. If we confine our study of "overseas Chinese literature" to a handful of notable writers born in the 1950s, we risk neglecting a wealth of writers. This issue transcends just generational changes; it also calls for a broader geographical perspective. Our examination should extend beyond traditional centers of overseas Chinese literature in North America and Southeast Asia to encompass the entire globe. Wherever Chinese is spoken, there lies the potential to discover traces of "Chinese literature." Additionally, literary diversity must be acknowledged—"overseas Chinese literature" is far more than merely "overseas Chinese novels."

In this special topic, we spotlight writers such as Ni Zhan'ge and He Xiapin in the US, Hu Wei in France, and Wang Bang in the UK, alongside previously featured authors like Zhu Yi in the US and Mr. Man in Australia. This expanded view aims to reassess and reimagine "overseas Chinese literature" within a broader and more contemporary literary landscape.

One thing is clear: these young writers share in the benefits of China's reform and opening up. In the context of China's rise and globalization, the notion of "going global" has become commonplace, and writing "in the world" is increasingly seen as the norm. The allure of extraordinary writing often arises from isolation. Ni Zhan'ge offers valuable insights into the overseas Chinese literature of the young generation. She believes:

> Today's "overseas Chinese writing" (if we temporarily set aside how we define this term) bears resemblance to literature from Europe and America during the rise of capitalism. In the seventeenth, eighteenth, and nineteenth centuries, European noble young men, later joined by the middle-class and women, traveled across Europe to experience diverse cultures, with some venturing even further to the colonies in Asia, Africa, and Latin America. In the twentieth century, American writers like Hemingway sought out Paris, exploring or imagining North Africa and the Middle East. This era was characterized by Orientalist discourse, supported by the political and economic foundations of capitalist empires. In the 21st century, despite ongoing challenges, China has undergone remarkable transformation. With a vast population traveling abroad, either short-term or long-term, "new" overseas Chinese writing—whether pursuing serious themes or entertainment, innovative experiments, or reinterpreting traditions—gradually positions China as a subject rather than an object. It pursues an Orientalism or even

Occidentalism from the viewpoint rooted in China, targeting the new generation's vast middle-class population as the consumer base.

Indeed, "new" overseas Chinese literature is intertwined with contemporary geopolitical dynamics, the evolving perceptions of China by younger
generations, and the shifting relationship between "me" and China. Furthermore, the impact of new media on overseas Chinese writing has introduced
a completely different "world map" for young writers compared to their predecessors. On this new map, they redefine China's position in the world and
explore their understanding of "me," China, and the world—gradually positioning China as a subject rather than an object. Although young overseas
Chinese writers may grapple with themes such as "foreign land," "diaspora,"
"marginality," and "loneliness," these newbies, new youth "going global" are
also cultivating an unprecedented confidence. They are reshaping the image
of overseas Chinese while crafting new forms of overseas Chinese literature.
Changes are underway; in our WeChat communications, Ni Zhan'ge notes
that "new media is redefining time and space, with a tug-of-war between
national borders and the so-called boundaries of information society."

Observations reveal that all four writers featured here have extensive
online writing experiences, distinct from domestic online literature. Moreover, Ni Zhan'ge, He Xiapin, and Hu Wei have pursued doctoral education in
their respective countries, influencing their literary styles. And it is not just
their educational and academic backgrounds. For instance, Wang Bang's
gender consciousness is particularly emphasized in the UK. Compared to
their predecessors, the younger generation is more self-aware, and new media allows their readership to transcend narrow national boundaries, reaching across the globe. Despite their extensive writing careers, none of them
have become bestselling authors.

Last, let's talk about language. All four authors in this special topic come
from bilingual backgrounds. During the preparation of this special topic,
discussions with editors Yanling and Xiaoye revealed that Hu Wei's novels

often feel like "translated novels." In reality, this is a deliberate choice by Hu Wei, who explains:

> For instance, I generally avoid writing sentences that cannot be translated into Western languages. Sometimes, I even think in foreign languages before writing. This may be related to my gradual adoption of French in my writing studies. I have discussed this with authors and editors of Western works with overseas experience, and it is not unique. In fact, I find it an interesting attempt in Chinese writing. Integrating foreign language thinking helps me shape what I want to express more accurately. Chinese is very flexible; it allows writers to explore their own language.

Wang Bang's bilingual poetry also touches on the re-creation of the Chinese literary language. Wang Bang's sense of loneliness in language is distinct from the "backwardness" and nationalistic hierarchies of a hundred years ago. One could say that loneliness in a foreign land evolves with each era. I am particularly interested in how English influences Chinese in Wang Bang's process of writing first in English and then in Chinese. In debates about publishing Wang Bang's poetry in English and Chinese, young novelist Zhu Jing and I have had intense discussions. She worries that publishing English poetry in a Chinese literary journal might be seen as a gimmick. I hope to use Wang Bang's English poetry as a sample to highlight the difficulties and efforts of the younger generation in non-native writing and to provoke limited reflection on Chinese language, which resonates with Hu Wei's novel language practice. Around the time of the May Fourth Movement, discussions about "national literature language" and "national language literature" arose, with different languages becoming essential resources for "national languages." As these young "overseas Chinese writers" navigate between native and non-native languages, their impact on Chinese and Chinese literary language remains an ongoing and evolving topic.

While older overseas Chinese writers focus on exporting "Chinese stories," the youngest generation aims to become "cosmopolitan" writers. This shift is worth exploring. Even within "Chinese stories," is there a new way of telling them, as seen in He Wapi's *The Plastic Age*?

Murmur or Noise
(Issue 2, 2019)

The literary status of lyrics should, in theory, be a settled matter. Whether considering *The Book of Songs*, *ci* (a special literary form of lyrics) of the Song Dynasty (AD 960–1279), or dramas of the Yuan Dynasty (AD 1271–1368), the nature of these literary forms remains clear. Over time, the music comes with them may have faded, and only scholars may still be able to "sing" the "lyrics." Nonetheless, the literary essence of them remains undiminished. Classical Chinese poetry has always been intrinsically linked to music as lyrics. The division of poetry from song and the idea that the capability of being sung is not a strict standard for poetry is a modern phenomenon. As a result, poetry and song have diverged, with poetry establishing its dominance over the past century. This divergence means that modern Chinese poetry's history is also a history of the disappearance of lyrics.

Currently, there is a call within Chinese modern literary studies to address the issue of incorporating ancient poetry into historical records. However, I believe that rather than focusing on reviewing the damage the separation of poetry and song has done to modern poetry, it would be more productive to address the inclusion of modern lyrics in literary history. Although lyrics by musicians such as Cui Jian and Luo Dayou have been included in various anthologies of contemporary Chinese literature, these selections often feel like an attempt to fill gaps, carrying an undertone of literary charity. Lyrics in any Chinese contemporary literary anthology are not self-sufficient; their inclusion in anthologies or future literary histories should be supported by a broader historical perspective. Thus, placing lyrics within the larger framework of modern poetry (such as previous inclusions of rock and folk lyrics in *People's Literature* as poetry) requires an understanding of the prehistory of "poetry and song." Lyrics inherit from an older poetic tradition and show a more conscious integration and absorption of music. While lyrics can be seen as poetry, they do not fully equate with it. Therefore, within the broader realm of modern poetry, lyrics should be considered as "overflow" rather than "incorporation."

Regarding the extent of lyrics parallel to modern Chinese poetry, I am uncertain if a comprehensive survey has been conducted. For the lyrics in this special issue, the focus is on a specific segment of rock and folk lyrics. Even within this segment, further reduction is necessary, excluding "agricultural heavy metal," pseudo-literary folk songs, and much of the television variety rock and folk music. As Zhong Lifeng stated, "Most so-called folk songs have unoriginal melodies; they are repetitive and regressive. The lyrics lack depth, and many people, including musicians, believe that merely playing an acoustic guitar constitutes folk music." Therefore, from a spiritual stance, aesthetic quality, and rhetoric, I agree with him that folk music, and even rock, are most closely related to "style." "Style" is a rough, sharp blade used to cut through the "pseudo" rock and folk trends.

If further differentiation is needed, I have a reference book: Li Wan's translation of *Lyrics for World Rock' N' Roll*, which includes the term "rock poetry" coined by Li Wan. This anthology contains 316 works from the global rock music scene from 1963 to 1997. I use these 316 lyrics as a standard for this special topic. I agree with Yan Jun's preface:

> Lyrics are simply lyrics; they are a part of songs and do not elevate the writer simply because they resemble poetry. The significance of this collection lies in freeing readers from the elitist cultural atmosphere of poetry and exposing them to another form of more 'warm-blooded' texts. These texts challenge language rules, reveal reality and human nature, respect individuality, and explore the existence beyond order (such as pathology and

violence) worthy of contemporary acclaim." Similarly, I partly agree with Li Wan, who has consciously excluded "rock music closer to consumer literature and more pointedly political or extreme experimental elements.

In this special topic, bands like Tongue, Omnipotent Youth Society, and Wood Pushing Melon represent the legacy of 1990s Chinese rock, remaining vibrant even today. Two decades ago, the *1998 Music New Forces* event in Guangzhou was considered the first gathering of Chinese underground rock. Yan Jun recorded Wu Tun and his band Tongue in his book *Underground: Secret Notes of New Music*:

> Tongue performed for 40 to 50 minutes, or an hour, but it wasn't enough. The people of Guangzhou shouted and fell in love with them unreservedly. The rhythm was intense, dense yet rhythmically rich. The guitar either roared or sawed like a file. The bass danced, with a popping "solo." The keyboard was bizarre and flamboyant, running around and shouting. The drums were clear, a bit flashy but steady, never ceasing.

Twenty years later, Wu Tun reappeared in Guangzhou, this time in *Flower City*, a literary journal, without a performance, without his bandmates, just a few of his lyrics. I don't know if there is any inevitability in this, but Wu Tun was the last addition to this special topic that I immediately selected from the list of bands and lyrics provided by Han Songluo. I read his two poetry collections, *The Spectacle of the Passing Scenes* and *The Report Before Losing Humanity*, and listened to his two albums: one titled *Mom, Let's Fly Together, Rock Together*, and the other with tracks like "GMO," "Time Machine," "Primitive Man's Air Conditioning Association" ... Many years ago, Li Wan commented on some people and some songs, saying, "So nostalgic so early," and twenty years later, Wu Tun and Tongue have not "aged"; they are "forever unstoppable."

Wu Tiao Ren tells us about the everyday life of the lower classes from the album *A Tale of Haifeng* to *Canton Girl* to *Dreamy Lisa Salon* and their recent *Stories*. They reveal how literature can intervene in reality and what kind of reality it can address, showing the spirit and power of dialect. Omnipotent Youth Society is more than their hit "Kill That Man from Shijiazhuang." Many of their songs are dedicated to their hometown, the old industrial city of Shijiazhuang. Omnipotent Youth Society is usually shortened as OYS. Their new album *Inside the Cable Temple* offers a view of "entering and exiting Taihang, sudden rain over the mountains," reflecting the sharpness and expanse of our era and our landscape—the states of Yan and Zhao should be like this.

Song Yuzhe was recommended by Yan Jun, a witness to Chinese rock and my pen pal during university days. We corresponded nearly thirty years ago and have yet to meet in person. He listened to my idea for this special topic and said, "Song Yuzhe is perfect for it." As an outsider, I recognize that the most suitable people to handle this special topic are Yan Jun, Han Songluo, Li Wan, Zhang Xiaozhou ... Moreover, this special topic should have been published earlier, even as the first issue of *Flower City Interest*, but was postponed due to Bob Dylan's reception of the Nobel Prize for Literature in 2016 and delayed for two years. In these two years of Flower City Interest, I have gained much literary and external friendship, guided by many friends into unfamiliar territories.

Zhong Lifeng is a contemporary poet and an example of a folk musician. In an interview, he recalled an old story. Juliette Gréco, in the 1950s and 1960s, performed in Parisian taverns and attracted the most famous writers, poets, and artists of the time, becoming their muse. Jean-Paul Sartre and Raymond Queneau wrote lyrics specifically for her, with Sartre praising: "Her voice itself contains a million poems!" Today's poetry, even extending to a broader literary scope, and its relationship with the world, readers, and critics, often carries a "massage-like" sweetness, sentimentality, and a comforting, drowsy ambiguity, like a prelude to euthanasia or the effect of some hallucinogen.

Rock poetry and folk music may seem like murmuring, or even noise, but their real significance lies not just in their literary recognition and differentiation but in their pure and naive spiritual stance, which can remedy today's literary scarcity. For this reason, we need to distill true rock poetry and folk music from ordinary lyrics—they are grounded in the prefix "folk" of folk music; they are the "style" that can be sung; they are also the reunion of poetry and song.

Travelers Between Translation and Writing
(Issue 3, 2019)

F lower City Interest has been running for over two years now, and in our regular interactions, many friends have noted its most striking feature: "crossing boundaries" or "transgressing borders." However, if such boundary-crossing or border-transgressing indeed exists, I hope it is not simply understood as an emphasis on writers' "non-professional writer identity" or "multiple identities," even though Flower City Interest has featured novels by directors and anthropologists, and poetry by artists. In China, the "professionalization" of writers is often more a product of the literary system than of individual choice. Our literary system naturally adds and subtracts from the imagined community of writers as if it were a real "unit," requiring a constant influx of "professional" writers.

We should recognize that the "professionalization" of writers has significantly improved in contemporary youth writing. Even if writing is their "main job," many young writers also engage in editing, screenwriting, or even unrelated "side jobs," and for some, writing itself is their "side job." The rise of the internet and new media has democratized literature, breaking the monopoly once held by a few so-called elite oligarchs and providing the possibility for universal writing. This has realistically changed the literary perspective, dispelling the mystical aura of writing as some arcane art and making it accessible to ordinary people. The aspirations of the May Fourth New Literature to overthrow "aristocratic literature" and "forest literature" and establish a "national literature" and "social literature" now seem achievable in the context of the present powerful egalitarianism and sharing ethos brought by the internet.

Thus, merely switching between different identities does not necessarily bring about literary "crossing boundaries" or "transgressing borders" today. It is only through self-reflection and re-examination of different identities during these switches, and the ensuing realization of their differences, that the potential of literature can be activated. And precisely because of this, for example, even though I have done a special feature on novels by directors, I do not believe that the novels or other forms of literary creations by directors necessarily expand the boundaries of literature. On the contrary, as literary intruders, they may be more conservative, more imitatively following, and more subservient to literary dogma. There are many similar examples, such as critics writing novels. Of the novels by many critics that I have read, only a few, like Wu Liang, Li Jingze, and Zhang Ning, who were already secretly novelists, manage to break free from existing constraints. Expecting a critic to become a novelist might result in losing both the critical edge and the possibility of becoming a successful novelist or poet. Thus, writers known for their other identities being showcased through "literary curation" ultimately aim to break through literary barriers and dismantle the inherent superiority and unnoticed hierarchies within the literary circle, such as the spatial imagination of "overseas" and "borderlands," which are actually natural outcomes of "central" worship.

Translator-writers, traveling between translation and writing, exemplify this concept.

But it seems that's not entirely the case. Over the century since the May Fourth New Literature, "translation" has always been a pivotal force in shaping "writing" from the very beginning. Without the translations of Lin Shu and others, the establishment of new literature would have been challenging. Even today, as Huang Yuning noted, "We cannot ignore the role of translation in the development of modern Chinese fiction. Through translation, we constructed the framework of the novel in a relatively short time, but the accumulation of native Chinese novels has not yet matched it."

In addition to the battling moments between old literature and new literature, throughout the significant moments of the new literature's progression, translation has often provided the most robust support and shelter. During the early stages of new literature, some writers even replaced "writing" with "translation," making foreign works their own creations. Unlike the traditional literature, new literature started from scratch when there were no established professional translators for literature as today, making it natural for writers with overseas study experiences to combine translation and writing.

For a long time, we believed that the driving force behind Chinese literature lay abroad, resulting in a rare importation of top-notch to even non-mainstream foreign literature into "national language." This has led to a tendency to refer to Chinese writers as the "Franz Kafka of China," "García Márquez of China," "Jorge Luis Borges of China," down to the "Raymond Carver of China," and beyond. Being a "knockoff" version of these figures was acceptable, with the notion of "creative transformation" being virtually undetectable even with the most sophisticated plagiarism checkers. Recognizable traces of this mimicry are often seen as "tributes."

Unquestionably, new Chinese literature has developed into a grand spectacle by paying homage to foreign literatures.

However, a century has passed since the birth of new Chinese literature, and we no longer live in its formative years. Today's native writing by translators no longer aligns with the era when translation and writing were inseparable. This might be a transitional period. Writers born from the mid-20th century to the early 1980s experienced a gap in foreign language proficiency, making them different from both their predecessors and younger writers. They could only acquire foreign literary experiences through translations, meaning their "homage" should first be to the translators. Starting from the late 1970s, translators became more professional, meaning that translation could exist independently without serving as an entry point to writing.

Poetry might be an exception. Poets and poetry translators have historically often been the same people, seamlessly integrating both skills. This tradition has remained unbroken since the inception of new Chinese literature.
In contrast, fiction has seen fewer such dual roles. Among the older generation, Han Shaogong stands out as a novelist-translator. Though there are
others, unlike poetry, where this practice has reached clinical usage, fiction
still seems experimental. Of course, if we acknowledge that it is a fact that
novelists in the first 30 years of the new Chinese literature were also translators, it is apparent that today's translator-novelists belong to a tradition.
However, today's translators are more professional than their predecessors,
and they are known more for their translation work than their novels, like
Huang Yuning.

In this special topic, we feature three translator-novelists. English translator Huang Yuning has engaged in novel-writing for the shortest time.
Japanese translator Mo Yin has pursued both translation and writing simultaneously, while another English translator, Yu Shi, began with writing and
later turned to translation. They are different, and particularly noteworthy
is that, as translators, they do not exhibit the usual divide between highbrow
and lowbrow literature that we often see. Huang Yuning translates both Ian
McEwan and Agatha Christie, as well as Janet Winterson, Chuck Palahniuk,
Flannery O'Connor, and Stephen King. Mo Yin translates both serious Japanese literature and light novels. When reading their novels, we can sense
how foreign genre literature influences their narrative styles, which is a natural outcome.

Though they have produced mature novels like *Jiama*, *Eight and a Half*,
and *A Historical Story of Daddy Boy*, I cannot predict whether their future
success as novelists will surpass their achievements as translators. Nevertheless, translators who delve deeply into foreign literature and then turn
to native writing open themselves up. This blend of translation and writing
creates valuable insights into how this practice might form a new literary
tradition, and into examining these "lab rats" of literary experimentation,

their practices, experiences, challenges, and limitations. As Huang Yuning put it, "From the perspective of translator Huang Yuning, novelist Huang Yuning attempts to express contemporary and future daily life using the concepts and techniques of world literature rather than the superficial 'translationese.'" Even just to correct the "translationese" in new literature, these translators' small-scale practices are meaningful.

New Desires, New Conquests: A Self-Examination
— on Creative Writing in Chinese Universities —
(Issue 4, 2019)

The title is derived from Zhang Yiwei's response to the question "What is 'creative' in creative writing?" in the Ask Me Anything column on *The Paper* (*Surging News*). Zhang Yiwei answered, "'Creative' is also about how artists discover and handle human desires, and illuminate the human soul in narrative art. In my understanding, 'creative' means the will to change the world or the way we view this will, new desires, new conquests." This statement closely aligns with what Yan Lianke said at the opening of the first Creative Writing Graduate Class at Renmin University: "Promoting the formation of literary views and worldviews." Both Zhang Yiwei and Yan Lianke are practitioners of creative writing in Chinese universities in the twenty-first century, with Zhang Yiwei having received a creative writing education at Fudan University.

I discussed this special topic with the young novelist Zhu Jing, a writing instructor in the traditional Chinese language and literature discipline at a university. She has deep interactions with many students who dream of writing. Each year, many inquire whether a creative writing graduate program can help them achieve their literary dreams.

What that needs contemplation is whether writing, or narrowly speaking, literary creation, must ultimately lead to becoming a professional writer. Yan Lianke, Zhang Yiwei, and Zhu Jing believe creative writing education should go beyond this. The prefix of creative writing is "creative," so the motivation for creative writing should be an individual's desire to expand their inner world and explore various possibilities with the world. Receiving creative writing training should be a moment when desires are activated, and one yearns for conquest.

Two or three years ago, I wrote a few words for the university poetry column of *Youth* magazine, discussing the poetic sentiment, and unity and coherence in writing of modern Chinese universities. I am not familiar with the Western university tradition, but modern Chinese universities have a literary tradition.

Modern universities in China have a history of just over a hundred years, and modern literature followed a decade or so later. Speaking of history, it is all new. Specifically, regarding modern poetry, if we trace its origins, we naturally refer to *New Youth* and Peking University. If we go further back, we reach the overseas study experiences of people like Hu Shi. No matter how we view it, the poetic sentiment, and unity and coherence in writing of universities should be an important part of the modern university tradition. The youthful spirit of May Fourth New Literature is certainly inseparable from the campus poets of that era. Therefore, as we commemorate a century of new poetry today, we see those institutions like Peking University, Tsinghua University, Nankai University, and the wartime National Southwestern Associated University were once gathering places for young poets. Poetry naturally aligns with youth and universities.

In certain stages of the century-long history of new poetry, universities declined, and the university spirit vanished, coinciding with the disappearance of poetry. At those times, true poetry thrived among the people. From the "Baiyangdian Poets" to the "Today Poets," this is an important thread in new-era literature. Poetry became a tool for young intellectual communities to reflect on life and society and to cut through the hard constraints of the times. It is important to note that the "Today Poets" represented a convergence of grassroots and university campus poetry forces. This leads to the revival of university poetry in the late 1970s after the resumption of college entrance examinations. We should view the poetry of the 1980s within the context of the university campus's spirit of liberation at that time. In a sense, without poetry, the universities of the 1980s would have been much dimmer. Or university campus poetry supported half of the poetry history of the 1980s. The poets who debuted in the 1980s and became classics in contemporary poetry history almost all wrote their famous works during their university years.

Today's university education is criticized for producing "sophisticated egoists," and the spiritual tradition of universities as the birthplace of new ideas and new literature in modern China is fading. However, concluding that the entire campus culture is crude, and barren might obscure many realities and truths. In fact, the literary prosperity of individual or "fan fiction" campus literature may far exceed our imagination. New media has allowed their gatherings to go beyond traditional university literary societies.

Therefore, even if one claims that university Chinese departments do not cultivate writers, considering that university education is now the standard education for all citizens, it is clear that almost all writers start writing in university. This is evident from the growth experiences of today's writers born in the 90s.

From the perspective of the university education system, contemporary creative writing in China has roughly four models, based on Fudan University, Renmin University, Beijing Normal University, and Shanghai University. The graduate program co-hosted by Beijing Normal University and the Lu Xun Literary Institute can be seen as an upgraded version of Lu Xun Literary Institute's advanced class or a formal education version, connecting with the "writers' workshops" that sprang up in the 1980s, offering a "green channel" for degree-seeking writers. In 1985, Wuhan University pioneered a writers' workshop by admitting transfer students, who, after passing the entrance examination, could directly enter the third year of undergraduate study, enjoying the same treatment as on-campus undergraduates. Graduates who passed the final exams received undergraduate diplomas and bachelor's degrees. Subsequently, Northwest University in Xi'an also collaborated with the China Writers Association to relocate the short-term writers' training class of Lu Xun Literary Institute to Northwest University, renaming it the Northwest University Writers' workshop. The program lasted two years, with graduates eligible for a Bachelor of Literature degree and the best allowed to pursue master's degrees in other Chinese language and literature majors (See Gong Shifeng and Xu Jie, "A Probe into the Writers' Workshops in the 1980s Universities"). Around the same time, Shandong University, Nanjing University, and Peking University also offered various forms of writers' workshops. In 1989, Beijing Normal University even offered a graduate-level writers' workshop. Nanjing University maintained its writers' workshop for over twenty years, the longest of all.

Writers' workshops are not strictly creative writing education. Most writers' workshops had the backing of various writers' associations or literary federations, and their course settings and training methods generally followed undergraduate Chinese language and literature education, such as the Nanjing University writers' workshop. A news report by Wang Yunlai mentioned that Nanjing University launched its writers' workshop in October 1987, with a three-year undergraduate program. Those who completed the required credits and graduation practice would be awarded a Bachelor of Literature degree by Nanjing University. The university formulated corresponding teaching plans based on the students' characteristics, equipped with a strong faculty, and systematically taught over twenty courses, including Chinese cultural history, Chinese and foreign literary trends, and Chinese language rhetoric and style. The program also integrated theoretical learning with creative practice, doing its best to provide conditions for their writing and setting a certain number of "creative credits."

The new-century university-based creative writing or master of fine arts programs began at Fudan University and Shanghai University. The creative writing master's program at Fudan University, which began enrollment in 2010, was tailored for Wang Anyi, who joined Fudan in 2003 (according to Chen Sihe). Similarly, Renmin University's creative writing graduate program was tailored for Yan Lianke. This means that the creative writing programs at both universities are centered on and aimed at cultivating writers. Shanghai University might consider more the professional training needs of practical writers. These tailored creative writing programs might lead to a wave of writers-on-campus.

There are subtle differences between the creative writing programs at Fudan University and Renmin University. While the former admits amateur students with some writing background during their adolescence but primarily those with literary dreams and desires, the latter's creative writing program admits mature young writers in their writing ascension period. For instance, Renmin University's first batch included Zhang Chu, Sun Pin, Shuang Xuetao, Zheng Xiaolü, etc. Yan Lianke thus led the writers' workshop under the literary system to a different path.

Therefore, this special issue features Zhang Yiwei and Shuang Xuetao, tailored for these two university creative writing programs. When Zhang Yiwei entered Fudan, it was a transition period from a master of arts in writing to a master of fine arts. At Renmin University, Shuang Xuetao was ascending in his writing from *Moses on the Plain* to *The Aviator*. My aim in this special issue is not to preemptively conclude the relationship between creative writing education and the growth of young writers but to raise questions. Before Zhang Yiwei and Shuang Xuetao, bestselling author Yan Geling and some Western writers had creative writing backgrounds. Although my research shows few graduates of Fudan University's first two creative writing cohorts became full-time writers, creative writing education undoubtedly transitioned many "amateur" writers into professionals, and established writers might also take a different path through creative writing training.

Creative writing in China is closely related to writing workshops, largely following the Iowa Writers' Workshop model. Fudan University, Renmin University, and Shanghai University all adhere to this tradition. Wuhan University almost became the precursor to creative writing in China but did not. According to Yu Kexun, "Although the Wuhan University Writers' Workshop was a product of the transfer student system, some fundamental ideas of the class were influenced by the International Writing Program at the University of Iowa. In the early 1980s, during a visit to China, the founders of the program, Hualing Nieh and Paul Engle, returned to Wuhan University and gave lectures. Engle recited his poetry, translated by the Chinese poet and veteran writer Xu Chi, creating a lively atmosphere. We had heard about their 'writing program' and seen some written materials before. Their visit to Wuhan deepened our impression. Later, when discussing the recruitment and training of transfer students for the Chinese department, the teachers and leaders who were informed about the International Writing Program of University of Iowa used it as an implicit reference for establishing our own writer's workshop. In my mind, our writer's workshop should be run in a similar manner." (Yu Kexun in *My Memories of the Writer's Workshop*).

Writing workshops bear some resemblance to the traditional apprenticeship model of Chinese artisans but with a modern, dialogic approach. They address the perennial debate: can writing be taught? Writing workshops provide a space, or a laboratory, where each participant is both an observer and a subject of examination. Within the overall process of literary production, a person in the workshop can simultaneously take on roles such as creative mentor, literary agent, critic, author, and editor. Here, writing is not a solitary contemplation but a collaborative effort. On the surface, workshops may teach techniques, but they go beyond that. As Zhang Yiwei talks about Wang Anyi:

> Teacher Wang's greatest influence on us wasn't in the writing itself but in the encouragement outside of writing—the aspiration that 'education changes fate.' What truly changes our fate through literature is not the royalties or the fame, but the literary life it bestows upon us, making us believe in a transcendent solemnity beyond the secular world. Through literature, we can become better people, better parents, students, neighbors, and colleagues. We can constantly overcome and transcend ourselves, forging genuine life insights, wisdom, and love from sharpness and pain.

Writing workshops are often small worlds built on personal charisma and tradition, such as Wang Anyi at Fudan University or Yan Lianke at Renmin University. In contrast, traditional "writer's workshops" and the newly rebranded "creative writing" programs often operate on a larger scale. Whether they can inspire individual writers' potential remains to be more thorough field investigations.

It is said that creative writing has entered the digital age. A book titled *Creative Writing in the Digital Age: Theory, Practice, and Pedagogy* specifically discusses this topic. The authors believe:

> Creative writing originates from print culture and is more dependent on it than other disciplines. Research shows that the literary genres involved in creative writing, such as poetry, fiction, non-fiction creative literature, and certain drama courses, are vastly distinct from digital genres. Digital genres include multimodal presentations, 'fan fiction,' social media posts, digital narratives, Wikipedia entries, and blogs. While all these genres involve similar writing technique issues, which creative writing teachers have already discussed in the classroom, differences between them still exist.

My aim for this special topic is to find cases of creative writing in the digital age. Although digital genres have long been an integral part of twenty-first-century Chinese literature, some literary elites or oligarchs still harbor doubts about the achievements of university creative writing in this regard. This should be a future direction for creative writing, which Shanghai University is exploring. The newly established creative writing program at East China Normal University should also be aware of it. In an era where everyone is constantly engaged in "writing" activities, questions about how to redefine "literature," how traditional literature and writers will evolve, and the significance of print-era writing workshops need to be answered through practices.

New Blood in Literature and Early Styles
(Issue 5, 2019)

B efore the internet, the "freedom to publish" for writers was governed by a comprehensive literary system centered around journals. This system encompassed literary imagination, policies, editing, publishing, criticism, and awards. The timing of a writer's debut and which journal published their work could mark significant moments in both personal writing histories and literary history. Most contemporary literary journals took it upon themselves to discover and nurture young talents, leading to an established evaluation system. For instance, literary journals founded during the reform and opening up era have celebrated their anniversaries every ten years by listing achievements, one key metric being the renowned writers who debuted or rose to fame or released representative works through their publications.

Good works are rare and hard to come by, and even in an era, outstanding authors and their works cannot be countless. If a literary journal fails to uphold literary standards and lacks basic aesthetic constraints, resorting to indiscriminately publishing writers' debut or early works to establish future prestige, it will inevitably foster vanity, extravagance, and unrealistic expectations outside the literary realm. This strategy of compromising aesthetics for future rewards is becoming the new normal for many journals. It seems that for future literary history, tracing a writer's debut or early works might exaggerate their significance. Therefore, any journal willing to claim the early works of renowned writers, such as Su Tong's works in *Youth*, Yu Hua's in *West Lake*, Ge Fei's in *Kanto Literature*, or Ma Yuan's in *Northern Literature*, could boast these as their former glories, even if these journals are now considered "weaker" or "smaller" in today's literary "food chain." (A question worth deeply exploring is how the hierarchy among Chinese literary journals—of course, not just literary journals—was formed.)

Another noteworthy issue is the abnormal ecology of contemporary Chinese reading and writing. For instance, in reading, we habitually substitute "recitation" for reading. As children, parents proudly have their kids recite Tang and Song poetry before guests. This practice continues into competitions like Chinese Poetry Congress. As for writing, in China, being able to write is considered a unique talent, and there is a "mysterious admiration" for those who can get published. Although I have not conducted research, it is unlikely that any other country manages its citizens' literary activities and writing from birth to death, as we do through school composition magazines, youth literary journals, and literary periodicals. Consequently, acceleration of literary maturation is happening at increasingly younger ages. I remember that during the mid-1980s when I was in high school, achieving a certain number of published compositions or awards could directly grant university admission. It would be interesting to investigate how many of these students (today they may be admitted through a preferential program for independent enrollment), now grown old, have continued to pursue literature as their lifelong career, and how many have succeeded.

In 2018, the inaugural Blancpain Imaginist Literary Prize was established by the publishing institute Imaginist in collaboration with the Swiss luxury watch brand Blancpain. When explaining the motivation behind the prize, Liang Wendao, the planner and head of the award office, emphasized "mature writing." He stated, "We hope to discover young writers with real potential, long-term creative expectations, and motivation, who have achieved considerable success, and introduce these serious, dedicated writers to more readers for the Chinese literary community, especially the novel circle." A more valuable concept he proposed was "early style" compared to the familiar "late style" theorized by Edward Said. Liang Wendao pointed out, "We seldom discuss early style in comparison." "There are also many authors who never reached middle or old age, such as the well-known French poet Arthur Rimbaud, who had only a youthful phase. Additionally, some authors produce work in their youth that is as remarkable as their later work, though the two phases are strikingly different." But the question remains whether "mature writing" and "early style" might become stale, adhering too rigidly to literary norms. In fact, many young writer models promoted by the current literary system are celebrated for producing works that align with preconceived notions of "mature" and "stylized" writing.

In a recent interview, Su Tong discussed his early works *The Eighth is a Bronze Statue* and *The Wandering Goldfish* published in *Youth*. He viewed his debut *The Eighth is a Bronze Statue* as an immature, yet fortuitous apprentice work written out of cleverness, unrelated to his inner self. Nonetheless, years later, Su Tong still believed that it provided him with tremendous encouragement and confidence to become a good writer. While he was less satisfied with *The Wandering Goldfish*, written around the same time as *Memories of Mulberry Garden*, he considered it "my own" novel, unlike his earlier, less heartfelt works. *Memories of Mulberry Garden*, one of Su Tong's earliest entries into literary history, represents his "early style," which is notably "my own" "early style."

Thus, "early style" refers to a writer's self-education and self-enlightenment from their formative and darkest periods to recognizing "my own" style. This "early style" in a writer's personal literary history does not necessarily correlate directly with biological age but can, as in the case of Han Dong praising Cao Kou, referring to him being in the "youthful stage of a master novelist." One must recognize that "early style" can be illusory and dangerous for a writer, potentially ending their literary journey prematurely. I recall accompanying Dong Ziqi from *Culture* in interviewing Han Dong, who remarked, "Zhu Wen wrote the best adolescent literature." This statement is worth pondering. If there indeed is youth writing, the challenge is how to transcend it ultimately. Zhu Wen's sudden departure from literature is often attributed to the allure of filmmaking, but the issue might be more complex. For some writers, the pursuit of "my own" style might remain unfulfilled throughout their lives, always writing under the shadows of others, let alone achieving an "early style." Yet, there is another possibility, that some writers, like meteors, achieve an "early style" with genius-like precocity and then perish in it. Contemporary Chinese literature has seen many such cases.

However, for today's young writers, the challenge is not how to avoid perishing in an "early style," but rather how to become aware of what constitutes "my own" and develop a unique "style."

The stories in this special topic, by Xie Qingpi, Qi Shimu, and Su Yixin, are their third, second, and first publications in literary journals, respectively. Since the inception of Flower City Interest, we have been cautious not to become "accelerators" of literary maturation, never categorizing authors by age but focusing on their aesthetic potential. Given this, is it against our original intention to feature Xie Qingpi, Qi Shimu, and Su Yixin in this special topic without predicting their literary futures? This is a deliberate risk because a healthy literary ecosystem needs new blood. New blood is the vanguard of an era's literature. Take Mo Yan, Wang Anyi, Su Tong, Yu Hua, A Lai, Lin Bai, and others who have become literary veterans as examples. In their "youth," they produced works with an "early style" that led the zeitgeist, a rarity among today's young writers. Unlike in Japan or Taiwan, in mainland China, for a considerable period, literary production centered around literary journals will continue to have its rationale and possibilities for existence. Physically young writers are often naturally seen as the providers of new literary blood. Thus, how young writers become this new blood, how they achieve "my own" early style, and how they sustain and regenerate their writing, should be continuously questioned and practiced.

Literary Expansionism
(Issue 6, 2019)

The texts by Jiang Fangzhou and Zhou Gongzhao featured in this special topic can still be read and interpreted within the traditional genres, literary forms, and genealogies of literature. *A Perfect Result* and *Reading 'Garden' in City N* are novels, while *We Placed a Giant Egg by the Sea* is a composite text blending non-fiction work notes, dialogues, and fictional elements (the embedded narrative text *The Gift of Civilization* is a novel, possibly an allegory or fairy tale). Since the enlightenment of the 1980s avant-garde literature, even ordinary readers today do not find hybrid texts offensive or abnormal. Therefore, while these are indeed independent literary texts, they transcend the bounds of independent literary texts. They travel, colonize, and continually invent literature, generating meaning in territories larger than literature. This "larger than" refers not only to the often-discussed relationship between literature and reality but also to the more concrete mutual support and inspiration between literature and other artistic practices. In this support and inspiration, literature is not merely decorative but a driving force in reality, even the soul of the entire artistic process.

The renewability of texts has always been an essential criterion for a classic to become a classic. Classic works and writers in literary history generally possess sustainable renewability. Hence, we often say that all writing is part of literary history. In fact, literature that absorbs and regenerates beyond the internal genealogy of literature contributes significantly to literature. Zhou Gongzhao's *Reading 'Garden' in N City* derives imaginative inspiration from traditional "non-literary" texts like *Jiangnan Garden Chronicles* and *Sui Yuan Kao*. Furthermore, by "renewability," I mean it extends beyond mere continuity and homage from the present to the past. Jiang Fangzhou and Zhou Gongzhao actively drive the renewal of their texts in their "here and now." This renewability involves not just the interpretation of the text but also the re-creation and dissemination of ideas and forms.

The version of Jiang Fangzhou's *A Perfect Result* we are publishing now is revised. Its original version was the narrative script for the art project "Casting Memories" curated by Wang Zigeng from the Central Academy of Fine Arts. The curatorial notes for "Casting Memories" are available online:

On September 22, 2018, an exhibition revolving around Shougang opened at St. Catherine's Church. The exhibition, titled "Casting Memories: The Achievements of Urban Renewal of Shougang Park and the Three Blast Furnaces Museum," aimed to present the history, present, and future of the Shougang industrial zone from the perspective of individual and family narratives. As the curator, after extensive field, we were deeply moved by the Shougang people and decided to approach the exhibition from a human perspective rather than simply displaying architectural renovations. The exhibition, coinciding with Shougang's centenary in 2019, utilized various media languages including architecture and stage design, graphic design, literature, multimedia, and photography to create an immersive experience that brought to life the historical and urban renewal journey of Shougang.

Jiang Fangzhou's *A Perfect Result* lays the foundation of the entire art project:

The exhibition is built on the story of a father and son at Shougang written by young writer Jiang Fangzhou, constructing multiple spaces representing the work and life of two generations of Shougang workers. Visitors explore the living spaces of the father and son within a box space, encountering detailed presentations of the father's diary, drawings, their chess table, bedroom, and study. Each room is unique and hides some mystery, immersing visitors in a special time and space where they become one of the story's protagonists.

We Placed a Giant Egg by the Sea, on the other hand, is a collaborative architectural competition that Jiang Fangzhou and her high school and university classmate Qin Sishi took part in, to make a design for a landmark in Qianhai, Shenzhen. Qin Sishi studied architecture in university and went on to graduate school at Harvard, later becoming an architect in a US architectural firm. As mentioned earlier, *We Placed a Giant Egg by the Sea* is a composite text blending work notes with the narrative text *The Gift of Civilization* embedded in the design proposal's implementation process.

If we do not limit ourselves to textual experiments alone, Jiang Fangzhou's "literary" participation in artistic practices, her "actions" and "activities" deserve deep exploration. This participation is not merely the mutual influence of literary circles or the crossing of multiple identities. For example, poet groups like Today Poets and The Stars Art Group had daily interactions, and some individuals had overlapping identities as both poets and painters. Similarly, novelist Liu Suola, who wrote *You Have No Choice* and *Blue Sky, Blue Sea*, is also a composer. Flower City Interest has featured several writers traveling across boundaries, such as a director's novel in the first issue.

Many such cross-identity writers have not received enough attention. For instance, the important long novel *The Epic of Wooden Horse* by art critic Li Xiaoshan should hold significant literary historical value at the end of the twentieth century, yet it remains little known in literary circles. Therefore, the relationship between literature and other arts is not just about the inspiration of novel techniques and structures from music, as some studies suggest, but about the overlap of multiple identities of writers or the coexistence of literature in various media language practice fields, empowering and inspiring each other.

In this sense, Jiang Fangzhou is expanding new territories. Similarly, publishing her *A Perfect Result* and "We Placed a Giant Egg by the Sea" separately would result in significant loss. It we observe these two art projects, it becomes clear that the literature that benefits from her is her reconstruction, imagination, and re-creation of reality, daily life, time, and space. In terms of presentation, "literature" yields the right to independent publication in exchange for "art's" expansion of literary boundaries. Today, this literary expansionism can manifest not only in architecture and spatial art but also in games, animation, picture books, photography, and cross-media contemporary art experiments.

More importantly, literary expansionism enlightens and initiates the consciousness and intellectual capability of youth to question and voice issues in contemporary China. Within the framework of grand literature and grand art, the collaboration and dialogue of young people ultimately expand the boundaries of thought. In the two art projects Jiang Fangzhou participated in, *A Perfect Result* addresses the industrial heritage, factory life, urban memory, and family experience of the People's Republic of China. According to Jiang Fangzhou's envisioned route, it is not merely a novel for ordinary readers but transforms into various media languages like architecture, stage design, graphic design, multimedia, and photography, with literature participating and witnessing, and leading and inspiring the joint "Casting Memories." "*We Placed a Giant Egg by the Sea*" proposes a grander "civilization" design, with broader visions of the future, the universe, and human exploration spirit, courage, and destiny.

On the surface, Zhou Gongzhao's *Reading 'Garden' in N City* appears as a "classical" text, but as Zhou Gongzhao mentioned, "The writing was initiated by an urban writing project by Pulsasir."

Established in 2007, Pulsasir is a youth academic group dedicated to writing practices, academic thinking, and artistic actions in divergent contexts. Their WeChat official account explains the "urban writing project" mentioned by Zhou Gongzhao: Pulsasir × Qingke Project: ten Cities, seven

Days, one Writing Journey: "Pulsasir × Qingke Project put the focus of urban travel on urban writing, aiming to explore youth's understanding and collaborative ability regarding contemporary cities and personal memory. Through field trips and participation in local networks, the project forms writing practices, constructing localized yet expansive urban strategies. Like a battle, the primary task of this urban writing mission is to immerse individual, creative internal labor into the tense relationship of contemporary Chinese urban spaces. Thus, the aim is not to produce an 'essay' with mature, clean language, elegant form, or refined thought, nor a few unique, captivating landscape photos, but to 'do hard labor,' 'do foreign work,' digging trenches between the city and the desert, facing the 'invisible cities.' As Italo Calvino revealed, we must not only question the city but also let the city question us. Therefore, this project can be understood as exploring what questions we can raise and answer in today's cities."

Thus, Zhou Gongzhao's *Reading 'Garden' in N City* is not a nostalgic elegy for ancient capitals and abandoned gardens but a process of illumination, opening, and revival:

> The remaining gardens in Nanjing have become fragments of urban sentiment and memory, like surviving poems and essays. They are incomplete but can be connected. I plan to investigate and write about the existing gardens and garden relics in Nanjing, mapping historical garden documents and images onto the city's surface texture, forming a multi-layered map. At this point, text and images (planned as photo collages) together create traces that have disappeared from contemporary maps. The landscape experience of present gardens, fragmentary memories, modern life, and documentary imaginings form an abstract and open memory, unfolding the city on paper.

"Writing practices, academic thinking, and artistic actions in divergent contexts"—are these individual cases or a noticeable trend in contemporary youth thought and writing? To draw conclusions, more field studies are needed. However, it can be hypothesized that if such writing practices become a conscious trend among young writers, the landscape of Chinese literature will undergo significant changes, and the state of contemporary youth thought will be profoundly affected, but how? We look forward to it.

Children of "My City"
(Issue I, 2020)

From October 26–27, 2018, the Shanghai-Nanjing Dual Cities Literary Workshop, which I co-initiated with Jin Li from Fudan University, centered on the theme "The City Being Observed and Displayed." This workshop discussed the contemporary urban expressions of young writers and artists from original cities in China. Novelists like Di An, Zhou Jianning, Chen Qiufan, Zhang Yiwei, Zhu Jing, Wang Zhanhei, Tangfei, Tang Rui, Chen Si'an, and Jiao Yaoyao attended. Some of them have joined us in this special topic, Records of Eight Cities. In the introduction to the workshop, I wrote:

> Since the opening of Shanghai, the modern city, a subject for literary "observation and display," has developed a history of over a hundred years in modern China. In the process of urbanization, it's not just recent that the 'city' has become a topic. Since the May Fourth New Literature, modern cities have been destinations and habitats for writers, naturally becoming subjects of their observation and display. Writers and artists create the urban literature and art they understand. Today, under this background, we are more concerned with how young people respond to the contemporary city. In the genealogy of cities being observed and displayed in modern times, what constitutes "my city" of the younger generation today? How do individuals write their unique "my city" that matches their gender, generation, and class? Considering the drastic changes between city and people in China over the past two decades of the twenty-first century, these changes reflect new ways of urban-rural relations and transformations within and

outside cities. Observing from within the city: each has its small traditions, and under the influences of contemporary Chinese politics, economy, culture, etc., a new urban tradition and "local identity" have formed.

These Chinese contemporary cities, with their distinct traditions and local experiences, enter the new century, bringing unprecedented changes to urban landscapes, spatial structures, the relationship between people and cities, the relationship among people within the city, and the living situations of individuals in cities. Such transformations in literature and art have already started at the end of the last century. For instance, the literary creations of writers born in the 1970s, 1980s, and 1990s provide new writing experiences for contemporary Chinese literature. Through the lens of 'the city being observed and displayed,' we can see the differences between the new generation of Chinese writers and the existing modern literary tradition. Their own literary and artistic creations also vary. New cities, new people, new experiences—what does logical new literature look like? My fundamental judgment is that the new transformation of contemporary Chinese literature should naturally occur among these people.

Reading this group of novels, we find that changes have indeed already occurred. New cities, new people, new experiences—does new literature naturally happen? This is the premise we imagined for this special topic. Taking mainland China as an example, the turn of the century's spectacle-oriented urban writing focused on cityscapes like bars, cafés, high-end hotels, shopping malls, and communities, in the novels of Di An, Zhu Jing, Guo Shuang, Ban Yu, Wang Zhanhei, and Yang Zewei, expands to suburban areas outside Beijing's Fourth Ring Road, universities, urban villages, apartments adjacent to cemeteries and villages in cities, small inns, RT-Mart (a large supermarket chain), etc. Even urban landmarks like cafés are not intentionally emphasized for their "urban fashionable enclave" label. Rebellious urban youth, petty bourgeois youth, and marginal people have transformed into the secular children of "my city," shifting urban writing from "abnormality" to a focus on these secular children's fates.

The concept of "my city" appeared early on. In 1975, Liu Yichang edited the supplement of *Express* and serialized Xi Xi's *My City*. The reason for revisiting and appropriating this old concept is the recognition that the "I" in "my city" can correct the "my" city writing, from the undifferentiated, plural "our city" to the distinctive, singular "my city." As an undifferentiated, plural "our city," it could be the so-called modern civilization's "flower of evil" in contrast to pastoral villages, the so-called metropolis of neon lights, the so-called nostalgic "Shanghai modern," the so-called "splendor of the fin de siècle," and so on. Simply put, the term "urban literature" in new century Chinese literature often does not reflect a deep understanding and contemplation of cities the writers live with daily. Instead, it is customized and pieced together according to some preconceived notions. The homogenized and formulaic cityscapes in new century Chinese urban literature are everywhere.

In 2011, I published "What is 'My City' and How to Write It" in the fourth issue of Shanghai's *Exploration and Free Views*. Seven or eight years have passed since then, and upon rereading that short article, the issues discussed still hold practical significance.

If we carefully sort through the urban literature of the new century in China, we find that these "literary city-building techniques" often follow traditional and modern, urban and rural confrontational thinking in their urban imagination. This is the most old-fashioned approach in contemporary urban imagination, echoing the conservative cultural traditions of modern China. Here, the city becomes the "foreign land" and "other" in the imagination of literati, with the countryside as their escape from reality. The city is the enemy of the past, disappearing, beautiful pastoral countryside and the source of all sins. Much of the so-called urban literature in the new century writes about the sins of the city and the evils of humanity within this simple urban-rural confrontation: the city, human and family fate, and daily life are awkwardly inserted into modern Chinese history, turning the city chronicles into a mere replica of modern political event history; the city is a place of pleasure, or it is simplified into a fashion symbol, with literary cities built from fashionable elements creating a mirage-like illusion; existing aesthetic conventions, especially Western modernist urban imagination, become the current urban imagination in China, etc.

Compared to the living Chinese cities, the imagined Chinese cities in literature have become "invisible cities" covered by various concepts. To the extreme, I believe that the writing of new century urban literature is becoming another form of ideologically correct replica. I term such urban literature as "non-my city" writing. In this "non-my city," there is no "my" original, singular, spiritual experience, reflection, and imagination between the writer and the city they write about.

So, what is "my city"? Broadly speaking, it questions whether there are differentiated "Chinese cities" in the rapidly globalizing era. If we only look at certain central business districts' architectural landscapes, luxury consumption in grand shopping malls, and popular lifestyles in Chinese cities, it may indeed be "one world, one dream." But the issue's other side is that beneath these urban surfaces and froth, there are precisely different undercurrents and shadows. The prehistory of Chinese cities before "modernity," the inter-city differences after "modernity," all make Chinese cities inevitably unique "alien" "my city."

Modern Chinese cities are products of the encounter between tradition and modernity. Compared to traditional rural China, modern cities are truly "others." Their uniqueness lies in that they are neither "a political center" of classical times nor communities based on bureaucratic landlords and wealthy gentry (Fei Xiaotong, *China's Gentry*). Nor are they simply new cities from the Western colonization. The growth history of modern Chinese cities has its historical and realistic aspects, issues, and experiences. These aspects are necessarily integrated into the character formation of modern Chinese cities.

Furthermore, looking within China, each city has its history, reality, is-sues, and experiences, with inter-city differences being extraordinarily sig-nificant. For instance, Nanjing and Shanghai, only a few hundred kilometers apart, taking an hour by high-speed rail to reach, are entirely different in spirit. Historically, Shanghai lacks Nanjing's old capital's decadent founda-tion, and Nanjing certainly doesn't have Shanghai's many colonial mem-ories. In reality, today's Shanghai is a veritable international metropolis, while Nanjing remains a city neither old nor new, neither rural nor urban. This can be seen in the city's art and ecological compositions. Nanjing is significantly behind Shanghai in terms of art exhibitions, performance lev-el, the vibrancy of art salons, and venue facilities. Hence, to some extent, "Shanghai baby" can only be the "baby" of trendy Shanghai. Zhu Jing's *Mr., Mr.* also sets the theme for the novel, with the character Mr. Ning, who stud-ies old knowledge, fitting naturally only in an ancient capital like Nanjing. In the dual-city narrative of traveling between Beijing and Nanjing, "Mr." and "ancient capital" form an elegy, where only the old days are worth cherish-ing, and those old days are slipping away.

Novels like *Mr., Mr.*, where new and old contrasts within the same city form a "dual-city narrative," include Guo Shuang's *Eight Hundred Meters from Xiao Hong*. "Xiao Hong" is the Guangzhou past in Guo Shuang's novel, with Xiao Hong's wandering life becoming the subtext of contemporary urban life in the novel. In Di An's *I Met Someone Kinder Than Me*, new "Beijingers" Zhang Zhitong and Hong Cheng are rootless drifters between Beijing and their small hometowns. Di An herself also has such a dual-city narrative between Beijing and Taiyuan. This kind of dual-city travel also appears in Wang Zhanhei's journeys between Shanghai and Jiaxing. However, unlike traditional migrations from the countryside to the city, these dual-city nar-ratives do not necessarily carry an undercurrent of homesickness. This is true for both the writers and the characters in the novels. In today's world, few countries can simultaneously juxtapose and possibly sustain so many different urban forms. It is not just the "localness" of cities but also the various literary traditions and genealogies. From the broader perspective of literary history, the urban literature of Taiwan and Hong Kong is the precursor to that of the mainland. The minor tradition of Chinese urban literature is worth cherishing. Hong Kong in Chen Yuanshan's *Standing on the Scale* and Taiwan in Lin Xiuhuo's *Banana Leaves Cover the Deer* both subtly reveal this minor tradition. The fantasy and magnificence of Taiwanese urban literature are the elusive sources of *Banana Leaves Cover the Deer*. Mainland China might also be this way. *Mr., Mr.* is written by Zhu Jing a writer from south of Yangtze, which comes as no surprise, especially considering that she was born in Yangzhou.

Even so, in works such as Guo Shuang's *Eight Hundred Meters from Xiao Hong*, Yang Zewei's *Daytime Selling Blue*, Di An's *I Met Someone Kinder Than Me*, and Wang Zhanhei's *Going to RT-Mart*, the localness of the city has significantly faded. Similarly, in Lin Xiuxiu's *Banana Leaves Cover the Deer*, the phenomena of online celebrity writers, fans, bestsellers, mobile games, live streaming, and LINE, all happening in a small town in China, also exemplify the youth subculture scene across the country. Cities are converging, yet the more subtle differences are being unearthed by young writers. The significance of "my city" lies in that everything about the city reflects my form, color, and emotions.

Therefore, each city possesses its personality, thus creating "my city." This personality can be related to the city's geographical space, regional culture, political or economic paradigms, and even social classes and ethnicities. The "I" in "my city" does not only refer to the differences between cities inside and outside or within. To an individual, a city provides not just a space for work and life but also spiritual and psychological harmony. Thus, in contemporary China, the relationship between the individual "I" and the different "city" must be that of a distinctive "my" "city." Thus, the so-called "my city" emphasizes not only the differences between ancient and modern, East and West, urban and rural in terms of urban form, spiritual temperament, and the spatial significance of geography, culture, and psychology in modern Chinese cities. For a writer, questioning what constitutes "my city" actually means considering how the cities they depict are imagined and constructed, how they are permeated with the writer's personal experiences, and what new possibilities they can offer to Chinese literature and even world literature.

It is worth mentioning that the "my" in "my city" should not be simplistically equated with the conceptual localness of the city. For example, Shenyang is known for its old industrial district, so Ban Yu and other young writers' works are often framed within the Tiexi District. When Ban Yu has already become one of the "Three Swordsmen of Tiexi," his *Wings* can be understood as a faint cry for help, rebelling against being disciplined and buried. For Ban Yu, Shenyang may indeed be the Tiexi District, but it could also be a secret music community of few people when he was a teenager. Such secrets can be many. In addition to Ban Yu, reading writers in this special topic, such as Di An, Guo Shuang, Wang Zhanhei, and Zhu Jing, we can also see their rebellion against being placed in a fixed frame and their efforts to rebuild the secret relationship between "I" and "my" city.

Based on this, I have reason to question and criticize the "non-I" and "no-I" nature of Chinese urban literature. Since we criticize and question the preconceived notions and conventions constructing the literary city imagination, we can further ask, how does "my city" become "literary"? Considering the composition of contemporary writers, those who became famous before the new century and are now at the peak of their creative careers mostly have the experience of moving from the "countryside" to the "city." We should recognize that viewing the city through the eyes of a "villager" results in both insight and blind spots. They see the differences between urban and rural areas but may overlook the unique aspects of different cities.

New century Chinese literature has techniques for "building the countryside" but lacks strength in "building the city." The key issue is that in their perspective, every city is the same, but every village is different. This is because the rural imagination in new century literature often represents the writer's emotional ties and shared glory and shame with "my countryside." What are the modern Chinese cities after the hybridization of tradition and modernity, East and West? What are Chinese cities in the context of new century globalization? Chinese writers do not seem to understand these issues as thoroughly and clearly as they understand modern Chinese villages. Therefore, if these writers engage in urban literature creation, they must adjust a conceptual city to their own sharply painful "my city" after the psychological shock and pain of the urban-rural confrontation.

How does "my city" become "literary"? Pondering on this question, just as they pour their souls into the countryside, modern Chinese writers' rural imagination can actually be a reference. They should not be ready to be mere passers-by escaping the city; whether they love it or hate it, they must entangle and stay with the city to possibly regard it as "my city." However, we must realize that the imagination of "my city" in new century literature is far more complex than that of "my countryside."

These are unprecedented cities. The rise of modern metropolises has revolutionized China's geographical space, cultural landscape, and people's emotions, psychology, and daily lifestyles. The current Chinese cities, with their mix of "chaos," "mashup," and "hybridity," are unprecedented "aliens" in human urban history. Facing such "alien" cities, existing literary experiences and single literary genres are powerless to complete the imaginative construction of "my city."

We must acknowledge that even if we admit that existing urban literary experiences can partially reflect in current urban literary writing, the "unprecedented" nature of the "issues" and "experiences" of contemporary Chinese cities dictates that the "literature" of "my city" is also "unprecedented." First is the emergence of new urban classes. However, from the reality of new century Chinese literature, these so-called new urban classes are often primarily focused on the weaker or marginalized groups in the city. Our writers have not sufficiently portrayed the broader and more complex new urban classes. Besides the rise of new urban classes in literature, writers also respect the mixing of old and new in Chinese urban history and reality, as well as the geographical differences and complexities of ancient and modern, East and West, urban and rural areas. Abandoning the conventional urban experience model of "everything outside Beijing is local, and everything outside Shanghai is rural," the experiences of small Chinese cities should also be part of the Chinese urban imagination.

The imagination and writing of "my city" in literature should not merely aim to expand territorial space and social class boundaries. The ultimate realization of the literary "my city" should be the emergence of "literary" urban landmarks infused with China's history and reality, issues, and experiences. These literary urban landmarks should bear the personal imprints of the writer's experience, rhetoric, structure, and style, just like Charles Dickens with London, Charles Baudelaire with Paris, Franz Kafka with Prague, James Joyce with Dublin, and Orhan Pamuk with Istanbul. We have reason to expect that the "my city" Chinese writers, situated in the global context of "alien" cities, will offer the world literature a series of literary "alien" "my cities." Since its inception three years ago, *Flower City Interest* has published 18 issues. We were basically making efforts to imagine the current literary landscape of China. In the inaugural issue of 2017, I wrote the opening words:

> Imagining the openness and possibilities of *Flower City*, the clamor of voices and the thriving of diversity is what we envision for the future of the Flower City Interest column. What should Flower City Interest contribute to Chinese literature? Given the current literary situation, only those with delusions would imagine they could create a grand literary era. So let's do what we can, what *Flower City* has always been doing, even if it is just opening up the contemporary Chinese literary scene as much as possible, seeing what individual, independent writers are doing as much as possible, even if it is just opening up and clarifying a little. The world we live in, whether

the best or the worst, indeed involves different genders and professions, en-countering different paths and times, being hurt, and possibly being made to succeed. As writers, we should naturally contribute different perceptions of reality, different literary experiences, imaginations, and different literary forms. Our column aims to let these "different" possibilities, diversities, and varieties surface together.

However, it require us to reflect that the expanding literary boundaries does not necessarily lead to literary "classics." I remember a phrase from *Chinese National Geography* when I was a child: "China is vast and holds abundant resources." For a vast and rich "China," a writer's life and literary expression are concrete and nuanced. Today's world is one where global-ization brings convenient transportation and information, while countless spaces, classes, and communities are fragmented. This is true for China and the greater world, as well as our personal lives and inner worlds. An individual, in this vast and expansive world and China, retreats to the small existence of the "most primitive" tribalization. Small to the extent that, like in one of the novels in this collection, a room in RT-Mart, a café, a rented apartment, a university, or even a small outdoor platform in a complex building can carry all the joys and sorrows of human life and the subtle darkness of humanity. Therefore, in a certain sense, given today's vast world, China, and human beings, literature should move from one's narrow self to the vast expanse. I still remember when Zhu Yanling, the editor-in-chief, and I imagined this column: How can young writers respond to Chinese is-sues and realities in a literary way?

Then, let us start from here, from the meeting and encounter of the small self and the small part of China, where honest perceptions of reality and love and pain for the world occur. Therefore, if we are to truly define the future of Flower City Interest, this is the direction we strive to head to. We hope the possibility of classic Chinese literature will be discovered in this direction and supported and protected by us.

Field, Ethnography (Personal Records), and Fiction
(Issue 2, 2020)

The choice of "intimate relationships" as the keyword for this special topic is rooted in the profound changes in Chinese society and family since the reform and opening up. Naturally, literature should respond to these changes, and Chinese writers should immerse themselves in portraying these changes.

Once, I asked Shanghai critic Zhang Dinghao if he had any recommendations for new writers. He suggested Dan Bao and a few others. At that time, Dan Bao was working at NoonStory and had not written much fiction. I was also compiling manuscripts for Yilin Publishing House and considered publishing a collection of her columns and non-fiction works. Over time, I intermittently asked Dan Bao for manuscripts, hoping to see her background in anthropology education and research reflected in her literary writing. I remember during last year's Spring Festival, Dan Bao, while in Shenyang, confirmed submitting a manuscript to Flower City Interest, and it was fiction. Several months later, probably in the spring, Dan Bao began teaching a course at Southeast University at a classmate's invitation. Upon seeing the course announcement, we had a clearer exchange about "what to write." During this exchange, we repeatedly discussed the changes in Chinese families brought about by the one-child policy since the mid to late 1970s. We both felt that this area hadn't been sufficiently expressed in Chinese literature, especially by writers of the one-child generation, and should become a new literary field.

A few months later, in August, writers Ye Yang and Lu Yuan of Wen Jing Publishing House held an event at Nanjing Pioneer Bookstore. Lu Yuan's

Childhood Beast and Ye Yang's *Please Don't Leave the Car Accident Scene* both offered unique literary expressions of contemporary experiences. We discussed Chinese-style families and intimate relationships and my commissioning of Dan Bao. They were contemporaries of Dan Bao. Shortly after, at an event in Beijing, Lu Yuan mentioned the Nanjing discussion to Dan Bao, who then sent me four of her novels: *Parents, Traveler, Mr.*, and *Oh Daddy*. I saw her detailed writing timeline, with the earliest starting in January 2018. This means it took Dan Bao over a year to write this set of novels.

From early 2018 to now, "intimate relationships" have been widely discussed in mass media, gaining more attention. Films and novels like *Marriage Story, Kim Ji-young, Born 1982*, and *The House on the Slope* have been introduced to China, enabling us to awaken and have an epiphany at a "historic moment," and then to reflect on our everyday familial and various intimate relationships, especially after several domestic violence incidents became public events in the past two years. However, "intimate relationships" are not limited to the dramatic presentations of domestic violence. They can be more microscopic, subtle, latent, darker, coldly violent, and habitually unnoticed. Dan Bao's novels do not escalate to domestic violence but depict seemingly mundane family life and intimate relationships, even if there are undercurrents. Without escalating to domestic violence, Chinese-style intimate relationships are still fraught with crises. Moreover, Chinese-style intimate relationships extend beyond the family.

In fact, the starting point of new Chinese literature, Lu Xun's *Diary of a Madman*, began with a reflection and critique of Chinese-style families and intimate relationships. Sociological researchers believe: "Every individual is born and grows up under the shadow of their ancestors and strives to give eternal meaning to their brief physical life through efforts to continue this legacy. Because the Chinese ethical system emphasizes that individual interests must be subordinated to the collective interests from family to the world, an independent, self-sufficient individual could hardly exist in traditional Chinese society." "Over the past century, the cultural revolutions in

China have been characterized by awakened individuals resisting the control of ancestral influence" (Yan Yunxiang, The "Transformation of Private Life").

As Yan Yunxiang points out, this indeed reflects the modern and contemporary social reality of China and serves as a prominent literary theme, evolving into a literary model and dogma. The question is, what happens after the "awakened individual resists the control of ancestral influence" today? What about after the modernization of the family? Dan Bao's recent novels are not about old-style Chinese families and intimate relationships, nor even the transitional period's complexities. For instance, *Traveler* portrays a "world-style family" traveling globally.

So, what can we gain from reading Dan Bao's novels?

It is certain that her novels possess a conscious "problem awareness." This awareness allows literature to engage with public events and attain literary publicness. Her novels touch on universal or traditional issues related to intimate relationships, such as gender and generational dynamics (in *Traveler*, a couple's thirteen-year age difference creates a generational gap, making gender issues also generational issues), the issue of non-marital children and their families addressed by *Oh Daddy*, explores transgressions, repair, and the trauma of intimate relationships explored by *Mr.*, and the specific "lost only child" issue (due to the one-child policy, the loss of an only child has become a common problem) in *Parents*.

A few years ago, Dan Bao had a column titled Looking Up at the Crows in *Vista* magazine. I searched and read these pieces online, finding that marriage, family, and intimate relationships are her writing keywords. When these magazine articles were transferred to the internet and WeChat official accounts, readers commented, describing Dan Bao as fearing family and marriage. Perhaps such writings influenced readers, as seen in the piece "New Definitions of Contemporary Intimate Relationship Terms," where Dan Bao offers her interpretations of these terms within familial intimacy:

Couple: Two friends who once had a sexual relationship.

Marriage: Other than making it difficult for me to get a boyfriend, it's fine.

This marriage: Its flaw is that it doesn't include a boyfriend—if it did, the marriage would be more harmonious.

Family: "Mom, is the festival for happiness?" "No, the festival is for being with family."

Sex: I want to know what you like. I want to know what else you might like.

Sexual pleasure: Time before metaphysics.

Love: At first, at least an ordinary dream. Perhaps it became a beautiful dream, causing the sleeper to relax and unknowingly slip into a nightmare. If it started as an obvious nightmare, the instinct to survive and seek pleasure would have made one open their eyes and wake up.

Love, again: A repeating machine must be the closest thing to a perpetual motion machine. When it appears in a remote village, it will terrify viewers like when people once believed cameras could capture souls.

Sex, again: Canadian poet Anne Carson said: "I will continue to study maps. Maps imitate reality in the way sex imitates desire—roughly, hastily."

Of course, we cannot conclude that Dan Bao is genuinely afraid of marriage and family based on her writings. There may be some overlap between her literary perspective and personal experience, but "fear" is an objective presence in her work. For example, in *Marriage Scenes*, she describes a couple's seventh wedding anniversary: "These strangers can imagine what happens next. On this night, this long-married couple will return home, back to their familiar bed. Sex has drifted away from them, with only occasional occurrence. Sometimes she thinks this might be the best kind of relationship. On this Saturday night, she lies in bed, saying things she has pondered for a long time. He is reading a magazine, turning the pages slowly. Until he reaches out and presses her temple. Whether this gesture signifies tolerance or concern is unclear. It feels more like pressing the stop button. She quiets down. He says, 'That's better.'"

In *Five Chinese Mothers in the Neighborhood*, Dan Bao writes:

The 52-year-old Zhang Yin began suffering from severe insomnia at the age of 51. She finally had a room of her own. Every night, after her husband's breathing turned into snoring, like an old, malfunctioning exhaust fan struggling to work, she would get up, tiptoe out of the room, pour a cup of hot water, and sit in his study reading magazines. Sometimes, she did nothing but sit in a wicker chair on the balcony, covered with a light blanket, gazing at the stars. Occasionally, she would fall asleep briefly, waking up in the cool air. Before long, the street beside the neighborhood would be traversed by water and garbage trucks, signaling the approach of dawn. Her room would no longer belong to herself, returning to a shared space with her husband.

In the first 26 years of her life, she lived with her parents, sharing a room with her grandmother and sister. After that, she lived with her husband in a dormitory provided by their workplace. At 28, she gave birth, her body belonging to her workplace during the day and to her baby at night. After her child started kindergarten, Zhang Yin lived a life segmented into blocks of time. Her most enjoyable moments were on work-organized trips or when she stayed in the bathroom by herself. Therefore, she insisted on installing a large bathtub when they moved, although she quickly discovered that her husband would enter the bathroom while she was bathing, to retrieve items, brush his teeth, relieve himself, and leave without closing the door.

Now, at night, she owns the entire house. Zhang Yin found rose-scented eye drops, bought colorful magazines on topics ranging from fashion to military, and did not mind them. Sometimes, she cleaned the room, polished the wardrobe doors, and made the walls shine. She no longer lay awake listening to her husband's snoring, resenting his untroubled peace. Now, in the dark, she felt a love for him that one might feel for the ignorant or strangers. In the dark, his body became part of the furniture, part of the home. And she was the only living person.

If we closely examine this, we will find that not only has the "fear" present in her magazine columns been carried into current novels, but some passages have also been directly transferred into novels, becoming small yet significant details within the narrative structure.

Dan Bao is an observer, and her background in anthropology influences her observations and writing. As she stated on her WeChat official account Zoology:

> My official account is called Zoology, which signifies observation. Previously, my studies were akin to anthropological observation. Now, I hesitate to label my casual writings as such, so I call it Zoology, where I place observation notes, drafts of novels, and column pieces. I don't consider the impact on the audience; I use it like a blog to document my daily observations and experiences, as well as for writing practice.

Based on this understanding, unlike many Chinese writers, Dan Bao's novels have an anthropological sense of "field" and "ethnography." For a novelist, "field" might not necessarily mean hands-on field investigations (referred to as "field trips" in contemporary Chinese literature), but rather the analysis, synthesis, and organization of relevant information. Today, with advanced information technology, one can conduct anthropological field and ethnographic writing without leaving home. A few years ago, Yu Hua's *The Seventh Day* faced criticism for being a "news potpourri." The issue is not whether novelists can begin their narratives with news reports—especially for reclusive novelists who may rely solely on news reports for inspiration—but rather how "facts" derived from news reports can transform into "fiction" in a novelist's narrative. Dan Bao honestly acknowledges the connection between her writing and news reports but has her unique approach. I believe this approach is influenced by her anthropological field and ethnographic writing training—"Traditionally, this involves long-term, meticulous fieldwork in a specific community to produce a detailed ethnography of everyday life." (Yan Yunxiang, "The Transformation of Private Life").

Therefore, she writes:

> I aspire to write novels, but my life experiences are quite limited. From home to school to just starting in the media, my primary activity has been sitting at a desk reading. The only slightly richer experiences come from brief periods of fieldwork. I'm not a social person, rarely going out or meeting different types of people, nor do I have the personality to gather stories over meals and drinks. Thus, when it comes to fiction, the necessary life details primarily come from the media. This is why I have a particular need to read newspapers.
>
> Nowadays, many artists use social news to construct their plots. *The Seventh Day* and *A Touch of Sin* are famous examples. Authors like A Yi, who was once a policeman, use cases they've encountered as the main plots for their novels. Li Yiyun, a novelist living in America, mentioned in an interview that she reads local town and city newspapers to construct her stories. However, such content requires exceptional skill to turn into novels, especially in an era where dramatic events in life are overly exposed.
>
> When I read reports, I'm not looking for highly dramatic, complete stories. Instead, I seek details unique to a certain type of life, allowing me to imagine the other aspects of that life. For instance, Mo Yan once said that when he was laboring on a farm in Xinjiang, "The mosquito bites were so severe that birds flying in the sky would fall down." Such details are literary, helping one understand what Ludwig Wittgenstein referred to as "forms of life."
>
> For example, last month [December 2016], there was a news story in *Beijing News* titled "Fallen Official Involved in 18-Year-Old Family Murder Case," which recounted a 1998 murder case in Guizhou. I wasn't very in-

terested in the conspiracy, murder, or relationships that could directly be turned into a movie. What intrigued me was a detail where a neighbor living below the crime scene told the reporter that alongside the child's cries upstairs, they could hear the sound of footsteps on the wooden floorboards. "Only chasing a child and hitting them would make such footsteps. We thought someone was beating a child badly." A certain kind of footsteps only occurs when someone is chasing and hitting a child, and the locals were familiar with this sound. Although they found it distressing, they didn't feel the need to intervene.

That familiar sound of "hitting a child" might soon disappear in a China that is becoming more middle-class, affluent, civilized, smoke-free, and latte-drinking. Such details are useful knowledge, soon-to-be-lost knowledge, knowledge of a segment of the population, and they can reveal the intricate details of an entire life, possibly forming the basis for understanding and empathy.

Therefore, I frequently browse social news to accumulate these details. However, I don't have any specific goals or consistent sources. These kinds of details are not easy to find in today's fashionable non-fiction "stories," which tend to be written like detective novels, omitting irrelevant details and making every sentence related to "solving the case." Thus, they are easier to spot in metropolitan or local newspapers.

(Dan Bao, "The Details Needed for Writing Novels,
I Obtain from the Media")

This is Dan Bao's "fieldwork," using media information as the source and field. As for ethnography, can her novels be seen as "ethnographic research centered on the individual"? In the introduction to her column Looking Up at the Crows, she writes: "Write a fictional biography of China for knowledge, in homage to Roberto Bolaño. These people's actions lie between national masters and villains; this series is a pirated hero's record, and every word here is fake." Regarding the relationship between ethnography and literature, Dan Bao discussed it in depth at a workshop at Yunnan University. For that workshop, she chose Chekhov's Sakhalin Island as the literary text. Dan Bao believes:

> Anton Chekhov, the renowned Russian writer, novelist, and playwright, authored *Sakhalin Island*. This non-fiction work provides valuable insights into ethnographic writing. Although it is not a typical contemporary ethnographic text, its nineteenth century origin, penned by a novelist rather than an anthropologist, imbues it with a sense of nationalism and humanitarian spirit rarely seen in modern ethnography. This quality can inspire us, particularly in conducting fieldwork and taking field notes.
>
> Ethnography has historically intertwined with non-fiction texts like missionary writings, explorer journals, government reports, and sociological surveys. These texts and ethnography have mutually influenced each other. By drawing from these various textual forms and gradually distinguishing their writing styles, ethnography evolved from the 1920s to a recognizable genre in 1940s and 1950s, and gradually into the texts we see today. While there is no uniform style, these works share an increasingly anthropological flavor, filled with anthropological jargon and insider language. Ethnographic writing perpetually oscillates between personal stories, social structures, and culture. In China, the relationship between ethnography and non-fiction has always been close. Since the 20th century, ethnographic writing has become deeply intertwined with social sciences, creating various derivative texts that nourish each other.

Dan Bao also discusses the relationship between ethnography and the texts of novels:

> Taiwanese anthropologist Huang Yinggui taught a course on Novels and Anthropology, aiming to "explore the socio-cultural characteristics of various cultural regions through representative novels." On the one hand,

he views literary works as representative texts of a region's culture, a typical text. On the other hand, he acknowledges the novelist's imagination, which may transcend cultural texts, challenge certain cultural notions, or consciously engage with them, revealing or critiquing the culture. These texts may also emphasize conflict, contradictions, and inconsistencies, using more intense and dramatic methods to highlight cultural absurdities. Thus, novels can be seen as both typical and transcendent, both documentary (resembling ethnography) and imaginative, challenging, and critical (where ethnography, beyond documentation, aims for interpretation).

Ethnography influences the style of Dan Bao's novels, which are marked by strong analytical elements, including psychological analysis of characters and logical analysis of narratives. Dan Bao once said: "I have always enjoyed reading modern and postmodern novels that challenge form, have strong analytical elements, and weak storytelling, such as Bolaño, Bernhard, and Musil. I also repeatedly read Tolstoy. As a child, I was deeply influenced by Jane Austen. Her works, like *Persuasion*, I read over and over, gradually forming my views on love, believing that the essence of love lies in waiting while growing."

It is worth noting the conscious gender awareness in her novels:

> A world described without a female perspective or stance is incomplete and one-sided. If all books only narrate political history—land reforms, liberation, cooperatives, anti-rightist campaigns, famine—under a patriarchal perspective, it becomes a mainstream narrative that has long been used as a reference, leading people to believe they see the entire world. But that's not the case.
>
> (Dan Bao, "Chekhov Could Well Be a Woman")

In her novels, the "strong analytical element" might compensate for the "weak storytelling." As in *Parents*, she writes:

Ancient Chinese stories often end without change or events after a strange encounter, just as Chinese families do. A farmer, carrying a basket of geese to sell in the city, meets a scholar on the road. The scholar insists on jumping into the basket to accompany him to the city, and so he does. The basket's weight doesn't increase. The scholar then uses magical skills to summon a few women, with whom they feast and drink, and then the scholar and women disappear, ending the story. The farmer continues his journey to sell the geese, with no change in their price or his life, unlike a Hollywood movie with dramatic turns. The story doesn't bring a climax or conclusion, just like in reality, where the farmer can only recount his experience to others.

She continues:

Is there a real story about oneself? We don't live in stories; we live in patterns—tiring, direction-changing, adventurous. So, what is the mission of a novel at this time?

In her ongoing long novel, Dan Bao explores why readers should read novels:

She thought, why should an ordinary person like her read novels? She doesn't write or particularly love literature. Perhaps novels are for moments like this, when an ordinary person realizes their life has turned into a soap opera. Novels make her feel a subtlety, a part of life that overflows the soap opera.

"Subtlety" and "overflow," along with "details" and "personal records," shape Dan Bao's unique style in observing and writing about Chinese family and intimate relationships, despite her relatively short novel-writing career.

It should be explained that this article heavily quotes Dan Bao's words because it substitutes for an intended in-depth conversation with her on the one-child policy, Chinese families, intimate relationships, anthropology, and literary expression. Due to publication deadlines, this comprehensive dialogue couldn't be completed, thus the simple and crude overlap of our viewpoints, perhaps not constituting a true dialogue, but a rough display, presentation, and record.

Twelve Fragments on County Towns and Literature
(Issue 3, 2020)

· *I* ·

This special topic commenced when Sun Pin interrupted her work on a mid-length novel to support me by writing a short story. The core concept "in the county town" then arose. Next, I immediately thought of the county towns in Zhang Chu and A Yi's novels. Although Zhang Chu later wrote many better novels, his 2003 work *Paperclip* remains particularly memorable to me—stark and unforgettable. I began reading A Yi from his *Gray Stories*. Sun Pin's county town is Jiaocheng in Shanxi Province, where she lived for eighteen years until she attended Lanzhou University. A Yi's county town is Ruichang in Jiangxi Province. He said that he left to escape the hopeless life of a minor civil servant. Zhang Chu has always lived in Luannan, Hebei Province. Last summer, when I went to Beidaihe and the high-speed train stopped in Tangshan, I knew I was close to Zhang Chu and sent him a photo of the station platform.

Zhang Chu is now a talent introduced by the Tianjin Writers' Association, and I'm unsure if he still resides in Luannan.

· *II* ·

This special topic was planned to consist of fictional texts by novelists and my visits to their county towns. Usually, I only read about their county towns in their novels, but I wanted to see these places for myself. Surprisingly, Editor-in-Chief Zhu Yanling was also interested in these visits. We immediately contacted the writers to confirm the timing, and I remember it was January 14, during the Nanjing Critics Association re-election meeting. Zhang Chu was in Luannan. Sun Pin returned to Jiaocheng every year for the New Year. A Yi went to his wife's hometown in Sichuan for the Spring Festival. Interestingly, visiting these three county towns required first arriving at their nearest major cities: Wuhan, Taiyuan, and Tangshan. In China, transportation affects not only logistics but also the political, economic, and cultural aspects of regions.

As planned, I would go to Ruichang after returning home before the Chinese New Year. On January 19, 2020, I returned to Nanjing from my hometown. On January 20, Wuhan went into lockdown. My plan to go to Ruichang via Wuhan fell through. As the pandemic worsened, travel restrictions kept me homebound.

Therefore, this special topic should include an unfinished travelogue.

· *III* ·

Regarding the relationship between county towns and China as a whole, I consulted Professor Zou Nongjian from Nanjing Normal University, who researches rural society. Professor Zou participated in Mr. Fei Xiaotong's research project on rural southern Jiangsu Province in the 1980s. Here's an excerpt from his WeChat message:

The county holds special significance in Chinese history, being the oldest administrative unit since Emperor Qin Shi Huang's establishment of the county system. Many prefectures and districts have disappeared over time, but the county has remained an essential administrative unit for over two thousand years. Literary figures perceive the depth of history, thus producing numerous literary works. However, amid the tides of modernization and urbanization, counties have lost their appeal and begun to decline. Particularly, our system treats counties as rural traditions. Though at the same administrative level, a county mayor is not the same as a city mayor,[2] which is quite lamentable.

Sociology often chases current popular trends, rarely leaving behind classics, producing at best some so-called practical works. In contrast, literary figures provide deep insights, especially those writing about the countryside, which invariably includes the county town. Considering this COVID-19 pandemic, we must seriously reflect on our development model, which excessively glorifies large metropolises and city clusters. Look at Wuhan, why did the pandemic break out here, and why has it been so difficult to control?

Indeed, as Professor Zou mentioned, there are numerous county towns in literature, with perhaps the most famous one from Lu Yao's *Life*. Going to the county town was once the dream of many rural youths. Professor Zou's literary memories likely date back to the 1980s and 1990s, but even today, the presence of county towns in literature is diminishing.

---

2   "City mayor" here refers to that of a county-level city.—Author.

· *IV* ·

My memories of county towns are linked to Hai'an and Rugao, both about ten *li* from the village where I was born in Jiangsu Province. I attended a rural school through junior high, the school standing solitary amid expansive fields. In the ninth grade, I moved to a school in a small town called Dingjiashuo, which had once been significant. In a 1970s Chinese atlas published in Japan, which I found in Professor Fujii Shōzō's lab at the University of Tokyo, Dingjiashuo was one of four names marked in Hai'an. However, following administrative changes, its functions waned, leaving it with just an old street and a few shops resembling scenes from old Republic of China films. Two years ago, when we visited, it was dilapidated.

A rural child cannot comprehend the smallness of a town without seeing the largeness of a county town. Because towns are small, county towns are the big cities. People living in county towns are the real urbanites. Gao Jialin perceived it this way, and so did I. In A Yi's *Meeting My Fiancée*, the father buys a house in the county town, leading the family on a grand move to the city. In Zhang Chu's *Several Moments with Xie Yunjin*, the dropout Xie Yunjin goes to work in the county town.

I spent three years in Hai'an for high school and ten years working in Rugao. My first trip to Hai'an was by boat along the Chuanchang River, which native poet Xiaohai wrote about. He has a famous poem called *Beiling River*, and in Hai'an, the Chuanchang and Beiling Rivers are equally well-known. During those three years, I became familiar with the county town's woven network of streets and alleys: the Xinhua Bookstore, hospitals, schools, bathhouses, restaurants, department stores, barber shops, county government offices, the post office where literary magazines are available, theaters showing movies, the workers' cultural center, and the cultural center hosting video screenings, billiards, and dances, etc. Factories and the train station were on the outskirts, like the desolate and chaotic areas described in Sun Pin's *General Cat.* During those three years, I wrote poetry and dabbled in literary clubs, barely touching the edges of literature. It is profoundly sad that the county town poets and novelists we revered in our youth ended up confined to the county town. One could in fact conduct a field study on how many literary youth county towns produced in the 1980s and 1990s.

My first trip to Rugao was before I started high school in Hai'an. After setting fire to the production team's haystack with a group of mischievous friends—a major offense at the time—my grandmother, inexplicably, took me to Rugao by bike, a place I longed to visit but had never reached. I remember entering from the north gate through stone-paved alleys. To my young mind, Rugao was a prosperous but declining large city, an old city. Indeed, compared to Hai'an, Rugao houses older temples and gardens.

County towns are not villages nor mere small towns. Rugao has long been a county-level city, and Hai'an also achieved county-level city status last year.

Until the turn of the millennium, county towns continuously supplied literary youth to Chinese literature. Many who began writing in the 1980s and 1990s remained in the county town. They formed the bedrock of that literary era. Even if they did not become excellent writers, they were at least excellent readers—county town clerks, teachers, workers, and so on.

However, the times have changed dramatically. I examined a survey conducted by *Literature* last year of 117 writers born after 1985. Among them, very few wrote in county towns, and even fewer originated from county towns. On the other hand, many are writing commercial online literature in county towns. Regardless, it is an undeniable fact that young writers of so-called serious literature have withdrawn from county towns. This may partly explain the current decline of rural literature.

· *V* ·

ounty towns are not merely the private domain of literature. In the album *A Tale of Haifeng* by the band Wu Tiao Ren, there are several songs about Haifeng, including: "Water Flows," "Changing Hong-kong Dollar," "An Unreasonable World," "Walking A Pig on My Bike," "I'll Tell You When Problems Come," "Green On Gray," "Dream Chemical Factory," "Daoshan Dude," "Uncle Lee," "Childhood," and "Bingyao." The song "Walking a Pig on My Bike" goes:

Alas, my friend,

Don't ask me,

If I've taken the Haifeng public bus.

I see it often, carrying air,

From Lian'an Intersection to Yunling.

Alas, my friend,

Don't ask me,

If I've heard the noise of Haifeng cars and motorcycles.

Even the deaf at the intersection are frightened by it.

I walk a pig on my bike,

(Standing at the East Gate, urinating violently, buying a tractor).

I walk a pig on my bike,

(Longjin Creek is a river, already crippled for thirty years).

I walk a pig on my bike,

(The countryside doesn't look like the countryside, the city doesn't look like the city, Haifeng Park has only one gate).

I walk a pig on my bike,

(When I was young, I asked my grandpa for twenty cents, he said better bring a hammer and a cup, I'll knock my nose to bleed for you).

Another song, "Water Flows" goes:

> They all say I'm sleep talking.
>
> Actually, it's Haifeng dialect I'm speaking.
>
> I don't know, I don't know,
>
> La la la la.
>
> Today globalization, tomorrow self-indulgence.

Wutiaoren describe themselves as "rooted in the world, with eyes on Haifeng." Their album *A Tale of Haifeng* was awarded the 2019 Album of the Year by *Southern Weekly*. Their acceptance speech read:

> *A Tale of Haifeng* is an album of stories: the story of "Changing Hongkong Dollar," the story of farmer "Uncle Lee," the story of single guy "Bingyao," the story of the guard at the "Dream Chemical Factory" ... These stories are as ordinary as the word "ordinary." Everyone has many such ordinary stories to tell, and every issue of *Southern Weekly* contains stories of such people. So, we interpret this "special tribute" from *Southern Weekly* not as an award for *A Tale of Haifeng* but as a recognition of every ordinary person living in big cities and small county towns. We hope that by saying this, we don't come across as pretentious ... *A Tale of Haifeng* is an album sung in your "foreign language."

· *VI* ·

Jia Zhangke might be the Chinese director who most frequently uses county towns as a backdrop. His films *Xiao Shan Going Home* (1994), *Xiao Wu* (1998), *Platform* (2000), *Unknown Pleasures* (2002), and *Moun-*

tains May Depart (2015) are all set in the county town of Fenyang in Shanxi Province. Jia Zhangke says:

> Life in a county town is very alluring, giving people ample time to feel the pleasures of life. For example, all the small shopkeepers and vendors on the street are your friends. The key maker, the shoe repairer, the tailor, the vegetable seller, the tofu seller, the newspaper vendor, the bank clerk, and the salesperson at the department store across the street—you know them all. After lunch, you take a nap until you wake up naturally, then ride a bike to a friend's place, chat for hours, and then go to a movie together, have dinner, play mahjong until you're exhausted, and then sleep. This life has its charm, being immersed in warm human relationships is especially comforting. However, if you never leave this place, it can become quite monotonous. Lying in bed in the morning, there's a sense of boredom seeping through the gaps.
>
> (Jia Zhangke, "The County Town and Me,"
> Tianya WeChat Official Account)

I resonate most with Jia Zhangke's depiction of the dusty county town. Fenyang is close to Sun Pin's Jiaocheng and far from my hometown's county town. But the idle street corner youths and pool tables are almost identical to my memories of the county town in the late 1980s, and similar scenes can be seen in Hou Hsiao-hsien's films. Many places, though far apart, feel very close.

· *VII* ·

In an interview with Xu Zhiyuan, A Yi talks about his county town.

Dandu: Over the years, you've been going back home frequently. How do you feel about the changes in the county town?

A Yi: Materially speaking, the county town is now better than even some big cities. There are just a few aspects that aren't great: one is the use of gas, as they might still be using gas cylinders, which I really hate; the other is heating, which isn't as convenient in the south compared to the north. But other than that, the living conditions are excellent: there's ample space—while you might live in a 50 square meters space in Beijing, you can get 200 square meters there; and the weather is beautiful. Yet, I still dread returning to the county town. I used to have frequent nightmares, dreaming that my father would grab a sack and drag me back to work at some local office. Recently, someone suggested that I go back home and work in the local cultural department, to help with promotions because I have some fame as a writer now. I didn't reject the idea at the time, but later found it absurd—if I really went, it would be quite depressing.

Moreover, a major reason for leaving the county town was the lack of books. There were only two places to buy books: newsstands, which updated quickly but only offered magazines like *Zawen Xuankan, Reader*, and *Sheshi Zhichu*; and Xinhua Bookstore, which didn't sell literary books. Now, I think, why do people in county towns prefer reading *Global Times*? Why are they interested in military affairs and political secrets? Why are essays so popular among county town intellectuals? Writers like Bo Yang, Li Ao, and Wang Xiaobo are insightful, but they've been talking about the same issues for years, stuck in a certain place. If I wanted to access more, I couldn't do it in a county town. China has many excellent intellectuals writing great articles, running excellent magazines, and publishing quality books, but their work doesn't reach county towns. In this situation, leaving is the only option. It wasn't until I went to Beijing that I encountered these diverse things. If you stay in the county town, you end up influenced by popular culture like Phoenix Legend and Wang Feng. My high school classmates in QQ and WeChat groups, including those who seemed more advanced in thought than me back then, now share shocking news every day, which is quite startling. People's consciousness is actually swallowed by the popular culture of the county town.

(A Yi, "Xu Zhiyuan's Dialogue with A Yi,"
Zhiyuan WeChat Official Account)

Literary youth who don't fit in with the county town become exiles in spirit.

· *VIII* ·

Among contemporary writers, few are as deeply intertwined with county towns while still residing there as Zhang Chu. He has two often-quoted writings, one being "In the County Town":

I moved from Datong to this county town called Bencheng in Hebei Province in 1983, and it's been over thirty years. In these thirty-plus years, except for a few years at university in Dalian and occasional business or personal trips, I have always lived here.

The county town has changed in the past decade. The changes are due to the opening of several private steel mills. Each steel mill is large, employing many workers, bustling and lively. The coal dust in the air settles on their faces, making their expressions look both proud and desolate. Gradually, more tall buildings appeared, and the county town finally saw buildings taller than twenty stories a few years ago. This was unimaginable before, as we often had earthquakes here, and people were afraid to live in tall buildings. But now, people seem fearless; with some money, they even buy fancy cars. Many of my childhood classmates now run various companies, greeting people warmly from their expensive vehicles. Like Macondo in *One Hundred Years of Solitude*, this county town is becoming increasingly bizarre and indulgent, and the air quality has changed significantly: it used to be dusty and dry but with a clean simplicity and brightness in essence that I believe stemmed from the people's hearts, not the climate. Nowadays, the town has KFC, various specialty stores, and different cars, but people have become more materialistic and mechanized. In conversations, adults can't avoid topics of houses, money, women, and power, as if only these discussions can make them shine brighter.

I believe this might not be unique to this county town; every county town in China is probably the same. This bustling, rosy-cheeked county town is nothing more than the most ordinary and typical county town in contemporary China. In such a place, new events happen every month. These so-called new things are invariably linked to affairs, poisonings, political conspiracies, and corruption, all tied to worldly desires. But because these desires are so blatant and commonplace, I can't help but pay attention to them. Thus, I discover many interesting yet sad stories.

(Zhang Chu, "In the County Town," *October* WeChat Official Account)

County towns are societies of acquaintances, but perhaps the "being acquainted" is more superficial. Seeing each other but not truly knowing each other might be the essence. Just look at the three novels in this special issue; each county town story has its own unique dark secrets, some even deadly. So, the literary impetus of the county town may not just come from its unique space and location but from its social samples and human nature.

Another famous piece of writing about county town literary youth by Zhang Chu circulating online is *Weeds Are Singing—Writers in the County Town*, published in Issue 12 of *Literature Harbor* in 2014 and later included in his short story collection *Love Stories of Middle-Aged Women*.

In 1999, Bencheng was like a sorrowful, simple symbol, a microcosm of all northern county towns. Since we moved there in 1984, it hadn't changed much over the years: the narrow, winding main street would get jammed with traffic at quitting time, and on either side of the street were low, shabby shops: Wenzhou people running barber shops, Chengdu people running Sichuan restaurants, Nanjing people selling dried salted duck, Guangzhou people running STD clinics, and Northeastern people selling cooked delicacy ... These outsiders with different accents opened their shop fronts, letting the straightforward sunlight pour in, casting bright or dim shadows on their fresh or greasy faces. Through years of trading, their waists hunched, their skin took on a sorrowful yellowish hue, and their fingernails absorbed the unique smell of the small town: the scent of paper glue, steel mill dust, and the fishy smell of underwater creatures from distant seas. Sometimes, I would ride my bike through Bencheng, watching the myriad faces of the world, and a trivial sense of happiness would fill my heart. I knew that, sooner or later, I would write their spiritual history, just like God creating man.

This is the elegy of literary youth in county towns, similar to Gu Chan-gwei's film *And the Spring Comes*. In terms of administrative divisions, *And the Spring Comes* might be set in a small city larger than a county town, but it is still a county town story. Sometimes, county town stories might be of aesthetic significance rather than geographically accurate county towns. Therefore, putting Yan Ge's *The Heartbreaking Stories from Pingle Town*, Zheng Zaihuan's *The Heartbreaking Stories from Zhumadian*, and other writings of small-town youth of aesthetic significance together might make

sense. The county town stories in contemporary Chinese literature are dedicated to those gray areas at the junction of urban and rural spaces.

· *IX* ·

If you search "Sun Pin" and "county town" together on the internet, you
will find many of her novels. Indeed, in her early works, county town is
a place her characters want to escape from; in her later works, it often
becomes the place where the escapees return in defeat. This shift is not just
a reversal of plot but also of mindset and aesthetic meaning. She once said:

> Last year (note: 2018), I returned to my hometown, a small county town
> to celebrate the Mid-Autumn Festival. Free, I wandered alone on the old
> street. There was a half-weathered millennium stone lion on the old street;
> it had been with me throughout my childhood and teenage years. When
> I was in middle school, I rode my bike past it every day without giving it
> much thought. But that day, I gazed at it for a long time in the golden au-
> tumn sunlight and recalled those clear and innocent times, full of dreams
> and confusion. Suddenly, I understood what changes over the ages and
> the passage of time truly meant. I felt something strange from it, some-
> thing akin to compassion or grace, which struck me deeply. The ordinary
> people passing by almost brought me to tears. I used to fear getting lost in
> the crowd, dreading becoming trivial and mediocre, never willing to easily
> forgive and accept my mistakes. But that afternoon, I saw the most brilliant
> side of the most ordinary people—not Lu Xun's critique of national char-
> acter, nor the condescending gaze of pseudo-intellectuals, nor the nihilistic
> pity and lamentation. I truly saw the extraordinary vitality in each individ-
> ual: fragile, splendid, diverse, struggling yet yearning to soar. The title of the
> novel appeared to me in that instant: *The Grace of the Lion*. Grace for all be-

ings, and also a form of grace and forgiveness for myself. Yes, over the years, I often felt powerless and disgusted, often unable to forgive a mediocre and emotional self. But in the end, I consider myself hardworking.

(Sun Pin, "The Ripples Between Reality and Illusion,"
Selected Short Stories WeChat Official Account)

I've seen photos of Sun Pin's county town she sent, desolate and decayed. Can such a place truly become a home to return to?

· *X* ·

Yuanzi became famous on Douban. In 2019, his *Daytime Wandering* was shortlisted for the Blancpain Imaginist Literary Prize. In the same year, he resigned from his job in Beijing, left the familiar literary circles, and returned to his hometown in the county town and rural areas of Hong'an, Hubei Province. There, he continued writing in a low-rent house with an annual rent of RMB 1,800 (2019 of Yuanzi: "Ten Years as a Beijing Drifter, Three Books Published, Returning to the County Town at 32," GQ WeChat Official Account).

Yuan Zi is one of the writers invited for this special topic. His county town, Hong'an, was severely struck by the pandemic, making it impossible for him to complete his planned novel. Who could calmly write at this time and place?

Earlier, Guangdong novelist Chen Zaijian also seemed to have returned to his county town, writing a series of novels about it.

· *XI* ·

In 2019, *A Worthy Life* by novelist Huang Xiaoyang depicted a brief history of a county town scoundrel. Earlier, *Foreign Land* by Fu Xiuying also set the county town as a station in the protagonist Zhai Xiaoli's life journey. Many writers born in the 1970s began by writing about villages and towns, about their original experiences. Such experiences have not been exhausted, and they have yet to produce great works matching their original experiences.

It is no longer common to observe writers and their relationships based on landmarks, but it is not entirely obsolete. For instance, in the past two years, Tiexi District (in Shenyang, Liaoning Province) has become a landmark of the "Northeast Renaissance." Expanding from Tiexi District to the Northeast, forming a new group of Northeast writers, and even creating "Northeast Studies," is something the mass media and universities are striving for. Whether it can be achieved and what this framework might encompass remains unknown.

But county towns are different. Different county towns sometimes share the same literary tone, such as the gray and despairing tones in the novels of Zhang Chu, A Yi, and Sun Pin. Or rather, all Chinese county towns share similar appearances, textures, tones, and innate qualities, like siblings.

"County towns" (possibly including suburban areas and small cities larger than county towns) as a literary space, a "place" in literature, is neither rural writing nor urban writing. Chinese modern literature research has focused more on the two extremes of city and countryside. Besides these two extremes, there might be a third literary tradition. I consulted Dan Bao, an anthropologist, about the county town issue. She provided nearly 10,000 words of material, offering valuable perspectives from various disciplines. Entering from a sociological path, she believes:

County towns may represent 'middle countries,' 'hinterlands,' cultural conservatism, stubbornness, and isolation, among other cultural characteristics. For a rural youth, a county town may not represent the 'first step toward urbanization,' but rather a depressing place. Its cultural characteristics are diametrically opposed to the progressive cities in their minds and lack the natural simplicity of the countryside. A county town may not be a stopover between rural and urban areas, but rather a different image of China, unlike the one imagined by intellectual or political elites in Beijing and Shanghai. How to understand geographical space as cultural space is not a standard, linear, progressive narrative of village—county—city.

For example, Dan Bao also mentioned *Orchard City Chronicle* by Shi Tuo: "This city is called Guoyuan Cheng a fictional small town in Central Asia, representing all such small towns." Not just *Orchard City Chronicle* but a large amount of new literature from the Republic of China is about intellectual youth saving the world and enlightenment, where the "space" and "place" of the stories should be "county towns" (small towns). These small towns were indeed the "middle countries," "hinterlands," culturally conservative, stubborn, and isolated. But since the reform and opening up, the cultural composition of county towns has become complex. For instance, in reform literature, county towns are both conservative and radical.

· *XII* ·

Looking at Zhang Chu's *Several Moments with Xie Yunjin*, A Yi's *Meeting My Fiancée*, and Sun Pin's *General Cat* together, one can see the urban-rural geography of China. Going to the countryside to Gujiazhuang and Jinyi Township, the county town is a city; going to Beijing, Zhengzhou, and Hangzhou, the county town is surrounded by countless villages. This is the spatial reality of Chinese county towns: chaotic, yet full of vitality. In their novels, the time in county towns corresponds to the growth history of small characters. Each of their county towns houses their own relatives. Facing their county towns and relatives, novelists naturally restrain their condescending sense of charity and overflowing sympathy, replacing it with a shared sense of destiny imbued with honest humanism. This is what makes their novels touching.

_ **Hometown, also a New Land** _
(Issue 4, 2020)

The first contribution to this special topic was *Village Museum* by Suo Er, which I received in November 2018. By May of the following year, this novel was shortlisted for the Pulsasir Award, among the 14 works selected. Inspired by *Village Museum*, I wanted to assemble young writers who write about the countryside, similar to the "Eight Cities" issue of Flower City Interest earlier this year, to create a snapshot of "literary countryside" on one literary genealogy through the lens of China's youngest novelists. However, Flower City Interest had already featured young rural writers like Zhou Kai, Ding Yan, and Qi Shimu, making it challenging to find three or four writers of the same caliber outside of this group. Thus, the project was shelved for almost two years. This special topic, now titled Village Museum, owes a debt of gratitude to Suo Er for patiently keeping the novel unpublished until now.

Suo Er is recognized among his peers for his extreme experiments with novelistic form. This is evident in *Village Museum* and his recent work *Wanderer in a Box* published in *Changjiang Literature & Art*, both of which are written without paragraphs, almost in a single continuous sentence. The decision to eschew traditional punctuation and segmentation may be seen as a display of technical skill but it also raises questions about the narrative pace and rhythm in novel-writing. Editor-in-Chief Zhu Yanling deliberated extensively and agreed to preserve Suo Er's "unique feature" out of respect for the writer's experiment and to provide a discussion point for readers. In fact, even before the era of fragmented, quickly consumed reading brought on by the internet, such an approach would have been considered "abnormal" or "reader-unfriendly." Thus, anyone specializing in narrative theory and literary form may find it fruitful to discuss the "form" of this novel in depth with Suo Er.

Although *Flower City* has a tradition of avant-garde literature, and Flower City Interest has embraced some extreme literary experiments, both Editor-in-Chief Zhu Yanling and I agree that we do not want to narrowly define avant-garde as mere formal experimentation, thereby limiting the broader possibilities of literary exploration to the potential of formal extremism. In reality, after the frenetic and compensatory lessons in modernism of the 1980s, pushing the boundaries of novelistic form has become increasingly difficult. From the 1990s to the present, it has been rare to label any writer purely as a literary formal experimenter.

Personally, I regret that due to space constraints, *Village Museum* was cut down from 36,000 to 27,000 Chinese characters, structurally "amputating" one of its characters. While this may not harm the issue's overall vision, it technically turns it into a different novel. Hopefully, this regret can be mitigated when Suo Er publishes the complete version in the future.

This year's previous issues of Flower City Interest have featured themes on cities, families, and county towns. Adding the countryside here, these "spaces" are transposed from reality into "literary spaces." *Village Museum* is constructed in Suo Er's novel as both an intrusion into and a dislocated outpost of the original rural geography and atmosphere. This aptly serves as a critique of current rural-themed literature, expressing dissatisfaction, questioning, and reflection on the "museum-ification" of the rural in contemporary literature. Much like many cultural and tourism projects that create rural building clusters to display objects, perform customs, and sell local specialties, many so-called "disappearing countryside" novels today resemble this form, as written in Suo Er's *Village Museum*:

> Does it truly, as its original intention and name suggest, restore and
> encapsulate those vanished, beautiful memories of the countryside? We

all know that our countryside is an aesthetic of disappearance, no longer as depicted by Wang Wei or Tao Yuanming. Our current countryside is not the same as before, as we put it into a museum, or rather, build a museum around it, treating it as a fossil, an art collection, and naming this museum Village Museum.

If the literary depiction of the "disappearing countryside" makes sense, it assumes cultural, emotional, and aesthetic presuppositions, as this vanished countryside we assume is "premodern," "Chinese," peaceful, and healthy. Notably, modern writers since Lu Xun have focused on the desolation of the "premodern" countryside, and this desolation cannot be entirely blamed on modernity but is rather revealed by it. Only the "literary countryside" represented by Fei Ming and Shen Congwen, recorded in the contrast between past and present, rural and urban, holds literary canonical significance, invoking modern emotions that cast a quasi-magical spell over readers. The literary establishment's excessive leniency and endorsement of the "disappearing countryside" narrative undoubtedly lowers the bar for such writing. Young writers generally abandon critical rural writing, partly due to this leniency and endorsement. For instance, Wei Wei's *Annals of Yanhe Village* far surpasses her earlier rural novels in both criticality and writing difficulty, yet her literary reputation still rests on those earlier, gentle, restrained, and lyrical works. This special topic warrants deeper exploration: why do writers born in the late 1960s and 1970s, with rural experiences, often choose the less transformative, more nebulous 1970s countryside over the dramatically changing countryside of the 1980s as their literary space? Perhaps the secret lies in the fact that post-1980s rural China is more complex, and the literary structure to grasp this era is still evolving. Conversely, the 1970s countryside has a rich modern literary heritage, serving as a "literary museum" for later writers to emulate.

I once privately discussed with Liang Hong: why has rural writing diminished among writers born in the 1970s, whose rural experience is far from depletion, why is it rare to find works with typical epochal structures, and why more and more writers leave the country writing? The answer might be that as a "museum," "fossil," and "artifact," the countryside is no longer growing, fluid, or alive. As Yuanzi says:

> Of course, many people are writing so-called realistic works. There are plenty of such works online and in literary journals. However, this foolproof realism is completely detached from reality. For instance, the rural areas they write about are actually "literary scenes" constructed collectively by a generation of writers. Older writers and their disciples painstakingly maintain these scenes. They have established standards for how peasants should speak, what workers should think, and how officials should act. If you don't write this way, it's considered unrealistic and out of touch. Ironically, their 'realism' principles are precisely the root of the lack of realism.

Existing literary history provides several "village museum" templates: Lu Xun's, Shen Congwen's, Zhao Shuli's, Liu Qing's, Lu Yao's, Wang Zengqi's, Mo Yan's, Yan Lianke's, Jia Pingwa's ... Young novelists replicate and imitate these templates, ignoring that each author's literary template arose from their respective era's realities and issues. Thus, the continually produced "literary countryside" is merely the "literary history's countryside." The key term of this special topic, "village museum," serves as a reminder that contemporary rural writing should not mimic the ubiquitous "village museum," reducing the countryside to simplistic symbols and spectacles. Instead, it should continuously uncover the realities and issues of our era's countryside, inventing new literary forms for our time.

However, some reality and issues have always been there. For example, the urban-rural divide has been a "Chinese problem" for over a century. Therefore, Yuanzi and Qiu Changting write:

Now I am walking this path, this one and not that one. These small roads, like natural gas pipelines, channel the energy of rural people away, converting it into money that flows back. When enough zeros accumulate in the accounts, they move out of the village and become urban residents. I once shared their passion for escaping the land, yearning to migrate to the big city. Now, I am walking the opposite path, returning from the city to the countryside.

(Yuanzi, *The Shaft*)

A pair of fusiliers, wild, unable to be raised in city aquariums, migrate to warmer eastern waters in autumn, and are thus caught.

I obediently shut my mouth. This was the only clue related to our origin, our shared hometown, the land we can never return to.

(Qiu Changting, *Glass House*)

Literature also reflects on and critiques history, as seen in Chen Jiyi's *Human-Faced Beast*, where the search for the "human-faced beast" inadvertently leads into the village's nightmarish past. This kind of writing, with its elements of crossing, magic, mutation, and allegory, is common among older writers from the 1950s and 1960s. It has become a safe passage for contemporary literature to delve into "contemporary history." In *Human-Faced Beast*, Chen Jiyi skillfully navigates the syntax of modern Chinese literature, depicting the relationships of vigilance, wariness, fear, and eventual violence between "I" and family members or villagers, which have roots in our literary history.

In recent years, Chen Jiyi's Jintang River Tales series has garnered attention in the literary world. This aligns with contemporaries like Lu Min, Xu Zechen, Wei Wei, and Fu Xiuying, who initially gained fame through rural writing but later shifted their focus. While many writers of their generation have moved from the countryside to the city, Chen Jiyi's "conservatism" in

Jintang River Tales stands out clearly due to its temporal and distinctive nature.

Chinese writers from mainland China and Taiwan also show significant differences. Born in 1977, Tong Weige's works, such as *The Research on Wang*, were published by Hinabook. For this special topic, he contributed *Event* and *Death*, selected from the collaborative writer project Alphabet Club. Tong Weige's use of rural experiences from his youth is not merely due to nostalgia or the significance of the "disappearing countryside." For him, the vanished, lost time forms a dim "labyrinth," where the gray areas of memory and forgetfulness are precisely what make narrative captivating. Comparing Taiwanese new countryside writers like Gan Yaoming, Wang Congwei, and Tong Weige, I particularly value Tong Weige's complex storytelling. Why are there differences within the same literary generation? It might stem from divergent literary traditions, reading preferences of the era, and global literary trends.

Suo Er's *Village Museum*, Yuanzi's *The Shaft*, and Qiu Changting's *Glass House* are notable for their writing based on the "rural scene." Yuanzi, a returnee to reality, moved back to his hometown from Beijing after years of residing there. His *The Shaft* reflects his personal experiences and life nuances with warmth and subtlety. In contrast, Qiu Changting's *Glass House* explores human legends and the darker corners of human nature.

Interestingly, three mainland Chinese writers in this special topic all coincidentally chose "returnees" as their narrators, following a narrative tradition initiated by Lu Xun in works like *Hometown*, *Blessing*, and *In the Tavern*. Notably, the returnees in *Village Museum*, *The Shaft*, and *Human-Faced Beast* all come from Beijing, offering a rich geography and political space for interpretation. In *Human-Faced Beast*, the route is Beijing–Jinhua–Tangxi Town–Wu Village. In Wu Village, "one night, I went to bed early and unexpectedly found myself longing for my days in Beijing. Though I hadn't been able to afford a house or find a girlfriend to consider marriage with, the city's bustling vibrancy, crowded streets, and constant noise had, in that specific moment in the remote southwestern mountains of Zhejiang, transformed into a cherished memory."

Yuanzi, in *The Shaft*, writes, "As long as I keep walking north, I can reach Beijing, a place I've never been."

Similarly, the returnee is also a stranger:

> Since I went to junior high school in the county, I have left this Fang-named village for 20 years. There are many people in the village I don't know, and vice versa. Previously, I was a stranger in the city; now, I am a stranger in the village. This estrangement has even been legally confirmed: when I went to university in Nanjing, my rural household registration changed to urban; after graduating, my household registration had no place to go. When I tried to move it back to the countryside, it was rejected because this idea contradicted modernization. Thus, I became a Chinese with neither land nor property, only able to temporarily reside somewhere.
>
> (Yuan Zi, *The Shaft*)

Which can better stimulate literary creativity: reality or imagination? It is hard to determine definitively. Some writers rely solely on real experiences to achieve literary success, while others become masters by creating purely from imagination. Often, literature is a blend and fabrication of both reality and imagination. Regarding the countryside, rural life, and literature, the tradition in modern Chinese literature seems to be that most writers start their literary journeys based on their childhood memories of their hometowns. Although their paths and destinations vary, the original homeland from which their lives set out remains a constant return point in their literature.

Chinese writers' deep entanglement with specific places didn't begin with Faulkner and García Márquez. Long before them, authors like Lu Xun, Fei Ming, Shen Congwen, Xiao Hong, Shi Tuo, Liu Qing, and Zhou Libo had already grounded their literary works in their native soil and rural settings.

This practice remained consistent among writers born between the 1950s and the 1970s.

The notion of summoning the spirit of the "disappearing countryside" with the craftsmanship of old novels begs the question of how to dialectically reconcile the disappeared with the regenerated. What is the current state of the Chinese countryside? How can literature accurately represent it? How should the heirs of literary history and the pioneers of literary future choose between them? These questions underscore the vastness, diversity, and ever-changing nature of China's countryside, which serves as both the homeland and the new land for literature.

The Illusion of the "Global Village" and World Travelers
(Issue 5, 2020)

W ang Bang drifted from Guangzhou in the UTC +8:00 to Lon-don in the GMT Zone. Her writing about Lewisham depicts her first stop in London, a destination for immigrants from around the world. Wu Yaling writes about Paris from Shanghai, where she once studied. Bo Lin writes from Beijing about Split in the UTC +1:00, while Chen Jizhou writes from Harvard in the UTC –5:00 about Jakarta, which share the same time zone as his hometown Chengdu, and Johannesburg in the UTC +2:00. These time zones divide time and create a temporal world map.

Besides Wang Bang, Wu Yaling, Bo Lin, and Chen Jizhou, others like Yang Meng, Xu Zhenfu, and Sha Qingqing were also invited to contribute to this special topic through introductions by friends. If categorized strictly, this special topic falls under travelogue, but not entirely. China has a long history of travelogue, with scholars lingering over landscapes, cultural journeys, mourning, and sentimentality, a tradition that persists today. Globally, travelogue can encompass works like *Hiroshima Notes* and *Okinawa Notes* by Ōe Kenzaburō, *Istanbul: Memories and the City* by Orhan Pamuk, and *The Middle Passage: Impressions of Five Societies—British, French and Dutch in the West Indies and South America, The Masque of Africa: Glimpses of African Belief,* and the "Indian Trilogy" by V. S. Naipaul. These works reflect the writer's untainted insight, intellectual creativity, and ways of understanding the world (what might be termed "travelogue as a method"), regardless of whether they are fictional or non-fictional. Any literary genre is an ancient

craft for today's writers. The later writers are both inheritors of literary heritage and self-saviors.

Wang Bang's Lewisham, a place densely populated with people of color,
is filled with individuals whose skin tones, appearances, clothing, and even
skin textures are entirely different from "me." Their languages, cultures, and
backgrounds are also vastly different. Almost everyone in Lewisham has a
"Ghanaian past," growing up in bodies shrouded in darkness, surrounded
by inky bile. Daylight is unseen, and only the moon and nightingale can
occasionally bring it out. Chen Jizhou's Johannesburg represents another
chapter of "Chinese past," chronicling the long history of Chinese immi-
gration to Johannesburg from the nineteenth to the twenty-first century.
If Wang Bang and Chen Jizhou write about the projection of "Chinese in
the world," Bo Lin's Split and Wu Yaling's Paris are personal and intimate.
Though their concerns may not seem grand, they are deeply personal. I had
little exchange with Wu Yaling, introduced to me by Fei Ying and contacted through Huang Dehai for this contribution. I met Bo Lin while she was
at *The Beijing News*, writing perhaps the best book reviews and interviews
on contemporary China. I once regarded her as a representative of media
literary criticism. She later resigned, possibly influenced by the allure of the
Balkans. But why the Balkans (Yugoslavia) and not somewhere else? Indeed,
Yugoslavia is part of the collective memory and spiritual past of contemporary Chinese people. However, the "Yugoslavia" remembered by those born
before the 1960s differs from the spiritual paths Bo Lin took.

> Yugoslavia is a very obscure and marginal issue, but I don't find it
> marginal in my heart. I believe that our attitude toward the Yugoslav issue
> reflects how we deal with our history. "We" includes not only Westerners
> but all individuals. If you cannot face your history and place it correctly,
> your future will inevitably be distorted, even if it might be superficially
> peaceful for a while. Now, people's focus is not on that place but on the US,
> Iran, Syria, and Turkey. However, everything is surging beneath the surface,

now it's just the fatigue and recovery after the war. The Serbs' sense of injury, grievance, and loss of dignity is fermenting internally, like the Germans in the 1920s. Blaming an entire nation because of Slobodan Milošević (former Serbian President) will trigger new hatred and wars.

(Yang Chen and Bo Lin, "Dialogue with Bo Lin: The Black Sheep and Gray Eagle of Yugoslavia")

Bo Lin's concern about "how we handle our history" reminds me of the "Blue Eastern Europe" translation series by Flower City Publishing House. The twentieth century's Eastern Europe was both Eastern Europe's "Eastern Europe" and China's "Eastern Europe," a member of the shared socialist family and a divergent path after the 1990s. For Chinese readers, different Eastern Europes exist.

By the way, Bo Lin's travels in Yugoslavia were funded by the One-Way Street "Sailor Project." The Sailor Project, initiated by the One-Way Street Public Welfare Foundation, aims to help young writers rediscover the world by sponsoring their overseas travel, assisting and guiding their writing, and promoting and exhibiting their final works, striving to bring new global imagination into Chinese writing. In my understanding, One-Way Street, including its affiliated *Dandu*, has always been committed to cultivating young thinkers, and seeing the world is an important step toward becoming a thinker. My consideration of this special topic was also somewhat inspired by the Sailor Project and *Dandu*. I discussed with Wu Qi, editor-in-chief of *Dandu*, hoping to present a complete issue of the Sailor Project's results in Flower City Interest. This special topic partially fulfills that plan, with Bo Lin coming from the Sailor Project and Wang Bang's most influential writing serialized in *Dandu*'s "British Observations." Bo Lin's Yugoslavia, Liu Zichao's Central Asia, and Guo Shuang's Nagasaki from the Sailor Project all delve into geographies worthy of reflection. These areas are not in the core zones of contemporary media storms or geopolitical centers. Wang Bang's London is no longer the London of the "Industrial Revolution." Yet, the periphery and alienation can often produce insights and intellectual power.

Wu Yaling's writing in this special topic is unique, resembling a broad travelogue—aesthetic stroll. Her *Jacob Wrestling with the Angel* is a "soul's encounter with the pain of beauty," as she discussed with Huang Dehai:

> Strictly speaking, I think I only saw some "appearances of beauty." The greatest charm lies in its incommunicability, like the experience of the figure in the painting. In such moments, one might encounter the "soul's pain of encountering beauty" described by Plato in Phaedrus, and that process is necessarily solitary. The painting precisely interprets the classical spirit's struggle between humanity and divinity. This evokes a subtle and genuine pain beyond the touch of emotion. For the same reason, this incommunicable process can sometimes be relieved, such as in moments of reading classics and feeling moved and pained, or in conversations like ours.
> (Wu Yaling and Huang Dehai, "I Don't Know Who Said It Better Than Plato")

Generally speaking, this special topic revolves around the writings of cross-border travelers navigating the world's time zones. To them, time zones symbolize more than just the passage of time; they represent the dynamic flow of time across the Earth, with its diverse landscapes, customs, and cultures. As young Chinese writer's journey through these various time zones, they become cultural "foreign travelers."

In 2005, Bi Feiyu published a short story titled *Rainbow*. It subtly presents a "time logic" that progresses concurrently from two perspectives: a retired intellectual couple, missing their three children who have emigrated abroad, whimsically sets up four quartz clocks in their home, adjusting them to the times of Beijing, San Francisco, Vancouver, and Munich, and hanging them on the wall according to their geographic sequence. In their home, four different times simultaneously emerge, each with its own logical rationale. However, the unexpected intrusion of a boy living next door disrupts the "rationality" of this internally consistent time logic. The boy, still in the nascent stages of conceptual understanding, believes that there should only be one correct time: "Beijing Time." The coexistence of four different times in the elderly couple's home clashes irreconcilably with the boy's understanding of "time logic," prompting the old lady to relay the boy's "protest" to her husband at the end of the story: "He said our clocks are broken."

Time zones delineate the realities of our daily lives. In another of Bi Feiyu's stories, *The Wang Village on the Earth* (published in *Shanghai Literature* in 2002), a father brings home a world map from the county town and pastes it on the gable of their main room, unexpectedly stirring considerable excitement among the residents of Wang Village: "After dinner, our house was packed with people, mostly young folks, all eager to see the world. Nobody spoke, nor did I, but that didn't hinder our fundamental realization about the world: it radiates out from 'China' at the center, like a piece of dough rolled flat, stretching outward in all directions, spawning seven continents and four oceans. China's contributions to the world are vividly clear on the map." This map simultaneously corrected a mistaken perception of the world held by the villagers, who had always believed the world to be a square plane with Wang Village at its center, extending uninhibitedly in four directions. Now, it was apparent that the world was much more expansive and elliptical, as indicated by the large brackets on the map's sides.

In fact, these narratives capture not just fictional elements but also moments of personal epiphany. The realization that "our clocks are broken" and the correction of a "wrong view" of the world signify moments of astonishment. This astonishment, as described by Chen Jizhou in his first impressions of Johannesburg, does not necessarily lead to the formation of new thoughts or inner transformation; often, it leads to mere curiosity. Our issue, however, intentionally avoids the superficiality of mere curiosity. These writers venture into foreign lands, and after experiencing profound soul-searching, they achieve deeper insights and gradual inner changes.

In the early 1990s, Han Shaogong wrote in his piece *The World* (*Flower City*, 1994, Issue 6): "National borders are becoming increasingly dubious. A nuclear power plant accident in the Soviet Union polluted several neighboring countries. Acid rain in Japan may have originated from China and Southeast Asia. Toxic gases eroding the earth's ozone layer affect not just one or a few countries but the entire planet. Furthermore, today, no single nation can solve challenges like information digitization, multinational corporations, and international drug trafficking. Expanding airlines and highways entangle even the most remote and tranquil places, thrusting people into journeys of migration, cultural integration, and hybridization. The world is growing smaller and closer. National identity is losing its distinctiveness and aesthetic basis." Han observed and felt a world increasingly interconnected, manifesting the slogan "One World, One Dream."

The "net" metaphorically captures what Marshall McLuhan predicted as the global village era in the 1950s. Around the same time, in 1956, Mao Zedong spoke of the "expulsion from the global community" during his speech "Strengthen the Party's Unity and Carry Forward Its Traditions" at the Eighth National Congress of the Communist Party of China. He said, "With so many people, so much land, and abundant resources, coupled with socialism's claimed advantages, if we cannot surpass the United States after fifty or sixty years, what does that make us? We must avoid being expelled from the global community! If we fail, we let down the world's people, and our contributions to humanity will be minimal."

In my youth—later dubbed the era of thought liberation in the 1980s—there were frequent calls to avoid being expelled from the global community. Today, we casually refer to reform and opening up, but we often overlook that openness was integral to these reforms. Extreme as it may seem, without openness, how can we talk about reform? It can be argued that as early as the Age of Discovery in the fifteenth century, the entire world was already swept into the tides of "globalization" and the "global village," and the "net" merely intensified this trend in the recent media revolution.

In Wang Bang's *Lewisham, London*, there is an epigraph: "Some say that the COVID-19 pandemic of 2020 will mark the end of the era of mobility, and humanity will return to its tribes, living a life of self-preservation, isolation, and hostility in caves. I think this is impossible, because I once lived in London, specifically, in Lewisham, London." Yet, it is worth pondering that the impossibility of returning to tribal and cave life signifies the powerful coercive force of "globalization." This immense force, however, highlights another possibility. The illusion of a "global village" bred by shared knowledge, emotions, and values masks the differences and even fractures among people caused by different traditions and secret paths of "time zones." Thus, the so-called "globalization" and "global village" might be just a layer or layers of froth. In another interview, Wang Bang stated:

> Selective reading, combined with various ingrained prejudices, inevitably leads to "limitations" especially in the era when big data takes advantage. Big data knows what you read every day and how to cater to your preferences: you browse a web page about "Chinese burial money" and your social page will tirelessly show various 'Chinese burial money,' enough to burn for years; you finish reading an online article, and you'll find a line below: "You might be interested" with a string of related links. Moreover, today's world has an information load like a multi-million-ton garbage dump. Information vendors, driven by political or commercial purposes to attract attention, first create clickbait headlines and then master the skill of casually labeling people, along with seductive emotional rhetoric, easily turning readers into "manual likers." It seems almost impossible to outwit big data and remain immune in this frenzy unless you strongly realize the limitations of your thinking in the uncontrollable chain deep in your brain.
>
> I am just a journalist, not a scholar. My non-fiction writing is aimed at the public, not academic journals. Rather than seeking an academic conclusion, I am striking sparks from flint, hoping that thoughtful and loving

readers will see the sparks and generously rescue me from the limitations of my thinking.

(Zhu Xiaowen and Wang Bang, "Dialogue with Writer Wang Bang: The Uncontrollable Truth")

The global COVID-19 pandemic in 2020 provided an opportunity to re-assess the illusion of the "global village." The issue, in fact, has long existed. Consequently, one way to escape the "net" is to restore walking the earth on our own feet, to see and think for ourselves. The progress of human history is often linked to geographical discoveries, and modern China is no exception. Looking at modern Chinese history, the so-called starting point of "modernity" is realizing that we are "in the world," not alone, and this begins with "world travel." Not to mention the earlier Silk Road and maritime trade, late Qing (AD 1644–1911) travelogues such as *Illustrated Treatise on the Maritime Kingdoms* and other Western and Eastern travelogues have already ushered in the epoch-making "opening of the eyes to the world."

At this juncture, travelogue as a genre is a spiritual map of Chinese people going global, not the later petty literati's show-off "been there, done that." Thus, we can understand the era from the late Qing to the 1930s and 1940s when modern intellectuals' travelogues were considered texts of thoughts. Yu Dafu said that the "liberation of literature" came from the "liberation of people." This connection can be used to envision the future: more time zones await young people to cross borders and walk the earth, paving the way for intellectual liberation and new territories; meanwhile, cleansing the already decayed and degenerate genres, such as travelogue and reportage. Even if it means returning to the modern starting points of these genres, let thoughts and texts support and invent each other, thereby restoring the dignity of the genres.

"I Want to Give You All, But I Have Nothing"
(Issue 6, 2020)

How many tree holes of such sizes exist online? There must be many. A quick search for WeChat official accounts named "tree hole" yields hundreds of results. While the internet is indeed flooded with ephemeral content, among the bubbles lie the desires, pains, cries for comfort, and even calls for help from tiny, helpless, and voiceless lives of the real world. On the internet, people shed their real-world armor and masks, expressing their faint voices and yearning to be heard. The internet becomes a faint light in their darkness. Since the advent of online media in the late 20th century—BBS, Q Zone, Renren, blogs, Weibo, WeChat—these writing platforms and social software, despite their differences, have consistently allowed for personal expression and extended social interaction from familiar circles to an infinite, unknown world.

Undoubtedly, "tree holes" are virtual spaces distinct from the real world, but they connect to the reality of human existence. It is the individual, weak calls of single lives that construct the myriad tree holes online, where they store the secrets of their lives. Thus, after covering cities, towns, the world, family, and other real-life themes that encompass our lives and spirits, I discussed with Editor-in-Chief Zhu Yanling the idea of dedicating an issue to "tree holes." This theme would honor those small, weak, hidden souls, helping them face the loneliness and fear in this world.

At this very moment, novelist Zhang Huiwen happened to give me a novel, *Memories of Nanjing*, which I found fitting for a "tree hole." The story recounts a middle-aged woman's reflection on a vague encounter during her youth. The act of remembering turns into a process of looking back and sorting out the past, leading to "repentance" (a term from the story) for possibly having hurt a humble and kind person.

I then invited Wen Zhen to contribute to this "tree hole" theme. I remember telling her, "Everyone has a bright side and a dark side of their life—parts they can show to others and social aspects bathed in sunlight, as well as secrets to hide in a tree hole." At the time, Wen Zhen and I also discussed urban literature and urban ailments, the anonymity and loneliness of city dwellers, and their fears and helplessness submerged in darkness. From mid-March to July, she completed the story *Mimi Peanuts*.

I did not inform Wen Zhen beforehand about Zhang Huiwen's novel. Now, putting the two stories together, it is quite surprising (or perhaps not?) that both depict the "more than friends, less than lovers" state of relationships. This emotional liminality, the darkest moment, might also be when a faint light appears. *Memories of Nanjing* ends at this critical point—the couple parts ways, never to meet again. On the other hand, *Mimi Peanuts* leaves open the possibility of a future.

Let us look at what the two stories specifically write about.

In *Memories of Nanjing*, the details of the city's landmarks and cuisine suggest that Zhang Huiwen has an accurate memory of Nanjing. Regardless of how long she stayed there, she likely has a deep affection for the city. I also want to thank her for embedding my alma mater, Nanjing Normal University, into her story. In *Memories of Nanjing*, planning to accompany her boyfriend to the US for his PhD studies, the protagonist, "I," lived in Nanjing for three months to prepare for my IELTS exam. Arriving in Nanjing before him, "I" rented a place and settled into my new routine. With the assistance of a college student who worked part-time as an agent and possessed a "gentle, non-threatening demeanor," "I" found an apartment with a balcony "bathed in pink or orange hues." During this period, "I" developed a vague and undefined friendship with this young man. Can such a fleeting encounter be called friendship in the usual sense? Let's call it that for now. This friendship began with the apartment rental and ended when the boyfriend's train arrived in Nanjing—fifteen minutes before he walked up to me. Years later, as "I" reflect on this friendship in middle age, "I" think of those middle-aged women who harshly criticize men. Perhaps they never encountered such a genuinely good man or experienced such warmth. The story concludes with a key word: "repentance"—a repentance for the cruelty of youth and the rough handling of that friendship.

Female writers often cautiously distinguish between their novels and their personal lives. Interestingly, this story boldly adopts a seemingly realistic first-person narrative from a female perspective. The narrative meticulously and candidly chronicles the gradual closeness between a man and a woman, unafraid of falling into clichés. They mistakenly board the wrong bus and spend some time alone, begin texting privately, have several meals together, talk without delving into anything profound, and even spend a night together when the power goes out in their neighborhood. Here, even the most mundane reader would have two questions: what happens next, and what do we learn? In fact, years later, this brief encounter becomes what the writers describes as a "precious gem." Readers looking for gossip might be disappointed; it heads toward the destination of lonely men and women in the city, a destination that has been greatly magnified by our media. Even when the man bathes and the woman brings him a towel, and despite spending a night together, the man is described as a "rare gentleman," and they both feel they have "passed a severe test, traversing a dangerous swamp." The story progresses naturally, maintaining a logical flow—is this the story's inherent logic, or the novelist's manipulation? The result can only be one thing.

This story serves as an apt sample, perhaps to explore whether first-person narration prompts readers to speculate about the truth, or to maintain the moral integrity of imagination, discussing the subtle restraint in female writing. Every era introduces new elements in female writing; for instance, this year both *October* and *Zhongshan* have focused on new female writing. However, certain inherent qualities in female writing remain unchanged.

Returning to the earlier question: in the real world, can we tolerate the critical feelings of friendships that verge on romance? This is a challenge for both the individuals involved and society at large. Honestly, what saddens me is the balcony in the story—a gendered and socially segregated space for "me," a place from which "I" can observe "his" residence but can only connect with my boyfriend indoors. This balcony holds the hidden pain and longing of a young woman, expanding and contracting, ethereal and un-guarded, shaded by tree shadows and touched by sunlight. "I" once drank there with "him"; "my" boyfriend also liked to linger there, but "I" lacked the courage to be there with the boyfriend. Afraid he would see it, "I" clearly un-derstood what this so-called friendship was. "I" indeed should repent, not for the cruelty of youth, as love or the lack thereof is a personal matter but taking without love is detestable.

The repentance in the story is about the unequal relationship and the heartless exploitation of the other person, or perhaps something else. It re-minds me of *Ikiru* by Kurosawa Akira, where Shimura Takashi sings, "Girl, life is short, you should try to fall in love." After all, the protagonist in her story has a decent boyfriend and grand prospects of an American dream with him. What does repentance mean? It signifies the passage of time, the realization of unintentional or deliberate harm inflicted by past actions, leading to a confrontation with honesty.

This story offers a reality check, prompting reflection and critique of our reality and humanity. Relationships are inherently about power. The protagonist's boyfriend is a future overseas PhD student; "I" desire someone who "can support me, so I don't have to worry about making a living." He is "a particularly ambitious person." Meanwhile, "he" is a nearly graduated, idle senior student, offering his only wealth—plenty of time, a bit of money, and youthful purity (or the "noble restraint" depicted in the story)—to "me." From past to present, "I" was always aware, this forms the prelude to mid-dle-age mourning and repentance. "I" later find happiness, and hope "he" does too, though readers might worry that "he" might never find happiness because one's emotional capacity is limited. "I" worry "he" might learn to be timid and obsequious toward women of higher status or exploit women of lower status. After all, this is human nature, the price of growing up, a lesson we are always taught.

Wen Zhen's *Mimi Peanuts* brings to mind a series of Japanese healing movies about cats. Stories where lonely people find solace through cats, such as the Gugu the Cat franchise or *The Cat in Their Arms* shown at the 2018 Shanghai Film Festival. In our times, what do cats signify? A common ground of online morality, aesthetics, and tastes, a quick way to identify like-minded individuals and evoke resonance. Raising a cat, establishing intimacy, and hoping for a relationship, this logic unfolds in these texts. Wen Zhen's handling of the subject is a meticulously crafted response to this form. This novel easily fits into such a sequence, one that could be endlessly extended.

Decisively, in this novel, Wen Zhen describes "him" as a "good-for-nothing," a solitary single dweller on the top floor of a thirty-story building. In *Memories of Nanjing*, the first-person narrative deliberately omits certain aspects of "him," naturally liberating the reader's imagination and even leading to ambiguous interpretations of the novel. In *Mimi Peanuts*, "he" is laid bare to the readers. However, it is not just about that. The text presents a clear, pure quality, serving not only a therapeutic purpose. The novel's depiction of "lonely living" and "lonely illness" seamlessly fits the backdrop of the era, where individuals, like stars in the sky, emit a faint yet enduring light, striving tirelessly in the vast human world.

The only expectation in the male character's life is a married woman from a client company, not very familiar to him, whose pleasant presence refreshes his mind and body like flowing water. He quietly names her "Jing." Jing is a cat-lover. However, her family does not allow her to keep one. He therefore adopts a stray cat he encounters, giving him a reason to call Jing and report on the cat's condition. On one occasion, Jing even bikes half an hour to help him bathe the cat. The novel refrains from over-explaining the characters' psychology in such moments and readers can sense the shift in the text's tone. If readers remember the beginning of the novel, where the protagonist idly observes in the bathroom, they can appreciate the same bathroom scene when Jing comes to his home to bathe the cat. There would be almost a moving symphony as background music at that moment. Later, on a rainy day when the cat goes missing, his confession to Jing on the phone marks the emotional peak of the novel: "I like you. I have always liked you. I got the cat to make you happy ... I actually always know he isn't nice to you ... There must be other cases than the time your wrist bruised ... How hard must one grip someone to leave such deep marks that your wrist turned purple?"

Life is inherently bitter, not inherently joyful, and some suffering cannot be spoken. Does it need to be spoken? Fifteen minutes after he loses the cat, the young woman appears, "lightly patting his shoulder, then gently calling out, 'Mimi, Mimi,' as she walked along the curb." It displays the lightness a contemporary urban novel can achieve. The novelist's skill lies in dwelling on these unclear, hazy moments, patiently extracting the most precious parts of human emotion. These precious and fragile things flow between hearts, understood by both him and her, and evidently by the cat named Mimi.

Thus, the so-called "tree hole," the chance encounters of urban men and women, are nothing but the countless souls swept along by the tide of the times, especially the parts of urban youth that cannot be illuminated. Specifically, the deceased's Weibo and the living's messages are mere dust. Perhaps for many, living is already a failure. The issue is that our literature should not only capture the vague shadows and voices of these failures. They have their warmth and heartbeat; they are real people of our time.

"I want to give you all, but I have nothing," is a line from Liao Yimei's song, "Amber." The men and women in Wen Zhen and Zhang Huiwen's novels are like this, and so are you and me. Sometimes literature should be dedicated to these deprived, failed, and voiceless people of our era, preserving

for them even a "tree hole" where they can pour out their hearts. After reading the novels, Zhu Yanling asked me, is it "tree hole" that they write about?
Yes, it indeed is "tree hole."

A Chorus of Whispers
(Issue I, 2021)

oday marks the second *Zhongshan* Star Literature Award, honoring young writers under the age of 35. As is tradition, the award ceremony is followed by a gathering featuring beer, barbecue, and conversation among the youth. Last year, this event took place on June 30. This year, due to the COVID-19 pandemic, the ceremony was postponed to November. Last year's gathering was held at the Jingshi Building on Ninghai Road, and this year it is the same venue but with a different group of young attendees.

November in Nanjing may lack the heat of summer, but it is arguably the city's best season. The leaves turn golden, and the wind carries a metallic sound. Comparing June to November in literary terms, it could symbolize the prime of a writer's life. Yet, how many writers today have a passionate beginning akin to June? Who among them can endure the seasons' forging to reach the mature robustness of November, the literary maturity with a metallic texture?

This special topic has been in the planning stages for quite some time. The title, *Youthquake*, is said to be an old term from the 1960s, but it was chosen as the Oxford Dictionary's Word of the Year in 2017. For some time, Chinese newspapers and magazines like *New Weekly* also enjoyed selecting annual keywords. The origin of the term and whether it was truly selected by Oxford is less significant. What matters is that this word encapsulates the impact or shock that youth bring to the future of an industry. In literature, can today's youth, including these *"Zhongshan* Stars," live up to this term?

Entrusting the future to the youth is often criticized by mechanical evolutionism, and rightly so. Looking globally, those who cause significant impact are not always young, and it is not uncommon for young people to falter. Nevertheless, the future inevitably rests in the hands of the youth, and literature is no exception. This is why we often attribute societal decay to the decadence and indifference of the youth. Regarding the so-called sluggish literature of our time (I have my doubts about this theory, but I am using the familiar language and logic to discuss it), we rarely blame middle-aged and elderly writers for their complacency. Instead, we often criticize the younger generation, forgetting that today's "youth" were once young themselves, striving and rising.

How many struggles and struggles did we have in our youth? We feel justified in blaming the youth's decadence because we have reached an age where we feel qualified to. Using our age as a credential, we condescendingly pass a bit of authority to the younger generation, then comfortably assume the role of critics.

But how do these young people, whom we criticize, actually live and write? Are the few who experience moments of glory truly representative of all young people today? Most young voices blend into a chorus of whispers, their faces blurred by similarity. Where does their uniqueness lie? This requires our careful observation and identification.

Therefore, when we chance upon putting together Xie Qingpi, Wang Suxin, Feng Yijin, Zhang Lingling, Lu Dekun, and Wang Moshu, there are many more young writers who stand alongside them, sharing their characteristics as subtle whisperers. Writers are particularly prone to isolation and helplessness. The so-called literary revolution of rebellion is often more illusion than reality. The so-called youthquake needs to be deeply immersed in their experiences, requiring us to listen and feel to truly understand.

This special topic is named "Youthquake" not to sensationalize a literary revolution. In today's context, literature is increasingly a private endeavor—so how can there be a revolution? Instead, the goal is to correct some prejudices against young writers, provide a few examples, and examine the literary "field." It is not merely to refute the accusation of homogeneity among young writers. What matters most is whether young writers can "criticize" each other constructively. Are they willing to publish such criticism publicly? From my interactions with them, young writers are never hesitant to criticize their peers fiercely when they gather. Now, let these voices meet on paper.

In 2020, Flower City Interest created six Chinese spaces—cities, county towns, families, towns, the world, and the virtual world—each represented by a "tree hole," with contributions from 23 young writers exploring these spaces from different perspectives, attempting to navigate these spaces. Their possibilities, and their helplessness, to some extent, are the various faces of literature's engaging with China's reality. This year, as a practitioner of literary criticism, I want to pose questions about contemporary literature. It is a question, not necessarily an answer. Xu Chenliang remarked that last year's six issues resembled six exhibition halls of a museum. I agree. In just a few years, Xu transformed *Literature* into the most contemporary "big literature" magazine. It is rumored that this magazine will be discontinued at the end of the year. I dare not exaggerate and say that this is the fate of literature in its time. After all, if a publication stops, our literature will continue.

Now, I begin to ask questions. The first question is, what is youth writing in our time?

Sometimes, Writers Break Out
— Merely from WeChat Moments —
(Issue 2, 2021)

I n discussing new Chinese literature, one must involve the revolution in modern printing technology, the publishing and remuneration systems, the creation of public spaces by literary journals and books, and how these public spaces have influenced contemporary writers and readers.

This history traces back to the literary reforms of the late Qing Dynasty and the literary revolution of the May Fourth Movement. It is said that *Fiction Monthly* represents half of the literary history of the 1920s. The other half is scattered across various journals and all sorts of newspaper supplements.

Over time, there has been a process of subtraction. We gradually removed the "reports" from "newspaper" and the "popularity" from "journals." Thus, our literature became what is called "pure" literature, stripped of its diversity and miscellaneous nature. For a long time, this pure literature developed its own mechanisms and modes of production—self-sufficient, closed, and exclusive. In simple terms, it became the literary enterprise of an inner circle. Aside from the strong intervention of non-literary factors, within this circle, we could produce the literature we imagined and cultivate our literary tastes. As one writer once said, mice in a cage end up smelling the same. We often take pride in, and sometimes lament, the scent and taste within this literary circle.

Regardless, I remain unequivocally supportive of journal literature, even tolerant of its seemingly "unlikable" elitist aesthetic stance. This stance is based on observations of the current state of Chinese national literary life and aesthetic standards. We still need literary standards and benchmarks for our times, which, for now, literary journals provide (although these standards and benchmarks might just be the tallest among a group of dwarfs). Furthermore, in an era driven by online sharing, egalitarianism, and the erasure of differences, the capital-defined aesthetic holds massive devouring power. Journal literature might be the last bastion of differentiated aesthetics. However, an "isolated island" can also be a place of growth, gradually expanding into the sea, thriving with life. Therefore, I oppose the long-standing narrow, self-righteous, and complacent journal taste fostered by journal literature. This journal taste often creates a false impression of prosperity due to its tradition and the support of various real-world forces.

Today, everyone talks about literature "known outside of a fixed circle" and "crossing boundaries." On the one hand, these terms have been replaced by the "attention economy" driven by mass media. Not only do news magazines and fashion publications focus on writers but also surviving print media and online platforms select writers with compelling stories as "selling points" to attract readers. Mass media consciously cultivates writers or intellectuals who fit their criteria. For instance, *Southern People Weekly* annually features "Young Leaders," often including writers. While mass media is interested in a writer's "literariness," it cares more about how they become writers with "stories." It is no wonder that writers like A Yi and Feng Tang frequently appear on the covers of popular magazines for a period. Their backgrounds—a small-town police officer and a gynecological oncology PhD working at McKinsey—make them inherently "legendary" media figures. Unlike traditional studio-bound writers, today's popular writers enjoy being public figures and consciously maintain a good rapport with mass media, cultivating a fan base as a potential readership market.

On the other hand, many writers' so-called "known outside of a fixed circle" and "crossing boundaries" might just be entering "WeChat Moments" or becoming a writer within a certain literary "WeChat Moments." In essence, journal literature is just a literary friend circle. Most of us use WeChat daily, posting various literary updates on WeChat Moments, creating the prosperity of our literary friend circle. However, we seem to ignore one thing: a friend circle is still just a friend circle. While not everyone in a friend circle is a true "friend," at least they are added after being approved as such.

Thus, "known outside of a fixed circle" and "crossing boundaries" in literature first requires awakening from the illusion of the prosperity of the literary "WeChat Moments" and from the illusion of mass media attention. Instead, we should focus on cultivating literary endeavors within our circle. My understanding of "known outside of a fixed circle" and "crossing boundaries" involves observation, understanding, dialogue, and learning between different worlds. It is about seeing myself in you, then becoming a better me—not about conquering or assimilating. It is about relearning how to create a contemporary literary journal and how to be a writer making conscious choices today, like Han Songluo regaining confidence as a journal novelist and returning to being a writer for journal literature.

Mu Ming, on the other hand, represents a different scenario. She is a literary immigrant, discovered by literary editors and transitioning from Douban to literary journals. In recent years, many so-called newcomers to journal literature were actually seasoned Douban writers. Publications such as *Youth Literature*, *Shanghai Literature*, *Fiction World*, and the recently discontinued *Literature* have all embraced numerous Douban writers. This trend is even more pronounced in literary books. Currently, these writers are primarily independent writers from Douban and similar online communities. However, in the future, will commercially drive online novel writers also migrate to literary journals? While there are precedents, these instances typically align with the tastes of literary journals. Yet, if commercial online novel writers begin controlling narrative lengths, the migration to and transition within literary journals could become more frequent, especially as major literary journals expand their novel sections with special issues and supplements.

We must first dismantle the fixed circles. Becoming known outside of a fixed circle should follow our innovation and renewal. The current challenge is how to accommodate these literary immigrants. How should their writing integrate into literary journals? In my view, this should not be based on the self-important illusions of literary journals, as if engaging in literary charity, or merely to showcase an ostensibly open-minded inclusivity by giving these literary immigrants a place. It shouldn't be about adding a few unfamiliar writers from different literary spaces to the table of contents. Instead, it should be about thoroughly cleansing the stagnant layers and introducing fresh aesthetics. This way, literary journals can be placed at the crossroads of our era's reality and literary life, revitalizing them for contemporary times.

Therefore, this special topic is not just about repositioning Han Songluo and Mu Ming in the literary landscape. It is about valuing their imagination, creativity, and their discoveries and inventions in literature and the world. Of course, we also anticipate the distant horizon of new literature, which is why I say: islands growing into the sea.

The Illusion of Place
(Issue 3, 2021)

In the fifth issue of *Flower City* in 2020, under the "Time Zone" feature of Flower City Interest, we explored how young Chinese writers traverse and observe different time zones, debunking the "global village illusion" of the globalization era. However, this "global village illusion" does not necessarily imply the viability of localness. Reassessing the "Time Zone" theme, the samples provided by writers like Bai Lin, Wang Bang, Chen Jizhou, and Wu Yaling reveal how a place persists and exists in various forms. Moreover, the localness that literature often highlights may merely be the localness of the "past tense." Bai Lin and Wu Yaling, for instance, are deeply fascinated by the places they focus on in their writing—be it the Balkans or France. In a sense, these regions have become their cultural "nostalgia," making them more inclined to unearth the "residuals" of the past within the present, those solidified in the flow of time, which might be retrieved through their "archaeological" efforts.

To use an imperfect analogy, writing as a form of cultural homecoming perhaps makes them "fans" of the cultures of the places they write about. This reflects a perspective of "others," similar to how the West has discovered China since the advent of modernity. In contrast, Chen Jizhou and Wang Bang have different experiences; Chen is merely a passerby in South Africa, while Wang is a guest resident in London. What they observe are the "mobile people" like themselves. Local elements such as food, customs, and dialects are uprooted from their native places, with some taking root elsewhere while most become mere baggage for migrants.

Modernity, cosmopolitanism, and globalization essentially lead to homogenization. Some places are defined as the world and its center, while the localness of most places becomes ineffective, turning into the periphery. Without considering Europe's own history of modernity, starting from the colonial expansion of old imperialist and capitalist powers like Britain and France, and through the era of globalization in the 20th century, homogenizing modernity has been around for two centuries. The global village is an illusion; the so-called localities have long been unrecognizable. In fact, the modern sense of "locality" is to a large extent a product of homogenizing modernity. Moreover, considering the improvement in material life, the necessity of locality itself is questionable. The future vision of development and a good life promised by modernity often comes at the cost of local landscapes, customs, and hereditary ways of daily life. In the context of population mobility in China, the necessity of hometowns is also dubious. It is easy for us to treat a foreign land as our home. In reality, the demand for locality that accompanies modernity is often an aesthetic need, commonly referred to as the need to "resist modernity." Extremists might argue that before modernity, locality was merely the history of the formation of places. The history of the damage and resistance of places emerged only after modernity. Thus, the hallmark of Chinese modern literature is the discovery of places: the realization that places are irretrievably lost under the crushing weight of modernity. And because they are about to disappear, places are redefined and savored in various forms of resistance.

A question arises, or a premise that should not be taken for granted: In today's world, where fluidity and change are the norms, is it possible for premodern hermits who hid away in seclusion to exist? Can premodern-style writing, such as local chronicles and clan genealogies, reappear today? The hermits of premodern era could remain ignorant to the changes of dynasties, but can they afford to do the same in the modern and globalized world? Without thorough field investigations into the composition of "stay-in-hometown" writers and their writing, it is difficult to reach a definitive conclusion. Hence, we can only say that when discussing the relationship between place and literature, the "stay-in-hometown" writers who have not crossed boundaries or engaged with the broader literary production have largely been ignored. They have always been the hidden and missing figures in our literary history. Even if Chen Zaijian temporarily withdraws to local living and writing, he is not an outsider to our era's literary production. Personally, I believe in the existence of "stay-in-hometown" writers outside our era's literary production, but what about a place outside civilization?

The discovery and definition of localities in the context of modernity are essentially about addressing the issue of "locality" under modernity. For instance, in this special topic, we selected several young writers from Chaoshan—Chen Qiufan, Lin Peiyuan, and Chen Zaijian—as examples. This list could extend further to include novelists like Chen Chongzheng and the Wutiaoren band we previously featured. The topic of "locality" under modernity, this extension of modern literature, was pioneered by generations of modern writers like Lu Xun, Fei Ming, Shen Congwen, Xiao Hong, Shi Tuo, Zhao Shuli, and has been transformed by writers of the People's Rebulic of China.

Notably, I once discussed the "hijacked and requisitioned places" to critique the misinterpretation and distortion of localities by writers for their purposes. In reality, whether depicting dilapidated places or pastoral ones, both are "illusions of place" produced by modernity and are subject to misinterpretation. The illusion and reality of places are juxtaposed, inseparable, and indivisible. Illusions are not mere surface labels and coatings of "places," but when the invention of places goes astray, deriving "phantom of place" from "illusions of place" becomes merely labels and coatings—such as feigned nostalgia or the belief that a place is the world. Unlike the juxtaposition and reversibility of the illusion and reality of places, the "illusion of place" is often difficult to restore and juxtapose to a concrete "place."

Therefore, our aim with this special topic is to recognize the nuanced differences in how writers engage with and construct their notions of place, and to explore the relationship between the reality and illusion of these places. Once this relationship is established, a place—whether shared by several writers or not—emerges as both unique and varied in significance. For instance, while Chen Qiufan, Chen Zaijian, and Lin Peiyuan all hail from the same region, Chaoshan, their individual experiences, perspectives, and writings diverge significantly. Today, it is challenging to assemble a cohesive regional cultural identity for writers. If such an identity could be assembled, it might only reflect a regional image-building exercise or the "illusion of place" perpetuated by mass media.

In another word, our focus on their common origins ultimately reveals the impossibility and fallacy of defining a writer group solely based on geographic or regional cultural significance. Even if individuals once shared a street or had parents working in the same now-defunct factory, in today's era of constant movement, literary paths and identities can vary widely. If everything seems uniform, it may either reflect the writer's mediocrity or be a spectacle crafted by mass media and literary studies, resulting in an "illusion of place."

Symptomatic Excess and the Loss of Elegance
(Issue 4, 2021)

If this special topic were to make an adversary, it would be the symptomatic excess prevalent in contemporary short stories.

The word count of short stories shouldn't merely be a numerical concern. Of course, in saying this, I am not entirely certain.

I consulted several writers and editors about this "short short story" special topic, asking why our short stories are getting longer and longer. More than one friend attributed this symptomatic excess to the remuneration system. Our standard practice is to pay by the word count, so naturally, shorter stories are less profitable than longer ones. A dedicated short story writer finds it nearly impossible to write one short story per month and make a living. If we look at the publication records of writers like Wang Zengqi, Su Tong, and Liu Qingbang, who established their literary status through short stories, we can see the output required. Calculating based on an average of 10,000 Chinese characters per short story, it takes about four to earn the same as one novella. Thus, writing shorter stories clearly results in a financial loss. Given that writing short stories is already not very economical, writers tend to extend them as much as possible.

Novels, whose length can be limitless, might face customary length expectations. Zhang Wei's novel *On the Plateau*, which won the Mao Dun Literature Prize, sparked controversy with its 4.5 million Chinese characters, far exceeding the usual expectations for novel length. If we consider online novels as part of literature, the ceiling of 4.5 million Chinese characters has long been surpassed. However, the case is different for short stories and novellas. Short stories are capped by novellas, and novellas by novels. These caps are quite rigid. Pushing beyond these limits changes the genre entirely. The issue now is that writers often aim for the upper word limits rather than conserving words within their respective categories.

Moreover, short stories inherently lack a lower word limit—they can always be shorter.

Nevertheless, I still believe that the word count and length of a story are not just about numbers or the corresponding payment. They are also matters of form and aesthetics. The charm of short stories should be evident in their word count and length. The brevity of short stories is both a constraint and a challenge, a display of skill within limits. With this in mind, I invited several writers to contribute to the "short short story" theme, setting a word limit of 5,000 to 8,000 Chinese characters without imposing any thematic, subject, or stylistic constraints. I understand that this request might be demanding for writers accustomed to their own comfortable pace and rhythm. Nonetheless, I am grateful that they accepted this unreasonable challenge and participated in this word-limited experiment. Special thanks to Yizhou and Xiaobai. Yizhou was the first to submit his work, while Xiaobai, due to a mistaken deadline and other commitments, couldn't finish on time for this special topic but will publish his piece later.

It is important to note that I do not oppose or deny the existence of "long short stories." In fact, we can cite numerous classic long short stories. Against this backdrop, emphasizing shorter short stories can be seen as a reminder of the current ecological state of short stories. I have *The Short Stories of 2019* compiled by *Selected Novels* from Lijiang Publishing House, which includes 20 short stories. Apart from Mo Yan's *Yidou Ge Notes*, which is exceptionally short, only Shao Li's *Festival* is under 10,000 Chinese characters, while the rest exceed 10,000, with half over 14,000. Among these, A Zhan's *Making Violins* and Wen Zhen's *Hedgehog, Hedgehog* each exceed 17,000 Chinese characters. Annual collections can somewhat represent the basic literary ecology, and the scarcity of short stories under 10,000 Chinese characters highlights a shift in the aesthetic of short story forms. Even if we refrain from making an absolute judgment on this shift's quality, the transformation in literary form due to changes in word count and length should be noted.

Indeed, the distribution of word counts in short stories has not always been skewed toward the long side. Looking through my books, *Object Lessons: The Paris Review Presents the Art of the Short Story* edited by Lorin Stein and Sadie Stein includes 20 stories, only six of which exceed 10,000 words. Two longer stories, Ethan Canin's *The Palace Thief* and Joy Williams's *Dimmer*, at around 30,000 and 20,000 words respectively, would be considered novellas by our standards. Excluding these two, only four stories exceed 10,000 words. Stories like Jane Bowles's *Emmy Moore's Journal*, Denis Johnson's *Car Crash While Hitchhiking*, Lydia Davis's *Ten Stories from Flaubert*, and Raymond Carver's *Why Don't You Dance?* are all around 4,000 to 5,000 words. Steven Milhauser's *Flying Carpets*, Donald Barthelme's *Several Garlic Tales*, James Salter's *Bangkok*, and Bernard Cooper's *Old Birds* are about 6,000 words each. In *Collected Stories of John Cheever* published by Yilin Press, of the 60 stories included, 22 are under 10,000 words, and another eight just exceed that length, making up half the collection.

Su Tong, in a conversation with Wang Hongtu, said, "I think various analogies can be made for short stories, and one can compare them to drama. If a novel is a multi-act play, a short story is a one-act play. Its story is complete, and the underlying theme must be fully expressed within one act." Regarding length, he stated, "My short stories are generally between 6,000 and 8,000 Chinese characters, or 9,000 at most. Rarely do they exceed 10,000, with the longest being around 12,000 to 13,000." (Su Tong and Wang Hongtu, "Poetics of the South: A Conversation between Su Tong and Wang Hongtu").

This is indeed reflected in Su Tong's self-favorite personal collection *Night Stories*, where 22 of the 42 selected stories are under 10,000 Chinese characters, making up 52.4%, with another six just over that mark, and 14 exceeding 12,000 Chinese characters. If we consider Su Tong as an example of deliberately writing short stories, let us look at Mo Yan, widely recognized for his novels. Randomly choosing two books, *Nine Pieces of Novels* and *Qiushui*, from the Mo Yan Short Story Collection series published by Zhejiang Literature and Art Publishing House, over half the stories are under 10,000 Chinese characters, with *Blue Castle* being less than 3,000 Chinese characters.

The *Writer* magazine has long focused on short stories, with its Golden Short Story column lasting many years. How do we understand "golden?" Perhaps it signifies brevity, like the saying "words are worth their weight in gold." In 2015, *Writer* invited novelists and critics like Yan Lianke, Ye Zhaoyan, Fan Xiaoqing, Liu Qingbang, Lin Nabian, Dong Xi, Shi Zhanjun, and Zhang Qinghua to discuss short stories. Notably, "How can short stories be made shorter?" was a central topic, with Yan Lianke citing two examples: *The College Student* and *The Bird-Eating Girl*, both around 5,000 Chinese characters and 300 Chinese characters respectively.

Regarding the symptomatic excess in short stories, I have not conducted in-depth research, but it is evident that some inherent charm and magic of short stories are being lost. This includes the beauty of conciseness and brevity. Jeffrey Eugenides commented on Denis Johnson's *Car Crash While Hitchhiking,* saying, "By definition, a short story must be short. This is what makes short stories so difficult to write. How do you keep the narrative concise while still fulfilling the functions of a novel? Unlike writing a novel, the primary challenge in writing a short story is determining what to leave out. The content within the story implicitly contains everything that is omitted." (*Object Lessons: The Paris Review Presents the Art of the Short Story*). Similarly, Harold Bloom in *How to Read and Why* wrote, "Short stories best deal with isolated individuals, especially those on the social margins," and short stories "are not allegories or parables, hence cannot be called fragments." "Most adept short story writers minimize moral judgments just as they do with narrative continuity and the details of characters' past lives." Observing the symptomatic excess in contemporary short stories suggests that it stems from a lack of restraint and a relaxation of narrative rigor.

Furthermore, short stories are increasingly resembling anecdotal local news rather than "the art of narration." As a result, the precision and elegance of the short story literary form are being eroded. Regardless of the emphasis on the folk literature tradition of Chinese novels, modern short stories, especially contemporary ones, should be refined and sophisticated. Without such differentiation, how do short stories differ from *Stories*, a general storytelling magazine? Frankly, many of our current short stories have become undisciplined *Stories*.

Critic Hugh Kenner suggested that "perhaps starting from Hemingway or Joyce, short stories have elevated from a primarily entertaining tradition to a form of high art" (*Object Lessons: The Paris Review Presents the Art of the Short Story*). Although modern Chinese short stories may not have experienced the same development, they ultimately accepted the progression of short stories from "Hemingway or Joyce onward." Even if not entirely, our short stories cannot entirely follow the classical traditions of "San Yan Er Pai"in the Ming Dynasty (AD 1368–1644), legends, and anecdotal notes. Even if they grow in the lineage of San Yan Er Pai, legends, and notes, it is rare to see writers purely engaging in "ancient" writing. This is an era of "Chinese literature" within contemporary world literature.

In the preface "The Physics of Short Stories" written for the "Short Classics" series, which began in 2011, Wang Anyi states:

> A good short story is like a sprite, extremely elastic, akin to soft matter in the realm of physics. Their vitality does not depend on quantity but on internal structure. As a narrative art form, a story must be structured, and in the confined space of a short story, there is no escaping the duty of storytelling. In the case of a novella or novel, there may be room to maneuver, allowing the story to make sense within a broader context. A novel is about making a self-consistent narrative, developing a premise born of imagination into a conclusion. During this development process, novellas and novels have the opportunity to add new conditions, continually supplement or

revise the path, and even allow for minor digressions or pauses. But short stories do not have this luxury; once they start, they must be meticulously planned, with no room for pointless meandering. This does not suggest any shortcuts or omissions, as doing so would diminish their vitality, which goes against our creative intent. So, it is not about simplification. What is it then? Borrowing a concept from physics, there is a principle from the Einstein school of thought, which considers the highest criterion of a theory to be its "elegance." How is "elegance" defined in theory? Einstein's opinion was: "As simple as possible, but no simpler." I believe this explanation can also be applied to fictional storytelling. Thus, a good short story can be defined as elegant.

Currently, short stories tend to be longer rather than shorter. If this is not due to a revolutionary adjustment of their "internal structure," the longer result can only be a "symptomatic excess," which means that the internal structure of short stories goes unnoticed by writers, leading to the loss of the elegance of short stories in the sense of their literary form. In short, short stories are becoming increasingly low-quality. In fact, novellas are also becoming so.

Now I would like to examine, with an almost compulsory requirement to control the word count of short stories to between 5,000 and 8,000 Chinese characters, what are the results of these stories within this "word count space"? I will not provide any preconceived interpretative guidance. Read them, read the short short stories. And I look forward to more "short short stories." I even hope there are literary journals bold enough to refuse short stories over ten thousand Chinese characters. Of course, for good short stories, should we reconsider our payment method? What if we did not calculate remuneration based on word count? What would the result be? Perhaps I am being too idealistic; after all, sometimes calculating payment by word count reflects the fairness of mediocrity.

— Machine Writing, Not Literature, Neither to Replace Writers' Creations: On the Technical Issues of AI writing Today — (Issue 5, 2021)

The two novels in this special topic were co-created by humans and machines. Although humans were credited as the authors, we have used different fonts to indicate the parts completed by the machine. Chen Qiufan collaborates with the "AI Science Fiction World" from Sinovation Ventures to write *Dayou*. He and Wang Yonggang, the developer of this product, hope the machine can imitate Chen's writing style. Thus, the machine is trained on various types and styles of Chen's novels. On the other hand, Wang's collaborator is the widely used writing software, "Dreamily." Unlike a customized AI writing product, it is a public AI writing tool.

The involvement of machines (AI) in literature, art, and other activities that require human high-level thinking and imagination has become a popular topic in mass media. Examples include singing by virtual idol Luo Tianyi, poetry by Xiaoice, and chess by robots. Some researchers, sensitive to trends, interpret these elementary literary and artistic activities, which currently rely on big data and algorithms, as machine (AI) writing that is replacing human literature. However, this is not the case.

For instance, contrary to the literary world's enthusiasm, Xiaoice's developer, Song Ruihua, Chief Scientist at Microsoft Asia-Pacific Research and Development Group, explicitly stated in his speech at the China National Computer Congress Technology Forum on October 26, 2018, "Natural Language Generation: Enabling Machines to Master Writing Skills," that machine poetry will not replace human poetry. He concluded his speech by citing an impromptu poem by his kindergarten daughter, emphasizing,

"When humans create poetry, it is a miraculous process beyond AI's reach; thus, there is still vast space for us." I interpret Song Ruihua's "vast space" as referring to two aspects: one is the potential of human writing and other aesthetic arts; the other is the prospects of machines (AI) engaging in aesthetic arts. Both aspects have expansive possibilities.

Ordinary people's curiosity, anxiety, and fear of AI are closely related to technological progress and the promotion by humanities and social science researchers and mass media. Another influence likely comes from science fiction's imagination of the near-future world, typically manifested in space travel and AI. In the film industry, from the 1980s' *Blade Runner* to the twenty-first century's *Ghost in the Shell*, there have been many explorations of AI's potential. *Blade Runner* was adapted from Philip K. Dick's novel *Do Androids Dream of Electric Sheep?*

AI is also a hot topic in contemporary Chinese literature. Young authors Du Li and Zhou Wanjing's novels, published in Flower City Interest, have both explored this theme. AI not only focuses on enhancing the body, which has been achieved and is still developing via technology but also on the evolution of intelligent beings from human-like, near-human to "human" and even superhuman. These biological and mechanical hybrids are "both social reality and fiction" (Haraway), as known as "cyborgs." In the future world depicted in science fiction, intelligent beings evolve from being used by humans to escaping human control and enslavement, becoming self-sufficient "other beings." These "others" share, occupy, and compete for living space with humans, growing and evolving. The most worrying aspect is not just the many ethical issues in human "other beings" interactions but the possibility that these "other beings" may turn against and enslave humans.

At least for now, AI writing, whether it is Xiaoice, Dreamily, which collaborated with Wang Yuan's *Homicide*, or the Sinovation Ventures collaborating with Chen Qiufan, only provides technical assistance, and it is just preliminary technology. Regarding technology, we should attribute it to technology. Let us look at Chen's practice and opinions.

Chen Qiufan, born in 1981, one year before *Blade Runner* came out, began experimenting with AI co-writing in 2017. The result is *The State of Ecstasy* in his collection *The Algorithm of Life*, about the symbiosis between humans and AI. Here are Chen's views on machine writing technology:

Chat GPT is essentially a language model, akin to a physical model used to understand and describe the essence of the physical world. A language model is used to understand and describe the essence of language. Humans have worldviews and linguistic views, such as what language is and the relationships between words or phrases that constitute language.

In simple terms, a language model is used for two main tasks. One is understanding natural language, such as determining which of two sentences is more natural or the dependencies between words or phrases in a sentence. The other is predicting natural language, such as predicting subsequent words given the initial part of a sentence.

Traditional language models are mainly used in tasks like speech recognition, machine translation, and OCR (optical character recognition, the process of converting printed characters into electronic text format using optical methods) for predicting and judging target sequences.

One of the two most common uses is translating a Chinese sentence into different English sentences, where the language model scores each translation to choose the best one; the other, in speech recognition, predicting "talking" as the next word after hearing "we are tal ..." even if "talking" was not fully heard. The voice heard was the enhanced signal.

Training a model can be likened to educating a student, following a "pre-training and fine-tuning" method. First, we give the machine many books to read, known as unsupervised pre-training. Then, we provide many practice questions with answers, known as supervised fine-tuning. After this learning process, the model is trained and can be tested, for instance, by providing a sentence for it to continue writing.

The AI used in this collaboration with humans is from Sinovation Ventures' DeeCamp 2020 AI Training Camp, a large-scale pre-trained model trained on over 1,000 GPUs with 300 GB of Chinese text data, comparable in size to Chat GPT-2 Large. It was then fine-tuned with a small amount of story data. Features shown in Chat GPT-3 this year are also evident in "AI Science Fiction World," and it is in Chinese.

From an operational perspective, the interaction between human writers and the model is straightforward. By providing scene and character keywords, AI can generate several paragraphs for the human writer to choose from. The human writer can modify these paragraphs, and AI will continue creating based on the revised text, over and over. completing a "joint work" between them.

Today, for AI, writing simple financial news reports is no longer a challenge because these tasks involve structured sentences that can be systematically processed. However, literary creation is a different matter altogether. From a creator's perspective, understanding the different stages of AI text creation involves several steps. Initially, AI uses statistical methods to combine language elements, producing simple verses. The next stage involves AI learning various grammar rules and objective knowledge from web text data sets in an unsupervised manner, simulating human writing styles. Going further, AI might be able to take an image or a sentence and develop it into a coherent, character-driven story with a typical narrative structure.

Therefore, at least for now, AI writing only offers a technical approach and fragmented experiments in text combination. It has not achieved what can be considered true machine-generated literature. Wang Yuan shares this viewpoint. Regarding *Homicide*, on July 13, Wang Yuan and I had a discussion on WeChat.

He Ping: I have a question: How were the scenes completed by Dreamily in *Homicide* (Senbei and Xuanli, me and Jing, Photon and me) chosen? Other parts first and then Dreamily completes the unfinished sections? Also, if a point is chosen in the middle to let Dreamily write freely, can it maintain logical coherence? (I sent Wang Yuan a discussion from the Douban group about a short story completed by Dreamily and a discussion about Dreamily's writing.) Did Dreamily write the stories on Douban group?

Wang Yuan: First, writing is done on Dreamily's online page. I write a section, then randomly click to generate, which continues with several paragraphs. I can choose a satisfactory one, and if none satisfies me, I can click to regenerate. There was no special content generation by Dreamily. Since this online continuation software is not smart enough, I expressed dissatisfaction with the generated text in the article.

All blue parts are generated but have been modified; otherwise, the semantics are too disjointed. I tried to keep the original writing style for distinction.

I am not familiar with the stories on Douban and did not use them as references. I only used the online generation function to complete a human-machine interactive writing attempt and did not delve much into the software. It is not as user-friendly as Sinovation Ventures' program, and it is better suited for web content rather than producing genuine interaction.

I believe two points are important. First, Dreamily cannot input the author's text to generate a style close to the author's narrative, unlike Sinovation Ventures' writing software. Second, the generated text often diverges significantly from the existing storyline, which affects the experience.

I find human-machine interactive writing a fascinating attempt, but AI replacing authors is still a long way off. AI is more suitable for generating news releases and reports, which have repetitive wording and can completely avoid sensitive words.

He Ping: Was *Homicide* written using Sinovation Ventures' software?

Wang Yuan: *Of Greatest Fulness, Deemed a Void* was written using Sinovation Ventures, while *Homicide* was done with Dreamily. When Sinovation Ventures subscription expired, I sought for free continuation software online.

He Ping: So, I think *Homicide* precisely proves Dreamily's formulaic nature.

Wang Yuan: Yes, it is fine for fun but not enough for serious writing. There are no surprising developments. The machine parts in Chen Qiufan's *Dayou* are more complex than those in *Homicide*.

He Ping: So, this type of writing is still experimental. *Homicide* proves that current writing software cannot produce literary content.

Wang Yuan: Creativity is more suitable than literariness, which is relatively vague. Creativity is easier to define: given a theme or existing content, what can the machine produce?

He Ping: Online literature might adapt to this type of writing software. Can machines create "literature"? Is this the right way to discuss the topic?

Wang Yuan: Interactive writing is a collaborative and competitive process between humans and machines, needing clashes to work. In two writing experiences, the clashes were insufficient, with Dreamily being less effective than Sinovation Ventures. Online literature and news releases are simple and have clear types, needing less creativity.

From this, we can see the current boundaries of AI writing. Practitioners involved are clear-headed, while noisy spectators often are not. For me, this was a technical enlightenment. Initially influenced by front scholars and mass media, I had high expectations for AI writing, hoping for complete narrative units rather than just poems by Xiaoice. However, the practical results demonstrated by Chen Qiufan and Wang Yuan prove that, so far, algorithm and corpus-based AI writing cannot independently complete "literary" texts. Even partial fragments in novels cannot be perfectly integrated into the narratives of Chen Qiufan and Wang Yuan. This imperfection, or even failure, contrasts with the exaggerated perfection and success of Xiao-ice's poetry, highlighting the significance of this special topic.

Xiaoice's poetry's literariness comes from the ambiguous nature of poetry itself, providing space for interpretation, meaning it is not Xiaoice "writing" poetry but interpreters "saying" it. If there is any literary achievement, it belongs to the interpreters. This does not mean that the global discussion and concerns about "cyborgs" and machine writing are meaningless. On the contrary, if elementary machine writing already stirs up anxiety and fear, are humans ready for the "cyber" space depicted in science fiction to come true one day?

Just a Scene Change Maybe
(Issue 6, 2021)

On May 19, 2000, Chen Cun published an article in the *Jiefang Daily*, in which he wrote, "Original literature born from the internet is the new growth point for literary creation." Yet, in the same piece, he also wrote, "The peaks of literature are always built by individual geniuses and efforts, not by the number of participants." For three to four years following his statement, and for a significant time thereafter, the number of participants was almost the sole reason cited in various annual reports and academic research papers to argue that online literature represented the aesthetic pinnacle and advanced productivity of contemporary literature.

It is only in the past one or two years that this perspective seems to have shifted—we have come to realize that the number of participants or the industry's scale and the advancement of aesthetics do not equate. Moreover, the literary audience, gained through constant aesthetic exploration, can be diverted by short videos on platforms like Kuaishou and TikTok, as well as by video games, online dramas, among other media. As a result, the presumed aesthetic bottom line of online literature has become elusive. At this critical juncture, can online literature, having thrived on the literary audience boom, turn inward to deeply cultivate and expand the aesthetic territory of Chinese literature—at least Chinese genre literature? Can it become, as Chen Cun described, "the new growth point for literary creation?" Online literature should not merely serve the entertainment industry. Even if imagined as a supplier of IP products for the entertainment industry, it needs to activate and boost its commercial creativity for sustainable development.

This is the context and background of discussion in this special topic. A common feature is the deep connection between the writing of Liao Jing and Yang Zhihan and the internet. Liao Jing's *Outside the Door* was commissioned by Xu Chenliang of *Con-Temporary Monthly* magazine, and Yang Zhihan's *Serial Collection* was passed along by editor Xu Zehong. Both manuscripts have been here for over a year.

I asked Liao Jing and Yang Zhihan to provide their writing resumes. Liao mentioned that from 2017 to 2019, she was an author on Douban Reading, where she published dozens of stories with hundreds of thousands of views. Since 2020, Liao Jing has also published several stories in traditional literary journals such as *Fiction World* and *Lotus*. Liao Jing has already published story collections, *Late Marriage* and *Wedding Night*, whose titles suggest the themes and target readers. Most of these stories were published on Douban Reading.

Few writers for print literary journals identify themselves based on the publication, as it would be unusual to call someone a *Harvest* or *Flower City* author since authors do not exclusively submit to one journal, nor do journals exclusively buy out any author. However, it is different online, where authors choose platforms that suit them, and platforms may buy out authors, leading them to gradually become identified with a specific type or style.

Douban is regarded as a hub for "artsy and fresh" content, contrasting with major online platforms like Qidian, Chuangshi, Jinjiang, Zongheng, Chinese Online, and 17K Novel, which publish long stories. Douban Reading is a literary site known for being "small and delicate," referring either to its offerings or its target audience. The products on Douban Reading primarily consist of short and medium-length fiction and non-fiction, often reflecting the ecology and mentality of contemporary urban youth—topics that might be considered "light" when expressed in literary terms. The Seventh Douban Reading Novella Contest, which included categories for women, suspense, literary, and fantasy, indicates the organizers' intention to foster a "young" urban literary trend aimed at young urban readers with some literary tastes, rather than the much larger group of readers who consume online literature to "kill time."

But this is not absolute. While Douban Reading intentionally caters to "lighter" reading tastes, it also accommodates broader literary possibilities. For instance, Liao Jing's novels address contemporary issues of women's fate with a significant sense of reality that, though seemingly light, is actually weighty. Yang Zhihan's experience with Douban Reading reflects the early, unrestrained writing history of many young authors before they become part of the traditional literary journal publication sequence. Her work *Serial Collection* was available on Douban Reading as early as December 2018. After comparing *Serial Collection* with her recent works, such as *The Temple Endures Without Snow*, which ranked sixth on the 2020 Chinese Novel Society's list, I decided to have Yang negotiate with Douban Reading so that *Serial Collection* is published in *Flower City*. This is because *Serial Collection* showcases a raw, untamed force in her early writing.

Although younger than Liao Jing, Yang has been involved in online writing for a longer period and has explored a variety of styles and changes. Before Douban Reading, she published commercially valuable online novels like *Born Lonely*, *Shen Qingxun*, and *A Tale of Dreaming* on Cloud Literature and Polar Bear Reading. *Shen Qingxun* even made it to the quarterly list of the 2015 Chinese Writers Association Online Literature Rankings and is still available on the major online novel platform Jinjiang Literature.

According to current standards for recognizing online writers, Yang Zhihan is more of a "online writer." Following the typical growth path of online writers, if she had continued from 2015 to the present, she might have more IP influence than many popular online writers. Though I have not had in-depth conversations with her, observing her trajectory from commercial online platforms to "Douban Reading" to literary journals such as *Shanghai Literature*, *Youth Literature*, *Lotus*, and *People's Literature*, she seems to be on a reverse path as a "contrarian." I cannot predict the future direction of her literary career, but what is clear is that, like a good actor, she possesses a broad and versatile "range of roles." I hope to see more new-generation writers with such a wide and diverse "range of roles."

Now, let us examine the relationship between online writing and traditional literary journals. In recent years, traditional literary spaces centered around journals, whether in publication, awards, anthologies, or rankings, have labeled click-attraction from the internet as a mark of "literary tolerance." Flower City Interest is no exception. For example, Liao Jing and Yang Zhihan, featured in this special topic, won the second prize in the literary group and the best character award, respectively, in the Seventh Douban Reading Novella Contest with *Saturday* and *Night Falls in an Instant* in 2020. Liao Jing's *I Am to Tell My Mother* also won a special award—the Most Unforgettable Character Award—in the sixth edition.

A search of Flower City Interest authors reveals many have connections to the Douban Reading contests. *Murder Television* by Datou Ma and *Sister* by Shen Shuzhi won first prizes in the Second Tell a Good Story Contest, *It's Always Raining When I Hit You* by Ban Yu won the first prize in the comedy story category in the fourth contest, and Mu Ming's *Twists and Turns*, *Sand and Stars*, and *Forging Sword* won the Sci-Fi Core Award, the Special Judge's Choice Award (awarded by the writer Han Song), and the third prize in the fantasy category, respectively, in the fifth, sixth, and seventh contests. In fact, in the early years of online writing, *Tianya* magazine published *Live Like a Human* in its fifth issue in 1999. Starting from "a little messy" in 2001, the unremitting promotion of new-generation writers in The Quartet column shifted focus to online writers. During the same period, Annie Baby was a quintessential amphibious author of both online and traditional print journals.

Even so, the publication of the special issue "Life · Future · Mirror Image," the seventh issue of *Youth Literature* in 2019 deserves to be seen as a landmark event marking the transition of online literature to traditional literary journals. An earlier milestone might be the 2005 rebranding of *Fangcao* magazine to *Fangcao Online Literature Selection*, although it did not last long. The contributions for this special topic of *Youth Literature* came from new media of online literature such as Future Affairs Administration, Douban Reading, Soulker, YASHL, NetEase's The Livings, and Bedtime Poem, all of which are online literature platforms.

If this special topic is merely viewed as an exhibition of online literary works, it would underestimate the creativity and ambition of *Youth Literature*. It is not just printed copies of online writings or "duplicates." Instead, it is a result of migration, editing, and recreation by a traditional literary journal, leading to an outcome that exceeds the original text. It demonstrates the limits of mutual circulation between online and print literary journals, much like the offline publication of online literature.

What kind of online literature can seamlessly transition from online to offline without losing its essence? We can see the exchangeable parts, but what about those hidden and unexchangeable parts? These might be specific authors and writing styles. I once proposed that authors accustomed to writing long online novels try their hand at short pieces suitable for journal publication, which was proved to be a challenging task. I want to take this opportunity to thank Jiutu. A few years ago, he accepted my invitation and wrote the short story I needed. However, it never got published because I couldn't put together a complete column. I believe that with more attempts like his, we could appreciate the unique strengths and weaknesses of both super-long online novels and short pieces in traditional journals.

With this issue of *Youth Literature* as an example, other new literary media that have transitioned from online platforms to print journals include apps like One and Substack. We can further question if there is any difference in the literary definition and aesthetic imagination between these and traditional literary journals since the May Fourth Movement. I think there is little difference; in fact, Douban Reading is a transition of traditional literary tastes to online platforms. Let's look at the judging panel for the Douban Reading call for contributions. The invited judges for the latest seventh edition were Bad Rabbit Pictures, Zhou Haohui, Ji Yaya, and Chen Qiufan. Except for Bad Rabbit Pictures, a film and media company, the other three are all related to traditional literary print media. The expert judges for the First Revival Novella and My Non-fiction Writing Writing Competitions included Chen Xiaoming, Shao Yanjun, Hong Qingbo, Yang Xinlan, Kong Lingyan, Shi Yifeng, Liang Hong, Zhuang Yong, and Zhou Yi. Four of them were editors of *Con-Temporary Monthly* and three were literature professors in college. Douban Reading does not dream to foster new literary tastes.

If those involved do not recall and narrate their experiences, will future researchers of online literature assume that it has always been dominated by a few giant online novel platforms from the beginning? One crucial difference between online publication and print publication is that many once-important websites become inaccessible over time, making it impossible for future generations to reconstruct historical scenes. We can say that every major online novel platform that survives today had its "tiny" times. During their "tiny" times, communities or BBS forums flourished. As historical relics, we can look at Tianya Community for an intuitive impression. These communities and BBS forums might have transformed into apps, WeChat official accounts, or public writing and publishing platforms like Douban.

In 2001, the China Social Sciences Press published Annie Baby's *Farewell Vivian*. She wrote in the preface, "Internet, Writing and Strangers," that "The internet is a mysterious garden for me. I know the way to explore it and let myself grow into a wild and lonely plant, rooted in the moist and fragrant soil." And "Many people do various things online: chatting, writing emails, playing video games, designing, falling in love, reading, or working. And I write." Small scale, individuality, free writing, and non-profit nature are some important traditions of early online literature that have been overshadowed by today's capital-driven industry. At the turn of the century, during the early days of online literature, what attracted the first writers to the internet was the freedom of expression. At least until 2004, the online literary ecosystem was still thriving wildly, with poets writing avant-garde poetry and novelists exploring various types of novels, while capital had not yet found a quick way to monetize.

At least during the Rongshuxia (the Chinese literature website with the longest history) phase, writers' understanding of online literature was more about the recognition of writing freedom rather than just a change in the medium. As Annie Baby put it, "Traditional media today is not free and personalized enough, too constrained by orthodox guidelines. As one netizen told me, without the internet, he wouldn't have been able to see my wild and melancholic Chinese novels." So, she wrote on the computer, on the internet, in the dark, and in silence, about desperation, loneliness, "falling and seeking escape." The readers she imagined in the internet age "exist online, perhaps with freer and alternative mindsets, and they also tend to feel lonelier." During Annie Baby's era of online writing, both writers and readers formed a small aesthetic community and social circle.

However, as the profit model of online literature, like all Chinese internet businesses, aims to convert the population dividend into economic benefits, this inevitably leads to sacrificing literary quality for a large readership, and then connecting to online literature platforms. Unlike early online literature, today it is an internet business. Hence, it relies on "pleasure points" to attract consumers and avoids setting aesthetic thresholds, thus encouraging aesthetic adventures. Most online writers today are not concerned with literary standards but with avoiding censorship to ensure financial gains. Like TikTok and live streaming, commercialized online literature is essentially entertainment, though it has literary qualities. Therefore, I think it is more suitable to study the so-called online literature discussed in mass media and public discourse as an industry rather than as literature. The internet era gave birth to so-called online writers like Annie Baby and enables traditional print media writing to seamlessly integrate into online literature without any discord.

In 1999, Wang Meng and Zong Renfa edited Online Literature Series, which included emerging writers born in the 1970s like Li Jingze, Zhang

Sheng, Li Er, Xia Shang, Li Feng, and Li Xiuwen. Zong Renfa wrote in the preface, "As a literature of 'human studies,' its rapid integration into cyberspace is closely linked to what cyberspace offers. The freedom of expression on the internet brings an unprecedented sense of release to writers, eliminating the potential constraints of writing on paper ... The freedom to write came true, so unexpectedly easy." The immediate result of this freedom was the surge in writing from communities, BBS forums, and personal blogs, especially the popularity of "blogs." Miao Wei said, "Blog writing changed the state of discussing public topics in internet forums, moving into fully personalized narratives. Everyone has a space to showcase their ideals, talents, and interests." Despite internet censorship, "blogs" are one's own free kingdom, unlike the enclaves carved out by print media. Flipping through Han Han's *Miscellaneous Texts*, Liu Yu's *A Bullet for You*, and A Yi's *Lonely*, the freedom of online writing feels tangible.

Chen Cun, whom we mentioned earlier, gave a speech titled "So-called Online Classics" at the Shanghai Library on October 17, 2004. He said, "The best period of online literature has passed." "The obvious sign of the decline of online literature is that online writing is becoming increasingly utilitarian, with online writers seeking offline publication, and independent and free online writing is waning."

Looking back, Chen's observation and judgment serve as evidence for "online writers seeking offline publication." In 2005, Shu Jinyu, a reporter for *China Reading Weekly*, wrote in a report, "Major literary websites are aggressively planning large-scale publications. *Fantasy World* magazine quickly entered a profitable state due to the serialization of *Novolands*, showing the publishing value of such works." Whether the first year of online literature is marked by *First Intimate Contact* in 1998 is still debated. Some believe it should be marked by Luo Sen's *Shape of the Wind* in 1997, Zhu Weilian's Rongshuxia or the Jin Yong's Inn forum, *Huaxia Digest*, or Shaojun's *Struggle and Equality*. Regardless of the tracing, the origin of online literature won't be earlier than 1991. From 1991 to 2004, in over a decade, and from 1998 to

2004, in five or six years, "the best period of online literature has passed." It was also around this time that Qidian began charging for reading, followed by the maturing of the tipping mechanism. The strong entry of capital from companies like Shanda, Tencent, Baidu, Alibaba, and iReader continuously redefined "online literature," shrinking its broad beginnings into genre stories constantly producing pleasure points.

Looking back, Chen's observation and judgment—"online writers seeking offline publication"—was only a phase. Even now, with "online writers writing online," online literature can never return to its so-called "best period."

We once naively believed that "writing online" could reshape and expand the landscape of contemporary Chinese literature. However, in hindsight, if it had any impact, it was merely the past. Today, when we migrate our audience from online to offline, we might think we are crossing new boundaries, but in reality, it is just a scene change.

Platforms like Rongshuxia, Tianya Community, Heilan, Sick Child, and Hometown Original Literature, along with the flourishing poetry forums and personal blog writing, have all become relics of the past. I believe that preserving the online writing scene and ecosystem from that era through rescue-styled research is crucial. In a short article for the *Hot Wind* online magazine, I used the title "Testimonies About to Vanish." It should be noted that parts of this article are a revision of that piece.

The once daring online writing spaces have now dwindled into "small yet beautiful" literary websites, apps, and official accounts, barely surviving under the pressure of enormous commercial online novel platforms. If these entities only inherit a fragment of the early online writing's "bourgeois" and "literary youth" spirit, then imagining "writing online" as the source of a Chinese literary revolution is nothing but an illusion.

Literary Curation: Reimagining the Role of Literary Journals

The establishment of modern journal and remuneration systems has been a crucial foundation for the development of modern Chinese literature. In many ways, the history of modern Chinese literature is also the history of its literary journals, and vice versa. At the close of the twentieth century, after the revitalization and subsequent flourishing of literary journals in the late 1970s and their extraordinary prosperity in the 1980s, these publications began to struggle under the pressures of a commercialized literary landscape. With dwindling readerships and sharply declining circulation, the situation became so dire that some even proclaimed, "We must defend literary journals."

Indeed, literary journals are an integral part of the broader literary eco-system, and any discussion of their future must take into account the state of this ecosystem over the past two decades. As for contemporary Chinese literary ecology, after nearly twenty years of immersion in new media and the internet, "literature" in the form of universal writing is a reality happening around us all the time.

The general public has encroached upon literary territories once monopolized by a select few. What was once considered non-literature or low-grade popular literature has taken root and flourished among ordinary readers, forcing professional readers to confront, acknowledge, and define it, thereby continuously expanding the boundaries of literature. In this context, literary activities centered on communication have shifted away from the traditional, contemplative, private literature that was once focused on publication in literary journals. Online literature, with its immediate reading, liking, commenting, tipping, and a fully developed culture of forums, bulletin boards, and offline activities driven by fan mobilization, has created a new "writer-reader" relationship. Such relationship disrupts the traditional, relatively closed cycle of literary production and consumption, where literary journals once played a vital intermediary role.

Many accounts focus solely on the crisis faced by literary journals around the turn of the century. However, the survival crisis that they faced at the end of the twentieth century can also be seen as a conscious revolution aimed at transforming traditional literary journals into vibrant new literary media. The impetus for this transformation partly came from the rise of new online media.

"The emergence of the internet indicates that people's ways of narration and reading are quietly changing, and this has many implications for literary journals."

"Literary journals are products of the era of written text. This era has not ended, but the era of digital text and images is already here. People's methods of engagement and reception are facing new challenges. Traditional concepts of literature and literary journals must adapt to this new reality. Without losing the essential core of literary journals, their modes of expression (including writers' approaches to writing) must undergo effective adjustments. This represents a change in editorial policy and a shift in management strategy."

"The main component of literary activities is the literary journal itself, which is a form of subjectivity. It is not merely a compilation of literary works, nor is it just about publishing a certain number of good works. The key is that it is a comprehensive text, a form of cultural media. It should more forcefully engage with creation and criticism, the current state of literature, and the entire process of literary activities, effectively guiding this state and process."[1]

This renewed recognition of the "media nature" of literary journals is significant. Unlike the narrow concept of "literary journals," the influence of "literary media" has a more public impact. *Lotus, Writer, Mengya*, and *Science Fiction World* were among the earliest literary journals at the turn of the century to establish themselves as "media." More recently, newly founded publications like *Sinan Literary Journal* and the revamped *Fiction World* in Shanghai have also been highlighted as literary journals with a strong sense of "media."

Since the beginning of the 21st century, new literary journals, represented by publications such as *Chutzpah!, Party, Dafang, ZUI Found, ZUI Fount, NEWRITING, ZUI Novel, Thinker's Letters, Super Nice, The Novoland Fantasy World*, and new literary media reform represented by MOOK have had a significant impact on literature. Unlike traditional literary journals, these new media no longer adhere to the conventional structure of dividing content into units by genre, such as poetry, prose, fiction, and literary criticism. Instead, they seek to rebuild the relationship between literature, its

---

1   Xiaomai, "Status of Literary Journals," *Youth Literature*, No. 2 (2000).

contemporary era, and the general readership under the concepts of "grand literature" and "pan-literature," emphasizing "cross-border" and "transcendence." Additionally, literary apps like ONE, Kernovel, the digital magazine *Minimum*, platforms like Douban, Jianshu, NetEase's The Livings, and Tencent Dajia, as well as literary-themed WeChat official accounts like Soulker, MOOK, Pulsasir, NoonStory, Feidi, Future Literature, Words of Behemoth, Wangxiang, Xiaozhong, and Heilan keep emerging as new literary media distinct from large commercial online literature platforms. These new media are products of the internet era's "universal writing," with some focusing on thematic content and fan-oriented tastes. Their relationship with traditional literary journals is a topic worth exploring.

It is important to note that the significance of *ZUI Found, Thinker's Letters*, and *Party* extends further. Although there are journals like *Mengya, West Lake, Youth Literature, Young Writers*, and *Youth* that publish works by young writers, and journals like *Harvest* and *People's Literature* that aim to discover new literary talents, these publications are not strictly led by young people themselves and thus fail to fully realize their literary vision. The chief editors of *ZUI Found, NEWRITING*, and *Party*—Di An, Zhang Yueran, and Han Han, respectively—are influential writers born in the 1980s. The emergence of these journals has allowed the independence of "youth" to be fully realized. The "fandom" of *NEWRITING*, the "thought" of *Party*, and the open aesthetic of *ZUI Found* show that these three journals are not meant to replace each other but to excel in their respective strengths, striving to expand the literary reading and writing life of the younger generation in China.

NEWRITING is a themed publication with a strong sense of issue awareness, with each issue beginning with a contemporary youth's spiritual problem, forming a unique intertext between literature and the mental reality of youth. From a certain perspective, the dozen or so themes of *NEWRITING* from 2008 to the present form a long spiritual history of Chinese youth. For them, the journals are not merely platforms for publishing literary works in the traditional sense but are spaces that transcend the boundaries between literature and other art forms, between literature and life, mutually coexist-ing and proliferating. Di An named *ZUI Found* as a "literary chronicle." The shift from a simple "literary journal" to a comprehensive "literary chronicle" should inspire the transformation and reform of the vast literary journals in contemporary China.

In early 2016, when discussing the Flower City Interest column with Zhu Yanling, the editor-in-chief of *Flower City*, we wondered what Flower City Interest should do for contemporary Chinese literature and how it should be done. The practice of having column hosts has been adopted by many journals since the 1980s, such as *Eastern Chronicles, Master, Lotus, Flower City*, and *Mountain Flowers*. In fact, column hosts have brought a different atmosphere to these journals compared to traditional literary editors. Crit-ics have had a realistic influence on literary journals; what impressed me most was a certain period of *Shanghai Literature* and *Zhongshan*, where crit-ics such as Chen Sihe, Cai Xiang, Ding Fan, and Wang Gan influenced their taste and manuscript selection with their personal positions. Broadly, I also positioned the Flower City Interest column as one hosted by critics.

The special significance of the Flower City Interest column for me is that "hosting" is a form of criticism—expressing judgments about contem-porary Chinese literature through hosting and highlighting one's aesthetic judgment and literary perspective as a critic. Accordingly, each theme has specific critical targets addressing the present-ness and sense of presence of contemporary Chinese literature, with the possibility and futurity of Chi-nese literature being the criteria for selecting writers. Under these targets and standards, heterogeneous texts that deviate from aesthetic conven-tions naturally receive more "attention," while the possibility and futurity leave room for discussion and questioning of the column's "bias."

As for "literary curation," the concept occurred to me while reading *A Brief History of Curating* by Hans Ulrich Obrist. In 2006, when Obrist inter-viewed Anne d'Harnoncourt, director of the Philadelphia Museum of Art, and asked her to define the role of a curator with the phrase "the curator as a bridge," d'Harnoncourt said: "A curator should be a liaison between art and the public. Of course, many artists themselves are liaisons, especially now, when artists do not need or want curators and prefer to communicate directly with the public. To me, that's great. I see the curator as a facilitator. You could also say that curators are obsessed with art and are willing to share that obsession with others. However, they must always be vigilant to avoid imposing their own perceptions and insights on others. This is difficult because you can only be yourself, you can only see art with your own eyes. In short, a curator helps the public approach art, experience the joy of art, feel the power of art, and its subversive qualities and other aspects." Like artists, writers and the reading public in contemporary China no longer fully rely on traditional literary journals as intermediaries for their communication and interaction. More communicative online platforms, such as Douban and Jianshu, which are based on personal writing, and blogs, Weibo, and WeChat official accounts challenge traditional literary journals on multiple fronts. Even when traditional journals transform into "literary media," they still lack full communicative efficacy.

"Literary curation" draws inspiration from art exhibitions and activities. Unlike traditional literary editors, a literary curator acts as a connector, facilitator, and sharer rather than a rigid literary preacher. In truth, every literary publication, including the medium itself, functions much like a form of "curation." Just as museums and galleries serve as public spaces for art exhibitions, literary journals are "skywalks" bustling with the flow of ideas and readers. Just as art exhibitions rely on curators, literary journals, too, benefit from the insight of critics who are well-positioned to become literary curators. Envisioning the *Flower City Interest* column as a public art gallery with a curator aligns with my intention of bringing critics closer to the heart of literary production, advancing their role into the editorial process.

In this context, "literary curation" as an editorial endeavor involves literature drawing inspiration from other art forms and, in turn, breathing life into them. This is reflected in columns featuring novels by directors, plays, film poems, lyrics, and more. Literature actively engages with other arts, extending beyond the pages of literary journals, leading to its own expansion and enrichment.

A good curator, even if curating different themes each time, should fundamentally be a good critic—one who brings essential tastes, perspectives, and aesthetic judgments to every curation, even if each exhibition's expression and presentation vary. These foundational qualities determine whether each "literary curation" of Flower City Interest is truly cutting-edge. It is this very cutting-edge that forms the link between the curator—or critic—and the literary era, emphasizing the immediacy and relevance of literary journals, which sets them apart from book publishing. For instance, 2018 Issue 5 of *Flower City*, titled "From 'Old Tales Retold' to 'Fan Fiction,'" emerged from a sharp observation that parts of our literary age were manifesting through fan fiction. These literary phenomena, unfolding online, were already shaping the literary creations of the younger generation, yet they hadn't received the attention they deserved. Whether it is the community-driven worlds of anime and cosplay or the thriving genre of fan fiction (CP stories), such productions on new media platforms showcase a more diverse and complex form. However, in my view, most scholars have yet to recognize these as legitimate literary phenomena, seeing them merely as "entertainment."

It is crucial to note that being cutting-edge doesn't mean simply chasing the new; it also involves rediscovery through the lens of literary history. For example, the 2017 issue 6 Science Fiction special explored not only the realistic depiction of the world but also absurd and magical approaches to understanding our reality. Today, we might ask whether "science fiction" offers a way to envision our future world. Another example is 2018 Issue 1, "Multi-Ethnic Writing" special, which questioned how works by non-Han ethnic writers, not yet translated into Chinese, could be integrated into the narrative of contemporary Chinese literary history.

When viewed through the lens of "literary curation," the history of contemporary Chinese literary journals includes many successful examples:

Harvest's "Special Issue on Avant-Garde Writers" in the 1980s, *Zhongshan*'s "New Realist Fiction," *Shige Bao* and *Shenzhen Youth News*'s "1986 Modern Poetry Group Exhibition in China," the 1990s' "Realism Shockwave," "Quartet," *Lotus*'s "Reshaping Those Born in the 1970s," and *Mengya*'s "New Concept Writing Competition" and *People's Literature*'s "Non-Fiction Writing," among others. In this sense, "literary curation" aspires for literary journals to become the most vibrant spaces within the broader landscape of literary production, ecology, and life. However, the reality is that among the numerous literary journals in contemporary China, only a few have successfully evolved from being "literary journals" to "literary media," and even fewer have consciously engaged in "literary curation." As a result, the part of contemporary literature centered around literary journals is increasingly becoming a conservative, rigid, and self-referential "literature for the few."

Afterword

Most of the writings in this collection of reviews were penned over the past four to five years and are divided into Part I and Part II.

Part I primarily reflects on Chinese literature since the reform and opening up, particularly in the past two decades of the twenty-first century. It covers topics such as the overall perspective of Chinese literature during the reform and opening up, its global and local dimensions, literature and intergeneration, literature and media, youth writing and public life, multi-ethnic literature, and the literary community, etc.

Part II contains general reviews from each issue of Flower City Interest. Since the first issue of *Flower City* in 2017, I have been in charge of Flower City Interest for five years, a total of thirty issues. It was also in 2017 that I co-initiated the Shanghai-Nanjing Dual Cities Literary Workshop. My primary role is teaching modern Chinese literary history at the university. Lecturing, conducting research projects, and writing papers constitute my daily work. Flower City Interest and the Shanghai-Nanjing Dual Cities Literary Workshop are my extensions from the academic world to the contemporary Chinese literary scene. The opening column's title, "Being a Messenger from the Contemporary Chinese Literary Scene," speaks to my hope to delve deep into the current literary scene in China, acting as an honest observer, messenger, and recorder.

In 1998, having written miscellaneous pieces for over a decade, I tried to shift to literary criticism. This period was not long. From 2002 to 2005, ten years after graduation, I returned to university to study, focusing my doctoral dissertation on historical materials and literary history research. For the next two or three years, I attempted to pick up literary criticism again, but progress was slow. It was not until 2008 that I dedicated more time to literary criticism.

This was a "return to criticism" that occurred in my forties. The so-called "year of no doubt" was not about midlife transformation but about recognizing a bit of my future possibilities and many limitations. At this point, literary criticism had long transitioned from the literary scene to the academy. Its resources, interests, approaches, structure, form, rhetoric, and style consciously accept the transformation and shaping from academic knowledge production.

In January 2010, as the last critic born in the 1960s featured in the Critics Today column of *Southern Cultural Forum*, I expressed my understanding of literary criticism, stating that I wanted to be a "person capable of criticism" in the truest sense, living in real China and engaging in the practice of literary criticism. Rooting oneself in the literary scene and participating in literary production and the construction of literary history is an important tradition of modern Chinese literary criticism. Flower City Interest and the Shanghai-Nanjing Dual Cities Literary Workshop pay homage to the predecessors of this tradition. This is also a "return to criticism," which does not mean withdrawing from the academy but practicing the possibility of dialogue between academic literary criticism and the literary scene.

Compiling and selecting this collection of reviews took nearly a year. At one point, I thought of giving these writings a title—"A Life with Literature," to commemorate the friends who have enriched my literary life over the years. Thank you for your love and passion.

September 2021

Appendix

Chinese Names of Essential Works Mentioned in the Book

· ***Written Works and Collections*** ·

Note: Some of the names of works included in collections are not listed.

"I am Fan Yusu" 《我是范雨素》

"I Am Going to Dongting Lake This Afternoon" 《我下午要去洞庭》

"New Definitions of Contemporary Intimate Relationship Terms" 《当代亲密关系释义》

1986 《一九八六年》

A Bullet for You 《给你一颗子弹》

A Cherry on a Pomegranate Tree 《石榴树上结樱桃》

A Delayed Elegy 《迟到的挽歌》

A Dictionary of Maqiao 《马桥词典》

A Gold-Digging Story 《掘金记》

A Man from Manchuria 《满洲里来的人》

A Perfect Result 《完美的结果》

A Resounding Slap in the Face 《耳光响亮》

A Tale of Big Nur 《大淖记事》

A War of One's Own 《一个人的战争》

A Worthy Life 《人间值得》

Airs of the States 《国风》

All Nights in the World 《世界上所有的夜晚》

Amorous Everywhere 《遍地风流》

Annals of Yanhe Village 《沿河村纪事》

Bababa 《爸爸爸》

Balloon 《气球》

Banana Leaves Cover the Deer 《蕉叶覆鹿》

Banished! 《扎根》

Bao Town 《小鲍庄》

Big Bathing Woman 《大浴女》

Big Breasts and Wide Hips 《丰乳肥臀》

Black Steed 《黑骏马》

Blessing 《祝福》

Bombing Graves 《炸坟》

Brothers 《兄弟》

Buddhist Initiation 《受戒》

Cabin on the Mountain 《山上的小屋》

Call to Arms 《呐喊》

Childhood Beast 《童年兽》

China's Gentry 《中国绅士》

Chronicle of a Blood Merchant 《许三观卖血记》

Clumsy Flower 《笨花》

Coloratura 《花腔》

Corn 《玉米》

Cries in the Drizzle 《细雨中的呼喊》

Cross-Country Race 《越野赛跑》

Dadongxiang 《大东乡》

Daily Conventions in Hometown 《故乡相处流传》

Daughter of the River 《饥饿的女儿》

Dayou 《大有》

Daytime Selling Blue 《白日贩蓝》

Death 《死亡》

Diary of a Madman 《狂人日记》

Dog Head Gold 《狗头金》

Eight Hundred Meters from Xiao Hong 《离萧红八百米》

Empty Mountain 《空山》

Enemy 《敌人》

Escape in 1934 《1943年的逃亡》

Event 《事件》

Farewell Vivian 《再见薇薇安》

Feed Me 《哺乳期的女人》

Fellow Townspeople 《故乡人》

Festival 《节日》

Fiction 《虚构》

Five Chinese Mothers in the Neighborhood 《小区里的五个中国母亲》

Five Women and a Rope 《五个女人和一根绳子》

Flock of Brown Bird 《褐色鸟群》

Foreign Land 《他乡》

Four Ways to Die of My Hometown 《我故乡死去的四种方法》

Fragmented Stories of Mountain Trolls 《山魈考残编》

Frog 《蛙》

General Cat 《猫将军》

Glass House 《玻璃屋子》

Goddess of the Lhasa River 《拉萨河女神》

Going to RT-Mart 《去大润发》

Golden Pastures 《金牧场》

Grassland 《草原》

Ground Covered with Chicken Feathers 《一地鸡毛》

Gui Qu Lai 《归去来》

Having the Time of Life 《过把瘾就死》

Heartbreaking Stories from Pingle Town 《平乐镇伤心故事集》

Heartbreaking Stories from Zhumadian 《驻马店伤心故事集》

Heavenly Dog 《天狗》

Hedgehog, Hedgehog 《刺猬，刺猬》

Hometown 《故乡》

Hometown, Regime, and Blood 《故乡天下黄花》

Homicide 《他杀》

Human-Faced Animals 《人面动物》

I am a Young Drunk 《我是少年酒坛子》

I Met Someone Kinder Than Me 《我认识过一个比我善良的人》

Illustrated Treatise on the Maritime Kingdoms 《海国图志》

In the County Town 《在县城》

In the Tavern 《在酒楼上》

Inviting Women for Riddles 《请女人猜谜》

Jacob Wrestling with the Angel 《雅各与天使摔跤》

Jade Dynasty 《诛仙》

Jiangnan Garden Chronicles 《江南园林志》

King of Chess 《棋王》

King of Children 《孩子王》

King of Trees 《树王》

La Wu Huo Liu 《拉乌霍流》

Late Marriage 《晚婚》

Lewisham, London 《Lewisham的伦敦》

Life 《人生》

Life as a Zither String 《命若琴弦》

Lonely 《寡人》

Love in a Fallen City 《倾城之恋》

Love in a Small Town 《小城之恋》

Love in the Brocade Valley 《锦绣谷之恋》

Love on the Barren Mountain 《荒山之恋》

Love Stories of Middle-Aged Women 《中年妇女恋爱史》

Luokan Village 《罗坎村》

Making Violins 《制琴记》

Manchukuo 《伪满洲国》

Marriage Scenes 《婚姻场景》

Material and Spirit in Hometown 《故乡面和花朵》

Meeting My Fianceé 《遇见未婚妻》

Memories of Mulberry Garden 《桑园留念》

Memories of Nanjing 《关于南京的回忆》

Migration 《徙》

Mimi Peanut 《咪咪花生》

Miscellaneous Texts 《杂的文》

Monkey Cool Cat 《猴酷猫》

Mr. 《先生》

Mr., Mr. 《先生，先生》

My Distant Qingping Bay 《我遥远的清平湾》

My Emperor Life 《我的帝王生涯》

My Suleiman is Missing 《我的苏莱曼不见了》

Night Mooring on the Qinhuai series 《夜泊秦淮》系列

Night Stories 《夜间故事》

Nine Pieces of Stories 《小说九段》

No Barbed Wire in the Sky 《天上没有铁丝网》

Notes on Principles 《务虚笔记》

Novolands 《九州》

Oh Daddy 《爸爸啊》

Old Dog 《老狗》

Old Floating Cloud 《苍老的浮云》

Old Stories Retold 《故事新编》

On the Plateau 《你在高原》

One Kind of Reality 《现实一种》

Oneness 《不二》

Orchard City Chronicles 《果园城记》

Ordinary World 《平凡的世界》

Orphans of a Beautiful New World 《美丽新世界的孤儿》

Outside the Door 《门外》

Parents 《父母》

Peach Blossom Paradise 《人面桃花》

Pearls and Agates 《珍珠玛瑙》

Piaomiao Zhi Lü 《飘渺之旅》

Plain 《平原》

Please Don't Leave the Car Accident Scene 《请勿离开车祸现场》

Poetry Across Oceans 《四海为诗》

Private Life 《私人生活》

Qinghuang 《青黄》

Qingyi 《青衣》

Qinqiang 《秦腔》

Qiushui 《秋水》

Rainbow 《彩虹》

Reading 'Garden' in N City 《在N市读园林》

Record of Regret 《后悔录》

Records of Women's Idle Talk 《妇女闲谈录》

Red Poppies 《尘埃落定》

Red Sorghum 《红高粱》

Rice 《米》

Rivers of the North 《北方的河》

Rose Gate 《玫瑰门》

Ruined City 《废都》

Saint Tianmenkou 《圣天门口》

September's Fable 《九月寓言》

Serial Collection 《连环收缴》

Seven and a Quarter 《七又四分之一》

Several Moments with Xie Yunjin 《和解云锦一起的若干瞬间》

Shape of the Wind 《风姿物语》

Snow Falling on the Mountains and Frost on the Hollows 《雪落高山霜打凹》

Song of Everlasting Regret 《长恨歌》

Special Gift 《异禀》

Spectacle of the Passing Scenes 《走马观花集》

Standing on the Scale 《站在天平上》

Stories from the Countryside 《插队的故事》

Stories of the Tang Dynasty series 《唐人笔记》系列

Strange Tales from a Chinese Studio 《聊斋志异》

Strange Tales from a Foreign Land 《异乡异闻》

Struggle and Equality 《奋斗与平等》

Sui Yuan Kao 《随园考》

Swing Frame 《秋千架》

The Algorithm of Life 《人生算法》

The Ancient Ship 《古船》

The Baptismal River 《施洗的河》

The Bat Is Singing 《蝙蝠在歌唱》

The Bird-Eating Girl 《吃鸟的女孩》

The Book of Songs 《诗经》

The College Student 《大学生》

The Devil 《魔王》

The Eighth is a Bronze Statue 《第五个是铜像》

The Embankment 《河岸》

The Epic of Wooden Horse 《木马故事》

The First Intimate Contact 《第一次亲密接触》

The Flight to the Moon 《奔月》

The Golden Age 《黄金时代》

The Home of a Village 《一个村庄的家》

The Homeland of Wolves and Songs 《有狼有歌的故乡》

The Last Quarter of the Moon 《额尔古纳河右岸》

The Love Story of Mazhuo 《玛卓的爱情》

The Messenger's Letters 《信使之函》

The Passage of Time 《日光流年》

The Report Before Losing Humanity 《没有失去人性前的报告》

The Research on Wang 《王考》

The Robber Tavern 《强盗酒馆》

The Seventh Day 《第七天》

The Shaft 《地下的天空》

The Temple Without Snow 《大寺终年无雪》

The Temptation of the Kailas Mountains 《冈底斯的诱惑》

The Three Chapters of Shangzhou 《商州三录》

The Tiger and the City that Never Sleeps 《老虎与不夜城》

The Troubleshooters 《顽主》

The Unforgivable Tsavo Lion 《不可饶恕的查沃狮》

The Wandering Goldfish 《流浪的金鱼》

The Wang Village on the Earth 《地球上的王家庄》

The World 《世界》

The World's Best Lover 《世界第一等恋人》

The Yellow Mud Hut 《黄泥小屋》

Thick Soil 《厚土》

Three Sisters 《玉秀》

To Live 《活着》

Transparent Radish 《透明的萝卜》

Traveler 《旅行家》

Turbulence 《浮躁》

Uncle's Stories 《叔叔的故事》

Village Museum 《乡村博物馆》

Visit to the World of Dreams 《访问梦境》

Wanderer in a Box 《箱中浪客》

Wandering 《彷徨》

We Placed a Giant Egg by the Sea 《我们在海边放了一个巨大的蛋》

Wedding Night 《新婚之夜》

Wenjiayao Scenery 《温家窑风景》

Westward Notes 《西行笔录》

White Deer Plain 《白鹿原》

White Tower 《白塔》

Wild Beast 《动物凶猛》

Wives and Concubines 《妻妾成群》

Wolf Totem 《狼图腾》

Womanwomanwoman 《女女女》

Wu Ding's Journey to the West 《无定西行记》

Ximen Inn 《西门旅社》

Xizang, a Soul Knotted on a Leather Thong 《西藏，系在皮绳上的魂》

Xizang: The Secret Years 《西藏，隐秘的岁月》

Years, Months, Dates 《年月日》

Yellow Mud Street 《黄泥街》

Yidou Ge Notes 《一斗阁笔记》

Yuyang 《玉秧》

· *Plays* ·

Thunderstorm 《雷雨》

Teahouse 《茶馆》

The Bus Stop 《车站》

The Savage 《野人》

Sifan 《思凡》

I Love XXX 《我爱XXX》

The Death of an Anarchist 《一个无政府主义者的死亡》

Rhinoceros in Love 《恋爱的犀牛》

I am the Moon 《我是月亮》

Telemachus 《特罗马克》

The Face of Chiang Kai-shek 《蒋公的面子》

Sisters 《姐妹》

· *Movies* ·

And the Spring Comes 《春分》

Legend of the Demon Cat 《妖猫传》

Mountains May Depart 《山河故人》

Platform 《站台》

Unknown Pleasures 《任逍遥》

Xiao Shan Going Home 《小山回家》

Xiao Wu 《小武》

· *Albums* ·

Canton Girl 《广东姑娘》

County Town Chronicles 《县城记》

Dreamy Lisa Salon 《梦幻丽莎发廊》

Inside the Cable Temple 《冀西南林路行》

Mom, Let's Fly Together, Rock Together 《妈妈一起飞吧，妈妈一起摇滚吧》

Stories 《故事会》

References

Cao, Naiqian, *Can't Help Thinking of You at Night*. Changjiang Literature and
  Art Publishing House, 2007.

García Márquez, Gabriel. "The Fragrance of Guava," in *The Theory of Iceberg:
  Dialogues and Sub-dialogues*, ed. Cui Daoyi, Zhu Wei, Wang Qingfeng,
  Wang Yongjun. Beijing: Workers' Publishing House, 1987.

Guha, Ranajit. "History at the Limit," in *Research on the Common People*
  selected and translated by Liu Jianzhi, Xu Zhaolin, et al. Beijing: Central
  Compilation and Translation Press, 2005.

Han, Shaogong, and Wang Yao. *Dialogue between Han Shaogong and Wang
  Yao*. Suzhou: Suzhou University Press, 2003.

———. "The 'Roots' of Literature," *Writers*, No. 4 (1985).

———. *A Dictionary of Maqiao*, Beijing: Writers Publishing House, 1996.

Jenkins, Henry. "Quentin Tarantino's *Star Wars*? Grassroots Creativity Meet
  the Media Industry," in *Convergence Culture: Where Old and New Media
  Collide*. New York: New York University Press, 2006, 131–168.

Jia, Pingwa, and Xie Youshun. *Dialogues between Jia Pingwa and Xie Youshun*. Suzhou: Suzhou University Press, 2003.

Li, Fengliang. "The Concept and Operation of Chinese Language Literature—Interview with Professor Wang Dewei," *Flower City*, No. 5 (2008).

Li, Hangyu. "On 'Seeking a Way Out': On the Problem of Seeking 'Roots,'"
  Zhongshan, No. 1 (1986).

———. "Sort Out Our 'Roots,'" *Writers*, No. 9 (1985).

Li, Qingxi. "Rethinking Root-Seeking Literature," *Shanghai Culture*, No. 5
  (2009).

Li, Rui. *The Reward of Life*. Beijing: Peoples Literature Publishing House,
  2008.

Li, Tuo. "Cultural Consciousness and Aesthetic Consciousness in Chinese and Western Literature—Preface to 'Shangzhou Sanlu' by Jia Pingwa," *Shanghai Literature*, No. 1 (1986).

Liu, Zhenyun. "The Overall Hometown and Its Specifics," *Literary and Artistic Contention*, No. 1 (1992).

Mo, Yan, and Wang Yao. *Record of A Conversation between Mo Yan and Wang Yao*. Suzhou: Suzhou University Press, 2003.

Object Lessons: The Paris Review Presents the Art of the Short Story. Edited By Lorin Stein and Sadie Stein, translated by Wen Jing, et al. Beijing: China Remin University Press, 2019.

Su, Tong. "About or Not about Writing," *Yangtze Jiang Literary Review*, No. 3 (2009).

The Paris Review: Interviews with Writers, Vol. 5, ed. *The Paris Review* Editorial Board, trans. Wang Hongtu, et al. Beijing: Peoples Literature Publishing House, 2020, 33.

Wang, Meng. "Preface: Charm of Gechuan River," in Li Hangyu, *The Last Fisherman*, Beijing: Peoples Literature Publishing, 1985.

Wang, Xiaoming. "Disbelief and Unwillingness to Believe: On the Creations of Three Root-Seeking Writers," *Literary Review*, No. 4 (1998).

Wang, Zengqi, and Shi Shuqing. "Prose-Style Novels as Lyrical Poetry—a Conversation with Mainland Chinese Writers No. 4," *Shanghai Literature*, No. 4, 1998.

Wang, Zengqi. "Postscript: Reading 'Can't Help Thinking of You at Night,' Cao Naiqian," Cao Naiqian, *Can't Help Thinking of You at Night*. Wuhan: Changjiang Literature and Art Publishing House, 2007, 232.

Xiaomai. "Status of Literary Journals," *Youth Literature*, No. 2 (2000).

Yan, Lianke. "The Relationship between Novels and the World—Lecture at Shanghai University," *Shanghai Literature*, No. 8 (2004).

Zhang, Chengzhi. "Postscript," in *Old Bridge*. Beijing: Beijing October Literature and Art Publishing House, 1984, 304–306.

Index

About the Author

He Ping, born in 1968, is a professor and doctoral supervisor at the College of Literature of Nanjing Normal University and the chief expert of the National Social Science Foundation's major projects.

He is the author of *Prose Speaking, Selected Literary Criticism of He Ping*, and *The Life of the Unknown*. In 2017, he initiated the Shanghai-Nanjing Dual Cities Literary Workshop, and in the same year, he began to host the Flower City Interest in *Flower City*.